# A THEORY OF INCOME DISTRIBUTION

# A THEORY
# OF INCOME
# DISTRIBUTION

HAROLD LYDALL

CLARENDON PRESS · OXFORD
1979

*Oxford University Press, Walton Street, Oxford* OX26 DP

OXFORD LONDON GLASGOW

NEW YORK TORONTO MELBOURNE WELLINGTON

KUALA LUMPUR SINGAPORE JAKARTA HONG KONG TOKYO

DELHI BOMBAY CALCUTTA MADRAS KARACHI

IBADAN NAIROBI DAR ES SALAAM CAPE TOWN

*Published in the United States by*
*Oxford University Press, New York*

**British Library Cataloguing in Publication Data**

Lydall, Harold French
   A theory of income distribution.
   1. Income distribution
   I. Title
   339.2'01       HC79.15        78–41140

   ISBN 0–19–828415–2

*Printed and bound in Great Britain*
*by W & J Mackay Limited, Chatham*

# PREFACE

This book brings together a number of ideas which have developed over a considerable period of time. Some of the main elements of the model described in Chapter 9 were first outlined in a paper in 1971; Chapter 12 owes a great deal to my 1968 book *The Structure of Earnings*; and it would be easy to find examples of continuity with work which first appeared as early as the 1950s.

What was needed in order to bring all this together, and to add other components, was time. And this essential element was most generously provided by the Social Science Research Council, which gave me a personal research grant for the year 1976–77. The University of East Anglia very kindly gave me leave of absence for that period.

Sections of the draft manuscript were read by Tony Atkinson, Henry Phelps Brown, Paul Taubman and Peter Townroe, each of whom made valuable suggestions for improvement. Although I may not have followed their advice in all respects, I am most grateful to them for their assistance.

At the end of the book there will be found an extensive list of references to works which I have consulted in detail. But it would be appropriate at this point to draw attention to a few books which have been of more general importance. In the first place, I should like to acknowledge the possibility that some of the ideas for the model presented in Chapter 9 were derived from reading two early works by Steindl (1945 and 1952). I have also made use of the general surveys of income distribution theory contained in the standard works by Bronfenbrenner (1971), Davidson (1959) and Johnson (1973). The theory of the determination of employment incomes is examined in depth in an excellent new book by Phelps Brown (1977), and there is a good introduction to the empirical side of the problem in Atkinson (1975).

Finally, I should like to express my warm thanks to Tarun Das for his assistance in programming computer simulations, to Enrique Hernandez Laos for several suggestions, and to Jean Colman, Kika Raba and Pauline Speculand for first-class secretarial assistance.

Institute of Economics and Statistics,                               H. F. L.
Oxford.                                                           March, 1979

# CONTENTS

# I

# INTRODUCTION

The main purpose of this book is to propose a new theory of income distribution. The explanation of the division of the national income by 'factor shares' has always been an important objective of economic theory; and Ricardo, in a well-known passage, declared it to be the principal problem of political economy. Ricardo's dictum, however, was an expression of his methodology rather than of his substantive interests. Marx, who took over a great deal from Ricardo, although dropping some of his most fertile ideas, regarded the distribution of income between wages and other incomes as the key to the understanding of capitalism. But it would not be true to say that Marx regarded the explanation of income distribution as the principal purpose of political economy. The neoclassical theorists of the last quarter of the nineteenth century treated income distribution as one outcome of a general equilibrium system. If the system could be solved for all prices and quantities, one would know the distribution of income as well as everything else, given the initial distributions of tastes and resources. But this theory yielded no empirical predictions until it was extended by J. B. Clark, Samuelson, Solow, and others to include an aggregate production function. In this form neoclassical theory seemed to provide a coherent explanation of some of the observed facts of experience and to yield testable predictions. The theory has been subjected to fundamental criticism by Joan Robinson, Kaldor, and other Cambridge economists, who have also suggested an alternative approach. While the latter group of theories have some interesting characteristics, they are based on strong and, in my opinion, implausible assumptions. Thus the problem of the distribution of factor shares is still very much an open question.

The major theories of distribution have been concerned with the distribution of income between social classes, or the owners of the factors of production, categories which are often assumed to be coterminous. In the final analysis, however, one must

surely be interested mainly in the distribution of income between households, or between groups of individuals who share
their incomes and expenditures. The implicit assumption
behind traditional theories of income distribution has been
that, if a large share of total income is paid in rent or profit, the
distribution is likely to be unequal. While there is clearly some
truth in this assumption, it is a loose sort of truth; and in the
conditions ruling in the industrialized countries today it is
becoming even looser. Much property income, for example, is
received by retired people and widows, who are often less well
off than many families in employment. The distribution of
income between persons is undoubtedly related to the factor
income distribution, but it is necessary to build a bridge between the two. In this book the distribution of factor incomes
will be considered first; but the ultimate intention is to account
for the size distribution of personal incomes, and to show how
the two kinds of distribution are connected.

Despite variations in the explicit emphasis given in different
theories to the distributional aspect, it is a rule that some kind
of theory of distribution lies at the heart of every general
economic theory. It is for this reason that I propose first to
review the work of the major schools of economics, starting with
Adam Smith. In each case we shall look not only for the theory's
explicit model of income distribution but also for any aspects of
its behavioural assumptions or of its methodology which are
likely to be of importance in an alternative theory. Although it
would be inaccurate to describe my alternative theory as eclectic, it will be found that each major economic theory has made
some contribution towards it, even if not in an immediately
obvious manner. There are several features of the alternative
theory which mark it off rather distinctly from all, or almost all,
previous theories; and it may be useful to refer to some of these
features at this point.

Virtually all previous theories of income distribution—with
the notable exception of the theory of Kalecki—are based on
the explicit or implicit assumption of perfect competition. This
goes for Marx as much as for Adam Smith, for Kaldor as much
as for Samuelson.[1] All economists have something to say about

---

[1] Kaldor has often criticized the assumption of perfect competition. But
his model of income distribution depends on it.

monopolies or market imperfections; but when they build their general models they rely on perfect competition. Factors are assumed to be homogeneous and mobile; prices of products and factor services—including capital services—are assumed to be equal for all; and knowledge—including technical knowledge—is a free good. Models are built around a single wage rate of labour and a uniform rate of profit on capital (strictly, a uniform rate of interest) within a framework of competitive equilibrium. These assumptions are not always logically compatible with other components of certain models. For example, both Marx and Marshall gave considerable emphasis to the importance of increasing returns to scale, which are inconsistent with perfect competition and a uniform rate of profit.

The major objection to perfect competition is that it is an unrealistic description of conditions in most of modern industry—as Sraffa pointed out more than half a century ago.[2] Perfect competition implies not only infinitely elastic demand curves for the products of individual firms but also perfect competition in factor markets, and perfect knowledge of existing techniques. Factors cannot be paid the value of their marginal products unless they are available in freely competitive supply to all; nor can the hirer know what the marginal product of a factor is unless he has the same knowledge of technique as every other potential hirer. He must also have perfect knowledge of the qualities of the factor whose services he is hiring. These assumptions rule out imperfections in the capital market, as well as differences between entrepreneurs in their technical knowledge. The logical conclusion is that in a perfectly competitive equilibrium all firms of equal efficiency would make 'normal' profits, equal to the rate of interest on their necessary capital.

The first step towards a satisfactory theory of income distribution—as of economics as a whole—is to drop the assumption of perfect competition. Hitherto economists have been afraid to take this step, because it seemed to entail the destruction of economic theory.[3] But this does not follow if the equilibrium of perfect competition can be replaced by an alternative

[2] Sraffa (1926).
[3] Hicks (1946, 83).

kind of equilibrium, such as will be proposed in Chapters 9 and 10 below.

A second, and closely linked, feature of the proposed theory is that it dispenses with the usual assumption of consumer and producer myopia. Anyone approaching economic theory with an unprejudiced eye would surely be astonished to discover that virtually the whole of the microeconomic part of economics, and even a considerable amount of the macroeconomic part, is based on the assumption that economic agents—households, firms, and governments—respond only to immediate stimuli, in particular to their current incomes and to the prices 'ruling' on the market at the moment when they make their decisions. Perhaps the most distinctive feature of human beings, in comparison with animals, is that they are forward-looking, that their actions are influenced by expectations as well as by current events. Nowhere is this more true than in the field of economic decisions. But the standard theories of economics rule this out. Demand is determined by current incomes and prices; supply—including future supply—responds to current prices; and even investment is often assumed to be mainly influenced by current conditions. These assumptions have had a disastrous effect on the theory of the firm; and I shall replace them by a theory of expectations-influenced decision-making.

A third feature of existing economic theory is the assumption of homogeneity of factors of production. It is, of course, admitted that people vary in their levels of skill and productivity. But this aspect is usually left on one side—and never brought back into the discussion. Even worse is the assumption that all firms are equal in their technical ability, an assumption which strikes at the heart of any rational theory of profits. My theory of distribution will give a prominent place to differences in productivity between firms and to their effects on differences in profits and in the earnings of their employees.

Because of its commitment to perfect competition, most traditional theory allows no role for increasing returns to scale. The consequence is that such theories fail to account for the expansion of firms, for the continuous reinvestment of profits, and for the importance of internally generated technical progress. By dropping the assumption of perfect competition the door can be opened to the influence of economies of scale, without which it is impossible to account for the dramatic economic progress of the past two centuries. Despite these important changes in basic assumptions, the proposed model of distribution will remain an equilibrium model. The science of economics is concerned with the behaviour of groups of persons and enterprises which are at least partially autonomous units, and for this reason the concept of equilibrium must inevitably play a role in any economic theory. At its simplest, equilibrium means a point of balance between conflicting pressures or tendencies. What matters, however, is the content of an equilibrium theory. I shall not employ the static theory of perfect competition, in which change comes only from exogenous factors, unexpectedly, and without arousing expectations of any further changes. The equilibrium will be an equilibrium of forces continually in motion, containing within itself the seeds of its own development and transformation. It will be what Marshall might have called a biological equilibrium. A Hegelian or a Marxist might call it a dialectical equilibrium.

The plan of the book is as follows. The first six chapters of Part I are devoted to a review and critique of previous theories of factor shares. Major attention is given to the theories of Ricardo, Marx, the neoclassical economists, and the 'Keynesians'. But a special chapter is devoted to Marshall, an unorthodox neoclassical who believed in the importance of increasing returns to scale and, perhaps for that reason, was ambivalent about static equilibrium. A critique of neoclassical theory leads to a reconsideration of some of the fundamental assumptions of that theory, in particular the assumption of perfect knowledge, which is maintained largely for normative reasons. The abandonment of this assumption opens the way to more fruitful concepts of competition, growth, and equilibrium.

The final chapter of Part I contains a summary of statistical evidence about the distribution of income, both by factor shares and by size. The evidence suggests that, although both types of distribution have been fairly stable over short or medium periods of time, there have been important changes in distribution over longer periods of time. The facts described in this chapter constitute the *explicanda* of the theories which follow in Parts II and III.

In Part II a new theory is proposed to account for the distribution of income between wages and profits. Wages for this purpose include all labour incomes, while profits are defined as the rest of net value added apart from land rent. In Chapter 9 the economy is assumed to be competitive, not in the idealized sense of perfect competition, but with freedom of entry and with perfect competition in product markets. What distinguishes this form of competition—described as Entry and Product Market (EPM) competition—from perfect competition is the existence of imperfect markets for capital and for 'private' technique, or know-how.

It is assumed that additional supplies of capital and know-how are generated predominantly within firms, and that it is the limits on the supplies of these two factors, especially the supply of organizational know-how, which prevents firms from freely choosing an optimal scale of operation. Hence new firms usually start as one-man enterprises, and gradually expand as their profits permit an increase in their capital and as their accumulated experience increases their organizational know-how, which is the prerequisite for efficient operation on a larger scale. By introducing these constraints on expansion it becomes possible to achieve a competitive equilibrium, even when there are in all firms unutilized internal economies of scale. It is further assumed that the marginal cost of production for the industry is the average unit cost of labour and materials in a one-man firm (OMF) of average efficiency, and that this is the equilibrium price of the product. Although the average OMF in equilibrium makes no profit, average profits are positive for larger firms and the profit margin increases continuously with the size of firm.

If there is a steady, or steadily increasing, inflow of OMFs in a group of industries (or in the economy as a whole), and if all firms have a constant reinvestment ratio (the ratio of net investment to the previous year's profits), the model implies that at the end of a number of years the size distribution of firms will be widely dispersed and positively skew. These features are further accentuated if, as is likely, the OMFs in each annual cohort of new entrants vary in their efficiency, and if the least efficient firms in each cohort are obliged to close down after a period of time. If a fixed relative size distribution of firms is combined with functions which specify how the profit margin varies with size of firm, the over-all division of value added between wages and profits is fully determined. The addition of some stochastic variation in the annual profits of firms introduces a margin of uncertainty but does not change the fundamental relations of the model.

The extension of the model to conditions of imperfect competition, which are predominant in industrialized countries, requires a theory of price determination under these conditions; and Chapter 10 contains the outline of such a theory. The foundation of the theory is the assumption that under imperfect competition with free entry the behaviour of firms is largely determined by their expectations, especially by expectations of the effect of the firm's level of prices on the probability of new entry. The firm selling a differentiated product, or forming part of a small group of firms selling a homogeneous product, will—in effect—estimate a 'no-entry' ceiling price for its product, and will normally maintain that price unchanged irrespective of its own output. The methods by which the no-entry price (NEP) is determined are discussed at length, and the conclusion is that, with some exceptions, the NEP will approximate to the equilibrium price which would exist under EPM competition. The outcome of this argument is that, so long as there is legal freedom of entry, especially entry of OMFs, equilibrium prices will be approximately the same under all varieties of competition. Thus a bridge can be built between the theory of income distribution under EPM competition and the theory which is relevant for an economy in which product differentiation is the dominant feature.

Some of the implications of the model for economic theory as a whole are touched on in Chapters 9 and 10; but Chapter 11 contains a more detailed discussion of the implications of the model for the theories of growth and fluctuations, inflation, international trade, and public finance.

In Part III we pass on to consider the size distribution of incomes. Chapter 12 contains a model designed to account for the pattern of inter-country differences in the size distribution of income which was described in Chapter 8. That pattern suggests that inequality increases in the early stages of economic development and declines in the later stages. There are also other features of the pattern which require explanation. The basic assumptions of the suggested model are (1) the economy is divided into two sectors, defined by their levels of technique, and (2) average income in each sector is determined by average productivity in that sector. Then a process of transfer of population from the less productive to the more productive sector can generate a pattern of changes in inequality similar to that revealed by the cross-section analysis of country differences. The model is further refined to allow for changes over time in the level of productivity within each sector, as well as for income differences within each sector.

In Chapter 13 the focus of attention shifts from long-term changes in the size distribution to a consideration of theories of the distribution of employment incomes. This is a field which has been studied fairly intensively in recent years. Four main types of theory have been proposed: theories of chance, theories of choice, theories of personal characteristics and development, and theories of the job structure. A review of these theories suggests that each contains some elements of truth. But the type of theory which provides the most fruitful framework for analysis seems to be the third, which can also be used to embrace most of the special contributions of the others. There is scope for further development of this theory by including additional personal characteristics, such as non-cognitive abilities, and also cultural influences and hierarchy effects.

Chapter 14 is concerned with other sources of factor income—from self-employment and property—and with the size distribution of family income from all sources. Changes in the size distribution of income from self-employment and property are considered within the framework of the historical evolution of an industrialized market economy. Some special patterns of social life which influence the distribution of family incomes, such as the family life-cycle, are also discussed.

The final chapter is devoted to general conclusions about my theory of income distribution, including a brief discussion of some of its policy implications.

# PART I

## THE BACKGROUND TO THE DEBATE

# 2

# ADAM SMITH AND RICARDO

## Adam Smith

Although Adam Smith was by no means the first important economist, being preceded in Britain by such famous writers as Mun, Petty, Locke, and Hume, and in France by Cantillon, Turgot, and Quesnay, his great work *The Wealth of Nations* published in 1776 is a distillation of the wisdom of his age as well as containing many original contributions of his own. As is well known, Adam Smith's principal message was the advantages of a free market and *laissez-faire*. Partly, this was a reaction against mercantilist restrictions on trade and the granting of monopoly rights to groups of traders and artisans; but it was mainly a perception of the enormous potential effects on productivity of division of labour. Since division of labour could be extended only by widening the market, the free market was twice blessed: it improved the allocation of resources, and it opened the door to economies of scale. The policy of free competition would inevitably lead to a great increase in wealth, i.e. in output and real income.

Adam Smith was not much interested in the over-all distribution of income. This was not because of a lack of humanitarian feelings but rather because he felt that the way forward for 'everyone' at that moment of British history was through freedom of trade. In practice, of course, the breakdown of monopolies, or of trade and guild restrictions, would inevitably be disadvantageous, at least temporarily, to those enjoying the benefits of such monopoly rights or restrictions. If pressed, however, I do not doubt that Adam Smith would have used the same argument as that suggested by Professor Hicks to justify free competition, namely, that sooner or later everyone is likely to benefit from it.[1] While it is easy to find fault with such an argument, it is noteworthy that all significant advances in human affairs have been accompanied by the claim that

[1] See Hicks (1941).

everyone, except perhaps some small minority, will benefit. The claim may be exaggerated, but it is not necessarily false.

Adam Smith's major theoretical contributions were made in the area of what would now be called microeconomics. He traced out, often in impressive detail, the processes whereby partial equilibrium is established in the markets for individual products, the earnings of individual occupations, or the rates of profit in particular industries. Moreover, he sketched the outline of a theory of general equilibrium, the output-maximizing equilibrium to which society is led by the 'invisible hand'.[2]

Occasionally Adam Smith also took a macroeconomic point of view, as in the following passage (I, 248):

> The whole annual produce of the land and labour of every country . . . naturally divides itself . . . into three parts: the rent of land, the wages of labour, and the profits of stock; and constitutes a revenue to three different orders of people; to those who live by rent, to those who live by wages, and to those who live by profit. These are the three great, original and constituent orders of every civilized society, from whose revenue that of every other order is ultimately derived.

How are these three income shares determined? Adam Smith offered some suggestions, but he never pretended to have a complete theory of income distribution. As regards rent he argued that, with the progress of society, the value of primary produce rises in relation to the value of manufactures (I, 247). So the real value of rent increases. But he also believed that the *share* of rent in the output of primary produce increases. Adam Smith never gave any coherent explanation for this conclusion and a full analysis of the problem had to wait another forty years, for the work of Malthus, Ricardo, and West.[3]

---

[2] 'As every individual, therefore, endeavours as much as he can both to employ his capital in the support of domestic industry, and so to direct that industry that its produce may be of the greatest value; every individual necessarily labours to render the annual revenue of the society as great as he can. He generally, indeed, neither intends to promote the public interest, nor knows how much he is promoting it . . . he intends only his own gain, and he is in this, as in many other cases, led by an invisible hand to promote an end which was no part of his intention. Nor is it always the worse for society that it was no part of it. By pursuing his own interest he frequently promotes that of the society more effectually than when he really intends to promote it.' (I, 421).

(Subsequent references to *The Wealth of Nations* will be in this form, showing the volume number and page.)

[3] In another passage (I, 317), as Cannan pointed out in his editorial comments, Adam Smith seems to say the opposite.

Adam Smith's approach to the division of income between wages and profits was a macroeconomic application of the kind of supply and demand analysis which he used so successfully in dealing with microeconomic problems. The demand for labour is assumed to be dependent on the supply of capital (I, 71). But it is not the actual size of the capital stock in relation to the labour supply which determines the demand for labour. Rather it is the difference between the rates of growth of the supplies of capital and labour respectively.[4] The reason for this is not explained; but the conclusion is restated emphatically elsewhere (I, 73, 248). It seems that Adam Smith implicitly assumed what would later be called a Malthusian mechanism, namely that, whenever the wage is above 'subsistence', population tends to increase.[5] If, when the wage is above subsistence, e.g. in a rich country, the rate of growth of capital were to fall to zero, the labour supply would be growing faster than the rate of growth of the capital stock. It is easy to see that this might tend to reduce the real wage; but it is not clear why a country in this condition should have a *lower* real wage than a poorer country in which the capital stock was increasing. Actual historical experience provides no evidence to support Adam Smith's hypothesis. It seems probable, from the examples which he quotes, that he was confounding the separate influences of the supplies of land and capital on the demand for labour.

Adam Smith also maintained that a rise in wages necessarily reduces the rate of profit. 'The increase of stock, which raises wages, tends to lower profit' (I, 89), i.e. the *rate* of profit. Later he described the process, as he saw it, in greater detail (I, 335):

> As capitals increase in any country, the profits which can be made by employing them necessarily diminish. It becomes gradually more and more difficult to find within the country a profitable method of employing any new capital . . . The demand for productive labour, by the increase of the funds

---

[4] 'It is not the actual greatness of national wealth, but its continual increase, which occasions a rise in the wages of labour. It is not, accordingly, in the richest countries, but in the most thriving, or in those which are growing rich the fastest, that the wages of labour are highest.' (I, 71). As Cannan remarked, these two sentences are not mutually consistent, and the words 'a rise in the' in the first sentence should probably be replaced by the word 'high'.

[5] If 'subsistence' is defined as the wage at which population ceases to grow, this becomes a tautology. The difficulty with this whole approach is to find a way out of such circular reasoning.

which are destined for maintaining it, grows every day greater and greater. Labourers easily find employment, but the owners of capital find it difficult to get labourers to employ. Their competition raises the wages of labour, and sinks the profits of stock.

This conclusion would be valid only in the absence of technical progress and the effects of increasing economies of scale. Adam Smith emphasized the importance of these latter factors in another part of his book, but at this point he forgot about them.

The notion that a rise in the real wage must inevitably reduce the rate of profit was taken over by Ricardo, who made it a foundation stone of his theory; and it was transmitted through this channel to Marx. All three were agreed that there is a tendency for the rate of profit to fall, although Marx went further when he assumed that the rate of profit will fall even when the real wage is constant. Neoclassical theory also predicts that, in the absence of technical progress, an increase in the capital-labour ratio will raise the wage and reduce the rate of profit. But, since no theory has yet demonstrated a method of separating technical progress from a change in the capital–labour ratio, even conceptually, the validity of this theorem has not been established.

Although Adam Smith failed to provide a clear model of macroeconomic income distribution, this is hardly a cause for complaint. He opened up so many fertile new avenues of economic analysis, and offered so many suggestive empirical observations, that his place in the history of economic thought is unique. A careful study of *The Wealth of Nations* shows that it contains all the ingredients of Ricardo's later theory of income distribution, even if not so carefully specified and integrated as in Ricardo. It was not Adam Smith's method to construct neat theoretical models, which pretend to give simple answers to complex questions. Because of his unwillingness to make the extreme abstractions required for such models his work is still a rich source of detailed perceptions and insights.

The importance of Adam Smith's contribution to economic theory lies mainly in his emphasis on two great ideas: the enormous possibilities for increasing productivity through division of labour (i.e. through economies of scale), and the beneficial effects of free competition. Ricardo accepted the latter idea, and developed it further, especially in its application to international trade. But the significance of the first idea seems to have escaped him. Perhaps because of the prolonged dominance of Ricardian theory, the importance of economies of scale was obscured until Marshall brought them back into prominence (although Marx had relied on economies of scale in predicting a trend towards the 'centralization' of industry). Subsequent refinements of neoclassical theory, together with its increasing use of the static method, led economists to believe that competition and unutilized economies of scale are incompatible assumptions; and they decided to drop the latter. Despite the efforts of a few modern economists—notably Kaldor—to revive the role of economies of scale, this part of Adam Smith's message is still largely neglected. It plays a crucial role, however, in the model of income distribution which I shall develop in Chapter 9.

## Ricardo

The first analytical model of income distribution in a capitalist economy was created by the genius of Ricardo. Ricardo claimed on more than one occasion that income distribution is 'the principal problem' in economics.[6] But this claim should not be taken too seriously. Ricardo was essentially a problem-solver, not an academic system-builder. When he came to study the problem of the Corn Laws, he found that it led him into an analysis of their effects on the incomes of landowners and capitalists; and in this manner he was pushed into constructing a model of macroeconomic income distribution. The Ricardian model gave striking results, and it was found to have applications to taxation as well as to trade policy. It was not surprising, therefore, that Ricardo came to regard income distribution as the key theoretical problem of economics. But no other economist, except perhaps Marx, has agreed with that judgement.

Ricardo followed Adam Smith in dividing the total product

---

[6] See his preface to the *Principles* (full title, *On the Principles of Political Economy and Taxation*), reprinted in Vol. I of the Sraffa edition of Ricardo's works. See also the much-quoted letter to Malthus of October 1820 in Vol. VIII (pp. 278–9) of the same edition. (Subsequent references to Ricardo will be made to the appropriate volume and page of the Sraffa edition.)

of industry among three 'classes': landlords, capitalists, and workers. Implicitly, he assumed that no member of a class receives income from more than one source. Hence the problem was to account for factor shares: rent, profits, and wages.

The first, and in some ways the clearest, account of Ricardo's theory can be found in a pamphlet published in 1815, *An Essay on the Influence of a low Price of Corn on the Profits of Stock.*[7] The model which he expounded in the *Principles*, two years later, was essentially an elaboration of the model in the *Essay*, but with some important changes in assumptions. The *Essay* model has been summarized in modern language, and with the help of modern diagrams, in several places, notably by Kaldor (1955) and Blaug (1968); and I shall follow a similar method. When we have examined the 'corn' model of the *Essay*, we shall proceed to consider the 'value' model of the *Principles*.

### Ricardo's corn model

Let us, then, suppose that a closed economy consists of two sectors: a farm sector, producing a single product called 'corn'; and a non-farm sector producing 'manufactures'. Production of corn requires capital, labour, and land, while manufactures require only capital and labour. Labour is a homogeneous input in both sectors. Since land is in fixed supply, the output of corn is subject to the law of diminishing returns as the variable factors—capital and labour—are increased. In manufactures, on the other hand, there are constant returns to combined units of capital and labour. Ricardo implicitly assumed that, for technical reasons, the proportion of capital to labour is constant in each sector. Although it is not precisely clear what this assumption means, especially if the real wage—a major component of capital advanced—is allowed to vary, the crucial point is that each additional worker is assumed to be endowed with the same amount of capital equipment. Then the marginal product per worker in manufactures is constant over all ranges

---

[7] The *Essay on Profits*, as Sraffa has proposed to call it, is reprinted in Vol. IV of the Sraffa edition. The title of the *Essay* gives an accurate description of its contents, especially if we include an additional section which reads 'shewing the inexpediency of restrictions on importation'. The *Essay* was written as a contribution to the debate then in progress in Parliament on the question of restricting imports of corn.

of output, while the marginal product per worker in agriculture changes only as a consequence of changes in the amount of land per worker.

Although Ricardo did not recognize the fact, the *Essay* model requires two further important assumptions. The first is that workers' consumption consists entirely of corn; the second, that farmers produce all their farm buildings and equipment with their own labour force. With these two assumptions, both wages and farm capital may be said to 'consist' of corn.[8]

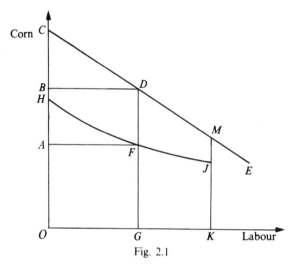

Fig. 2.1

The usual diagram to illustrate Ricardo's corn model is given in Fig. 2.1. The diagram refers only to the farm sector of the economy. Output of corn is measured on the vertical axis and inputs of labour (with complementary inputs of capital) on the horizontal axis. With a fixed supply of farm land, there are diminishing returns to labour-and-capital in the production of corn. Hence, for a given state of agricultural technique, the marginal product of labour-and-capital can be represented by a downward-sloping line, such as *CE*. At any point on the line,

[8] In the *Essay* (IV, 10) Ricardo included buildings and machinery in farm capital, without explicitly assuming that these items were made on the farm. In the *Principles* (e.g. I, 97, 103, 118, 224, 306, 406) he freely admitted that part of workers' consumption consists of non-farm products. He does not appear, however, to have recognized the significance of these facts for his *Essay* model.

such as $D$, the area under the line from $C$ to $D$, i.e. the area $OCDG$, measures the total output of corn. At this level of output, which corresponds to a volume of employment $OG$, the marginal product of labour-and-capital is $GD$.

Ricardo assumed that there is already a clear division of property rights between landowners, farmers, and workers. Landowners own the 'original and indestructible powers of the soil'; farmers organize production as capitalist employers; while workers hire themselves to farmers for a wage. Each class is in a state of perfect competition, both within the class and between classes. Hence, in full equilibrium, no piece of land receives a rent less than the maximum which will be paid by a willing farmer, and both wages and profit rates are uniform across all farms. In these circumstances, no farmer can retain more corn per worker than the amount produced at the margin, namely $GD$; and the entire surplus of output over this amount, given by the area $BCD$, will be paid as rent to landowners. Thus the first step in dividing total farm output between the factors of production is to separate out rent.[9] The remainder, represented by the area $OBDG$, is available to pay wages and profits.

The next step is to divide the corn available for paying wages and profits between these two types of income. If it is assumed that the corn wage per worker is given exogenously, e.g. by $OA$, the division follows immediately into $OAFG$ of wages and $ABDF$ of profits. Moreover, if the same wage is maintained while the volume of farm employment increases, the amount of profit per worker $(FD)$ and the ratio of profits to wages $(FD/FG)$ will steadily decline. And if corn capital per worker is also constant, as Ricardo assumed, the rate of profit will decline in the same proportion as profit per worker. This is the theoretical basis for Ricardo's conviction (e.g. I, 120) that, in a closed economy with fixed natural resources and a constant level of technique, the rate of profit must inevitably fall as the economy expands, until it reaches a stationary state.

But the validity of this argument depends crucially on the assumption that the level of the corn wage is independent of the marginal product of farm labour. Ricardo often wrote as if he believed this to be so; yet it is an assumption which is inconsis-

---

[9] As Ricardo made clear, this part of his analysis is based on the work of Malthus. See, e.g., IV, 9.

tent with an essential part of his own theory. The difficulty arises because Ricardo had two separate theories of wage determination. On the one hand, he held a theory of the *long-run equilibrium* wage, which he assumed to be a 'subsistence' wage. The subsistence wage is defined as a wage which will maintain the population (and hence eventually the labour supply) constant.[10] Since long-run equilibrium meant to Ricardo the stationary state, it follows that the long-run equilibrium wage is the subsistence wage. But what will be the wage when the economy is not in a stationary state? This brings us to Ricardo's second theory of wage determination—his theory of *short-run equilibrium*.

Ricardo admitted, following Adam Smith, that in the short term wages are determined by supply and demand. To be more precise, he argued (I, 95, 98) that, when the rate of growth of capital exceeds the rate of growth of the labour supply, wages will rise above their long-run 'natural price'. This is, in fact, an essential link in his model. For if the wage were always held at the subsistence level there would never be any increase in population, and none of the other consequences would follow. It is, therefore, not correct to argue, as some interpreters of Ricardo have done, that he assumed that the labour supply is infinitely elastic at the subsistence wage, if that statement is meant to imply that the wage cannot rise above subsistence in any circumstances. Ricardo himself did not make such an assumption. Indeed, he admitted (I, 98) that over long periods of time the wage might be above subsistence, and even increasing (although the latter conclusion does not follow from his model).

Consider, for example, the situation in a 'new' country, where employment in the farm sector is small in relation to the total supply of land but technique is relatively advanced. The marginal product of labour will be high and, if at the same time the wage were held down to the subsistence level, profit per worker and the profit rate in farming would be high. Ricardo maintained in the *Essay*, for reasons which I shall discuss later,

[10] The subsistence wage is not determined by purely biological factors but has a 'customary' element. Ricardo recognized (I, 96–7) that the customary minimum wage varies between countries and over time. But, since he failed to provide a theory to account for such variations, his model of income distribution in long-run equilibrium is indeterminate.

that the profit rate in agriculture determines the profit rate throughout the economy. So in these circumstances the profit rate would be high everywhere, there would be large savings out of profits and a rapid growth of the supply of capital. But with wages at subsistence the population (and hence eventually the labour supply) would be constant. The consequence must be, according to Ricardo's short-run theory, that the wage would rise.[11]

Thus Ricardo's short-run theory requires that the real wage should vary in the same direction as the marginal product of labour. This suggests that the path of the real wage may be represented by a downward-sloping line, such as $HJ$ in Fig. 2.1. When population pressure is low, the wage is substantially above subsistence, and this encourages the population to grow. But in this early phase profit per worker is also high, the rate of growth of capital is rapid, and the growing population does not immediately depress the wage to subsistence. Ideally, we may imagine that the wage will follow a smooth path, which will satisfy both the short-run equilibrium requirements, i.e. a wage which balances current demand and supply for labour (which depend in turn on the relative supplies of labour and capital), and the long-run equilibrium requirements, which are that the growth rates of capital and labour should be such as to keep the future wage moving along the same path. When the marginal product has fallen to $MK$, it will be sufficient to pay only a subsistence wage, $JK$, and a profit per worker, $MJ$, which is so small that it will not induce any further saving (see I, 122). Then both labour and capital will stop growing and the economy will be in a stationary state.

Once it is admitted that the real wage is positively related to the marginal product of labour, the basis for Ricardo's prediction of a falling rate of profit becomes insecure. It is true that

[11] In a newly settled country with free access to land at a competitive rent it would not be possible for farmers to hold the wage down by an open or tacit agreement among themselves. Workers would compare their wage with the incomes which they could obtain as self-employed farmers and, if the wage were held down artificially, many workers would move out of employment into self-employment. Cf. Smith (I, 85): 'In years of plenty, servants frequently leave their masters and trust their subsistence to what they can make by their own industry'. Similarly (in II, 67–8) Adam Smith argues that high wages in the North American colonies are due to the plentiful supply of good land.

profit per worker would probably be higher in the early stages of economic development than in the later stages; but the wage component of capital per worker would also be higher. Whether the profit rate would fall would depend on the exact relation between the marginal product and the wage in the different stages of development, as well as on the relative importance of fixed capital in comparison with circulating (wage) capital. All of this, moreover, is predicated on the assumption of unchanging technique. If technique is improving, the line $CE$ will be shifting to the right, and the rate of profit may rise even while farm output and employment are increasing.

To complete Ricardo's 'corn' model we must return to the question of the interrelations between the two sectors of the economy. As already mentioned, Ricardo expressed the firm conviction in the *Essay* (II, 12) that the rate of profit in agriculture determines the rate of profit in the rest of the economy.[12] The obverse of this rule was also that no changes in productivity or profit outside agriculture could affect the rate of profit in agriculture (see IV, 23–4). But how did Ricardo justify this view? The first element in his argument was that the output of corn depends solely on the size of the population (presumably also, although he did not say so, on the level of the corn wage). Hence, no improvement in profits outside agriculture can result in a withdrawal of capital and labour from agriculture. This argument prevents any influence on farm profit from the rate of profit outside. It remains to be shown, however, that (1) the rate of profit in agriculture can be established independently of conditions outside agriculture, and (2) that the agricultural rate is inevitably extended over the rest of the economy. The first of these conditions will be satisfied if both the agricultural wage and capital per worker in agriculture are fixed in terms of corn.[13] Then profit per worker, also measured

---

[12] See also his letter to Trower of March 1814 (VI, 103–4) where he wrote: 'in short it is the profits of the farmer which regulate the profits of all other trades,—and as the profits of the farmer must necessarily decrease with every augmentation of Capital employed on the land, provided no improvements be at the same time made in husbandry, all other profits must diminish and therefore the rate of profit must fall'.

[13] As we pointed out earlier, these two assumptions are implicit in Ricardo's *Essay* model.

in corn, can be divided by capital per worker to obtain a pure number, which is independent of relative prices in the rest of the economy. But if these two assumptions are not correct—as Ricardo would have been obliged to admit—changes in relative prices outside agriculture could affect the rate of profit in agriculture. For example, if the corn-price of manufactures were to fall, both the corn wage and the corn-value of farm capital would tend to fall, and the rate of profit in agriculture would tend to rise.

Ricardo believed that the second condition could be satisfied by an appeal to the laws of competition. In a perfectly competitive market, he assumed, the rate of profit will be equalized in all industries. Hence it is not possible to have a different rate of profit in agriculture. But here Ricardo was forgetting his earlier assumption that the output of corn is determined, not by the forces of market competition, but by the physical food requirements of the population. One cannot follow both lines of argument simultaneously. If corn output is fixed by purely technical considerations, the resources used by agriculture are not determined by the competitive market, and there is no reason why the rate of profit in agriculture should not be different from the rate of profit in other industries.

### Ricardo's value model

Between writing the *Essay* and writing the *Principles* (a period of less than two years) Ricardo must have recognized the weakness in his previous line of argument. In particular, he came to realize more clearly that wages do not consist only of corn, and hence perhaps that productivity in the non-farm sector may affect the real-wage equivalent of a given corn wage.[14] Nevertheless, he still firmly believed that 'in all countries, and in all times, profits [i.e. the rate of profit] depend on the quantity of labour requisite to provide necessaries for the labourers, on that land or with that capital which yields no rent' (I, 126).

It does not require any elaborate analytical apparatus to see that, if one component of the wage is a fixed amount of a

---

[14] But see below for a reaffirmation of the view that changes in productivity outside agriculture cannot affect the profit rate.

product of which the supply depends on a fixed supply of natural resources, and if population increases while technique is constant, a steadily increasing proportion of the total labour force will need to be employed in producing the fixed component. But the implication of these assumptions for changes in the rate of profit on capital are not so obvious. Since Ricardo was, for some unstated reason, especially interested in the determination of the *rate* of profit, and since in the *Principles* he had abandoned the strict assumptions of the corn model used in the *Essay*, he was obliged to find a new method of accounting for the general rate of profit. The method which he chose was to postulate a law of value, his famous labour theory of value.

Discussions of the labour theory of value are sometimes confused by failure to distinguish clearly between the views of Adam Smith, Ricardo, and Marx. Adam Smith believed that labour is an appropriate *numéraire* for measuring the values of other things. On this 'labour commanded' assumption, the value of anything is best measured by its market equivalent in terms of wage-units. For example, if $Y$ is the money value of the national product and $w$ is the (uniform) money wage, the labour value of the national product is $Y/w$. For Ricardo, on the other hand, the value of a reproducible commodity is determined by its labour cost (or 'labour embodied'). Ricardo often wrote as if the relevant labour cost were *average* labour cost per unit; but he also made it abundantly clear that in the case of primary products the relevant cost is *marginal* labour cost. Having 'got rid of rent', he was inclined to think of marginal labour cost in primary industries—especially in 'corn'—as if it were a fixed amount, independent of demand. But this, of course, is inconsistent with his model. In the special case where all industries in an economy operated under conditions of constant cost, i.e. if there were no primary industries using scarce natural resources, Ricardo's theory implies that the value of the national product would be measured by the size of the total labour force, $L$. Since $Y/w = LY/(wL) = L/S_w$, where $S_w$ is the share of the money wage bill in the money value of the national product, it can be seen that Ricardo's 'average' labour theory yields a value of the national product $S_w$ times the value estimated by Smith's method. As both Smith and Ricardo recognized, the two measures are equal only when $S_w = 1$, i.e.

when there is no surplus over wages. This was supposed by Smith (I, 49) to have been the situation in an 'early and crude state of society which precedes both the accumulation of stock and the appropriation of land'.[15]

We shall consider Marx's theory of value more closely in the next chapter. For the moment it will suffice to say that in Volume I of *Capital* he gave the general impression that he had adopted the Ricardian theory (in its 'average' form). In Volume III, however, published 27 years later, it became clear that this was a misinterpretation of his position. He had never in fact intended to explain relative prices by relative labour costs.

The major advantage which Ricardo derived from the labour theory of value was that it enabled him to substantiate his *Essay* theorem, without relying upon the extreme assumptions required for the 'corn' model. He now relaxed the assumption that all wages consist of corn but maintained the (realistic) assumption that the proportion of food expenditure in the wage is high.

The basic assumption of the Ricardian labour theory is that $p_{ij} = \lambda'_i/\lambda'_j$, where $p_{ij}$ is the price of good $i$ in terms of good $j$ and $\lambda'_i, \lambda'_j$, are the marginal labour costs per unit of $i$ and $j$ respectively. In the case of non-farm goods Ricardo assumed that marginal labour cost is constant, so that, if $j$ is a non-farm good, $\lambda'_j = \lambda_j$, where $\lambda_j$ is the average labour cost per unit of $j$. Now suppose that there are only two goods: good $i$ which is corn and good $j$ which is cloth, and that $\lambda_j$ is constant.[16] If the output of corn increases, with land and technique constant, $\lambda'_i$ will rise, and hence also $p_{ij}$. But this rise in the price of corn in terms of cloth means that, if the producers of cloth are to continue to pay their workers a fixed real wage (enough to buy fixed amounts of corn and cloth), they must set aside for this purpose a larger proportion of their output of cloth. Hence their profit margin per worker in terms of cloth (and also, even more, in terms of corn) is reduced; and, unless there is a corresponding fall in

[15] This state of society, which is entirely mythical, is the result of imagining a market economy with division of labour but without any private property or specialized skills. The entire construction is self-contradictory. In the absence of private property or special skills there would be no advantages in exchange.

[16] The implicit assumption is that corn and cloth are completely separate industries, which do not purchase any inputs from one another. Then their output values depend entirely on their direct labour inputs.

their capital per worker (also in cloth), their rate of profit will fall.

Even in the *Principles* Ricardo seems to have overlooked the influence of a fall in the corn-price of manufactures on the rate of profit in agriculture. If workers spend part of their wages on manufactures and the corn-price of manufactures falls, it is possible to maintain the same real wage with a lower corn wage. And, if the marginal product of labour in agriculture is constant, the effect of a fall in the price of manufactures will be to raise the profit margin in agriculture, and hence the rate of profit in that industry.[17]

Although Ricardo seems to have been satisfied with his use of the labour theory of value as a method of proving his basic theorem, he soon discovered that the theory is inconsistent with some empirical observations. The difficulty which he encountered, even in the first chapter of the *Principles*, is that when the profit rate falls in one industry (say, agriculture) there is no guarantee, if prices conform to the theory, that profit rates will move in the same manner in all industries; or alternatively that, if profit rates move together, prices will obey the labour theory of value. He discovered, in brief, that the exact outcome depends on the distribution of capital–labour ratios across industries. For example, if wages rise uniformly in all industries, but prices are unchanged, the effect on the profit rate of a capital-intensive industry (in which wages are a small share of value added) will be smaller than the effect on the profit rate of a labour-intensive industry. If, on the other hand, profit rates are brought into equality again across all industries, the prices of capital-intensive industries will need to fall in relation to the prices of labour-intensive industries.

This result worried Ricardo, and at one point (in 1820) he was tempted to abandon the labour theory of value altogether.[18] But in the third edition of the *Principles*, published in the following year, Ricardo steadfastly adhered to the labour theory, although admitting that it required some modification

---

[17] This conclusion is strongly contradicted by some remarks in (I, 133). For example: 'The rate of profits is never increased by a better distribution of labour, by the invention of machinery, by the establishment of roads and canals, or by any means of abridging labour either in the manufacture or in the conveyance of goods'.

[18] See his letter to McCulloch of 13 June 1820, in (VIII, 194).

when applied to the effects of a change in wages. Strangely enough, he never seems to have realized that, even when wages are unchanged, relative prices will not be proportional to relative labour costs unless capital-intensities are equal. The equal capital-intensity assumption, which is necessary to avoid differential effects on prices of a rise in wages, is also a prerequisite condition for the validity of the labour theory of value as a whole.[19]

*An alternative approach*

If Ricardo had had a knowledge of modern techniques of analysis, he could have established all the valid parts of his conclusions without employing the labour theory of value. For example, the effects of diminishing returns in one industry when population increases can be illustrated by a diagram such as Fig. 2.2. The line $AB$ is a transformation curve between corn and manufactures in situation 1, when there is a fixed total labour supply, $L_1$, and a constant amount of capital equipment per worker. In drawing the transformation curve it is assumed that corn production uses land but manufacturing does not. Then, if the total supply of land is fixed, $AB$ is concave to the origin. $OL$ is the vector of wage-goods, i.e. it shows the combination of corn and manufactures which makes up the (fixed) real wage. The total wage bill for $L_1$ workers is represented by the point $E$. For simplicity it may be assumed that landlords and capitalists consume no corn but only manufactures. Then the surplus of manufactures available to these classes (and hence their real income) in situation 1 is measured by the distance $EG$.

In situation 2 there are twice as many workers and twice as much equipment, but the supply of land is unchanged. Consequently, the transformation curve in situation 2, $CD$, intersects

[19] The 'average' labour theory is, as I have said, that $p_{ij} = \lambda_i/\lambda_j$. But, in equilibrium, the money price of $i$ is $p_i = \dfrac{1}{Q_i}(wL_i + rK_i)$ where $Q_i$ is the quantity of $i$, $w$ is the money wage, $r$ is the rate of profit, $L_i$ is the amount of labour used in industry $i$, and $K_i$ is the money value of capital in industry $i$. This can be written as $p_i = \lambda_i (w + rk_i)$ where $k_i = K_i/L_i$. Then $p_{ij} = \dfrac{\lambda_i (w + rk_i)}{\lambda_j (w + rk_j)}$ which is equal to $\lambda_i/\lambda_j$ only if $k_i = k_j$.

the manufactures axis at a point where $OD = 2\,(OB)$, while it intersects the corn axis at a point where $OC < 2\,(OA)$. (If all labour and capital were used to produce manufactures in both situations 1 and 2, the output in 2 would be twice as great as in 1; while in the case of corn the increase is smaller because of diminishing returns on the fixed supply of land.) The new wage bill is represented by point $F$, with $OF = 2\,(OE)$, and the new surplus of manufactures is $FH$.

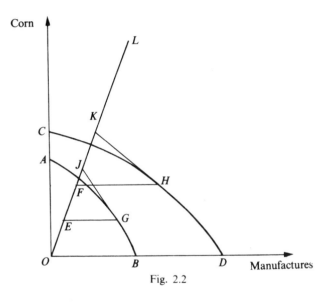

Fig. 2.2

According to the labour theory of value income shares should be measured by their labour costs. Since the labour cost per unit of manufactures is assumed constant, the labour cost of each income share can be measured on our diagram by its cost in terms of manufactures. The manufactures cost of total output is the maximum amount of manufactures which could be produced if all labour were employed in manufactures. This is measured by $OB$ and $OD$ in situations 1 and 2 respectively. The corresponding manufactures cost of non-wage incomes (indeed their physical composition) is given by $EG$ and $FH$. The ratio $FH/OD$ is likely in all normal cases to be less than the ratio $EG/OB$, since the slope of the straight line connecting points $H$

and $D$ is likely to be less than the slope of the straight line connecting points $G$ and $B$.

But the measurement of income shares by their labour costs is arbitrary, and may give different results from the more usual method of measurement in terms of current prices. Shares in current prices can be estimated in the diagram as follows. If we assume perfect competition, as Ricardo did, the manufactures–corn price-ratio in situation 1 is equal to the slope of the tangent at point $G$, and at point $H$ in situation 2. If these tangents are projected to cut $OL$, the points of intersection measure by their distance from the origin the corresponding values of total output in terms of wage-goods at current prices. Then the ratio of wages to total output in current prices is given by $OE/OJ$ in 1 and $OF/OK$ in 2. In general, $OK < 2\ (OJ)$ and the wage share in current prices will rise as we move from 1 to 2.

While it can be demonstrated in this manner that, on Ricardo's assumptions, the effect of an increase in population will normally be to raise the wage share, it is not possible without additional information to show that the rate of profit will fall. For example, in Fig. 2.2, as we have seen, there is a relative shift of labour away from manufactures into corn production. If the capital–labour ratio in manufactures is higher than in corn, this will result in a fall in the average capital–labour ratio in the whole economy. In some circumstances this fall in the capital–labour ratio might be sufficient to offset the decline in the share of non-wage incomes and *raise* the ratio of surplus (profit and rent) to capital. The effect on the rate of profit itself would then depend on the way in which the division between rent and profit was affected.

### Some additional observations

Ricardo used his theory for the very practical purpose of demonstrating that it would be advantageous to investors, and temporarily also to workers, if restrictions on imports of corn were eliminated. His model showed that the British population could grow without depressing the rate of profit, if the additional corn supplies were obtained from overseas in exchange for manufactures rather than by increased domestic production of corn. Britain could become 'the workshop of the world'. The underlying assumption, which was realistic at the time, was that diminishing returns in foreign agriculture were of small importance. In the modern world, however, where the phenomenon of diminishing returns on relatively fixed natural resources has become a general problem, the Ricardian model may have a renewed relevance. Applied on a world scale, the Ricardian model suggests that, in the absence of (sufficient) technical progress, the shares of rent and wages will rise and share of profits will fall. In a rough sense the effects of the oil shortage may perhaps be interpreted in this way.

In the chapter 'On Machinery', which Ricardo added to the third edition of the *Principles*, he introduced a completely new idea, namely, the possibility of substitution between capital and labour. Up to this point capital and labour had been strictly complementary; but he now raised the question whether the introduction of machinery could lead to unemployment of labour. His argument, as usual, was based on a particular arithmetical example (I, 388–90).

A capitalist is supposed to be simultaneously a farmer and a manufacturer of necessaries, i.e. to be a producer of wage-goods, implicitly in the right proportions. Normally he employs, let us say, 100 men on this work and they produce enough food and necessaries for their own subsistence plus a surplus for the capitalist. In a particular year, unexpectedly, the capitalist transfers half his work-force on to making machinery. During that year, the workers live on the wage-goods produced in the previous year, which the capitalist had stored up for this purpose. But with only half the work-force now engaged in producing wage-goods they will produce only half as much output (here Ricardo forgets about the law of diminishing returns). Consequently, the stock of wage-goods available to pay wages in the following year will be insufficient to employ 100 workers (especially after deducting, as Ricardo assumes, a fixed amount of surplus for the capitalist). Hence a decision to invest in additional machinery leads to unemployment.

This example is totally unconvincing; indeed, one may say that it is unworthy of Ricardo's normal analytical expertise. As he himself admitted later in the same chapter, the model would have no relevance if the capitalist saved up in advance of investing, or if he used current savings, either of his own or borrowed from others.[20] Nevertheless, Ricardo was touching upon a real problem. Investments in machinery, or indeed any improvement in technique, reduce labour requirements for a given level of output. Within a single firm or industry, the reduction in labour requirements may be greater than the simultaneous increase in output (whether associated with the new investment or arising independently). In that case, there will be at least a temporary displacement of labour from that firm or industry. The normal assumption of both classical and neoclassical economics is that sooner or later unemployed labour will be reabsorbed through a general expansion of activity.[21] The historical record of capitalist development shows that this prediction has in fact been fulfilled; but only, in some cases, after fairly long periods of transitional unemployment or severely reduced incomes for the displaced workers. The problem cannot, however, be analysed fruitfully by purely *a priori* methods, let alone by taking arbitrary examples. It requires a much deeper study of the factors which influence the balance of intensive as against extensive investments, especially the role of technical change. An important additional consideration is differences in the rates of growth of firms of different sizes, a matter which is central to the model of growth and distribution which will be proposed in Chapter 9 below.

*Conclusion*

A general assessment of Ricardo's contribution to the theory of income distribution must inevitably be rather mixed. While he showed a brilliant capacity to construct a meaningful economic model from a few simple—and empirically plausible—assumptions, the counterpart effect was to push economics into static

---

[20] 'The statements which I have made will not, I hope, lead to the inference that machinery should not be encouraged. To elucidate the principle, I have been supposing that improved machinery is *suddenly* discovered, and extensively used; but the truth is, that these discoveries are gradual, and rather operate in determining the employment of the capital which is saved and accumulated, than in diverting capital from its actual employment.' (I, 395).

[21] Marx, on the other hand, assumed that increasing capital-intensity inevitably swells the ranks of the 'industrial reserve army', hence keeping wages down to subsistence. I shall consider the role of this element in Marx's model of distribution in the next chapter.

methods of analysis, and especially towards sterile comparisons of stationary states. Ricardo's method of high abstraction tended to cut economics off from its real foundations in, to use Marshall's phrase, 'the ordinary business of life'. Landlords, capitalists, and workers appear as mere puppets, controlled by outside forces. There is virtually no room for anyone to show enterprise, initiative, or a desire to control his own destiny. The effect is particularly deplorable in the case of the capitalists, who are turned into automata, mechanically reinvesting their profits and collecting a surplus which owes nothing to enterprise or organization.[22] In effect, Ricardo's theory is a theory of two forms of rent: a rent of land which is determined at the margin, and a rent of capital which is a final residual. The capitalists' willingness to save and invest plays a role only at one point: when it suddenly ceases. Meantime, all investments automatically earn the same rate of profit, irrespective of any efforts or initiative on the side of the investors.

The consequence of Ricardo's methods was that he became the progenitor of two totally opposed streams in economics: the economics of Marx and static neoclassical theory. In neither theory does capital have any role to play except to exist. Marx drove Ricardo's assumptions to their logical conclusion in one direction: profits are simply a surplus, no different from rent; indeed the two can conveniently be treated under one heading. Neoclassical theory tried to provide some support for the role of the capitalist by appealing to the sacrifices involved in saving. But this support was feeble, and it missed the main point. The only social justification for profits is that they reward enterprise and organization which would not otherwise be forthcoming. But such qualities cannot be incorporated into a static framework.

[22] This stockbroker's view of capitalism has unfortunately had an excessive influence in its country of origin.

# 3

# MARX

Marx was not primarily interested in constructing a theory to explain the distribution of income. His purpose in writing *Capital* was 'to lay bare the economic law of motion of modern society', i.e. of capitalism (I, xix).[1] He planned to reveal its internal contradictions and the reasons for its inevitable collapse. Marx expressed hatred of capitalist exploiters and indignation at the poverty and bad working conditions of the proletariat. But he did not believe in bourgeois notions of justice and equality. He was convinced that the dialectical development of history required the overthrow of capitalism and the establishment of socialism, and his aim was to help history along its inevitable course by shortening and lessening the 'birth-pangs' of the new regime.

Nevertheless, the subject of income distribution is at the centre of Marx's theory. The society whose laws of motion Marx was attempting to describe was that of developed industrial capitalism. In such a society, Marx assumed, virtually the whole population is divided into two groups: the proletariat, workers without property; and the capitalists, employers and exploiters of the proletariat. Subsidiary classes such as land-owners, artisans, and peasants are allowed a shadowy existence; but they are of no importance in the general scene.[2]

## Marx's theory of value

Marx's first object was to explain the origin of 'surplus value': the source of rent, interest, and profit. Despite his large intellectual debt to Ricardo, he did not follow Ricardo's method of first separating out rent and then dividing the remainder between wages and profits. Instead, Marx took over Ricardo's labour

[1] Subsequent references to Marx's *Capital* will be in this form, giving only the relevant volume and page.

[2] There is a curious contrast between the proletariat–capitalist dichotomy in Marx's economic writings and the rich variety of classes which appears in his political writings.

theory of value and applied it, in its 'average' form, to all commodities, including primary products. The idea that exchange values are determined at the margin was rejected.[3]

In Chapter 1 of the first volume of *Capital* Marx addressed himself directly to the problem of how exchange values (i.e. relative prices) are determined. His answer, which I shall consider in more detail below, was the same as that given by Ricardo in the case of manufactures, namely that $p_{ij} = \lambda_i/\lambda_j$, where $p_{ij}$ is the exchange value of commodity $i$ in terms of commodity $j$ and $\lambda_i$, $\lambda_j$ are the average labour costs of producing $i$ and $j$ respectively. But Marx introduced at this point a new concept, namely 'value'. The value of a commodity is *defined* as its labour cost (strictly, as we shall see, its socially necessary labour cost in terms of unskilled-labour-equivalent units). Thus $v_i \equiv \lambda_i$ and $v_j \equiv \lambda_j$, where $v_i$, $v_j$ are the values of goods $i$ and $j$ respectively. It might seem, therefore, that Marx's theory was that $p_{ij} = v_i/v_j$. Indeed, this was how most people interpreted his theory for the next twenty-seven years.[4]

When Volume III of *Capital* was published in 1894, it became clear that Marx did not in fact subscribe to the Ricardian theory that exchange values are determined by relative

[3] The rejection is for the most part implicit, since marginal concepts and the law of diminishing returns are simply not mentioned, at least in Volume I of *Capital*, which was the only volume to be published in Marx's lifetime. In Volume III, published posthumously by Engels, there are many new ideas, e.g. about the relation between labour-values and prices. There is also an explicit rejection of the marginal approach to the determination of relative prices (III, 210–11).

[4] Marx himself was largely responsible for this misinterpretation of his intentions, as a consequence of his almost total failure to draw a clear distinction between values and prices in Volume I of *Capital*. There can, indeed, be some doubt whether Marx was ready to make such a distinction at that time. For example, in his report to the meetings of the General Council of the First International in June 1865, two years before the publication of Volume I of *Capital* (reprinted under the title of *Wages, Price and Profit* in the *Selected Works* of Marx and Engels) there occurs the following passage (p. 202): 'A commodity has a *value*, because it is a *crystallisation of social labour*. the *greatness* of its value, of its *relative* value, depends on the greater or less amount of that social substance contained in it; that is to say, on the relative mass of labour necessary for its production. The *relative values of commodities* are, therefore, determined by the *respective quantities or amounts of labour, worked up, realised, fixed in them. The correlative* quantities of commodities which can be produced in the *same time of labour are equal.* Or the value of one commodity is to the value of another commodity as the quantity of labour fixed in the one is to the quantity of labour fixed in the other' (italics in original text).

labour costs. In that volume exchange values were made to depend on relative 'prices of production'. The reformulation means that $p_{ij} \equiv p_i/p_j$ where $p_i$, $p_j$ are the prices of production (measured in terms of money) of $i$ and $j$. Hence the problem of explaining exchange values was now presented as a problem of accounting for relative prices of production or, in modern terms, long-run average costs. What remained, then, of the theory of value? Although exchange values were no longer directly determined by the ratios of labour-values, Marx maintained that prices of production could not be explained without first measuring *aggregate* labour values of output, wages, and capital. Only with this prior information could one deduce the average rate of profit which was needed, together with the money wage, in order to derive prices of production.

Although Marx did not use his theory of value directly to explain relative prices of goods, he did use it to explain the level of money wages, i.e. the price of labour (or, in his terminology, labour-power). It is necessary, therefore, to consider how Marx justified his labour theory of exchange values in Chapter 1 of Volume I of *Capital*.

Ricardo had made no serious attempt to 'justify' his labour theory of value. After citing a number of passages from Adam Smith about labour being the real or 'first' price of everything he added (I, 13): 'That this is really the foundation of the exchangeable value of all things, excepting those which cannot be increased by human industry, is a doctrine of the utmost importance in political economy; for from no source do so many errors, and so much difference of opinion in that science proceed, as from the vague ideas which are attached to the word value.' That was all. For Marx, however, the citation of earlier opinions was not a sufficient reason for accepting an assumption. Instead, Marx attempted to derive the labour theory of value by a logical process.

Marx's proof of his theory of value is based on five main axioms. He started by defining the problem as one of accounting for the exchange values of 'commodities'. What is a commodity? 'A commodity is, in the first place, an object outside us, a thing that by its properties satisfies human wants of some sort or another' (1, 1). Although we are not explicitly given any further list of defining characteristics of a commodity, it can be deduced by inference that Marx would have included two additional criteria in such a list: first, that a commodity is a product of labour, and second, that it is produced with a view to exchange.[5] On the basis of these additional criteria, land and other non-produced natural resources are excluded from the class of commodities, and hence from the operation of the law of value; and so are goods and services produced for direct consumption.

Given this definition, Marx now asked the question: why does one commodity exchange in a certain ratio with another? His answer (axiom no. 1) was that this can be explained only by the fact that 'there exists in equal quantities something common to both. The two things must . . . be equal to a third, which in itself is neither the one nor the other. Each of them, so far as it is exchange value, must therefore be reducible to this third' (I, 3–4). The next step in the argument (axiom no. 2) was the assertion that the only property which two commodities have in common is 'that of being products of labour' (I, 4). The relevant concept of labour is 'human labour in the abstract', which was now given the name 'value' (I, 5). 'Therefore, the common substance that manifests itself in the exchange value of commodities, whenever they are exchanged, is their value' (I, 5).

Before proceeding further, Marx made two important clarifications of the meaning of the word 'labour'. The first was a definition of what he meant by 'human labour in the abstract'. His problem was to reduce labour of different skills to a single unit of measurement. The unit which Marx chose was unskilled-labour-equivalents. If skilled labour of type $i$ is equivalent to $k_i$ units of unskilled labour, $h_i$ hours of labour by an $i$-worker count as the equivalent of $k_i h_i$ hours of 'human labour in the abstract'. For the group of unskilled workers, say group $j$, $k_j = 1$. But how do we know the values of the $k$-coefficients? Marx maintained (axiom no. 3) that they are proportional to the wage rates ruling in the market (I, 11). This, as Böhm-Bawerk and others have pointed out, is a major inconsistency in his theory, which is supposed to explain market phenomena by

[5] The first criterion is obvious from Marx's whole discussion. The second is referred to incidentally. For example: 'The mode of production in which the product takes the form of a commodity, or is produced directly for exchange . . .' (I, 54). Again '. . . an article destined to be sold, a commodity' (I, 166).

means of more fundamental non-market relations. In any case, no proof was given that relative values produced by workers of different skills are proportional to their wages.[6]

The second matter requiring clarification arises from the fact that workers of equal skill working in the same industry, or strictly on the same job, often produce different quantities of the same product. Does this mean that the more productive worker produces more value per hour than the less productive? Since Marx assumed perfect competition in product markets, and hence a common price for each product, it was necessary to define labour time in such a way as to exclude differential effects of this sort. Marx's formula for solving this problem (axiom no. 4) was that the relevant labour time is the 'socially necessary' labour time (I, 6). The use of this phrase raises some difficult questions, to which we shall return. In the meantime, it should be noted that, in order to transform actually recorded hours of labour into value-creating equivalent hours it is necessary to make two adjustments: first, the adjustment to unskilled-labour-equivalent hours; and second, the adjustment to socially necessary hours. The Marxian theory of value is, then, that the value of each product is equal to the number of socially necessary unskilled-labour-equivalent hours required for its production.

Up to this point, Marx's model was perhaps not very different in principle from many other economic models which incorporate an author's preferred definitions and assumptions. It is true that Marx's axioms are not exactly self-evident. For example, there is no law of science or logic which says that $A = B$ can be true only if $A$ and $B$ contain equal quantities of some

---

[6] In a later passage (I, 179) Marx slightly expanded his remarks on this question, as follows: 'All labour of a higher or more complicated character than average labour is expenditure of labour-power of a more costly kind, labour-power whose production has cost more time and labour, and which therefore has a higher value, than unskilled or simple labour-power. This power being of a higher value, its consumption is labour of a higher class, labour that creates in equal times proportionally higher values than unskilled labour does.' The first statement—that the cost of skilled labour-power, and hence its long-run equilibrium wage, is higher than the cost of unskilled labour-power—is clearly correct. But Marx offered no proof of the second statement, that relative *values produced by* different labour-powers are proportional to relative *costs of producing* those labour-powers. It is a possible hypothesis. But, since values are unobservable independently of labour costs, the hypothesis cannot be tested empirically.

third thing. Nor is it true that the only common property of commodities is that they are products of labour. The assumption that, as between workers of different skills, the value created per hour varies in proportion to the wage has no obvious justification and leads to results inconsistent with the theory. And the adjustment for 'social necessity' raises major theoretical problems. But the test of the model is, of course, the uses to which it is put.

The principal purpose of Marx's model was to explain aggregate surplus value. Surplus value—in the simplified Marxian economy—is the difference between the value of output and the value of wages. The labour theory of value gives a measure of the aggregate value of output: it is the aggregate level of employment, converted to unskilled-labour-equivalents. Alternatively, it is the aggregate money wage bill divided by the hourly wage of unskilled workers. If $L$ is aggregate hours of employment of unskilled-labour-equivalents, by Marx's third axiom $L = \dfrac{1}{w_0} \sum_i w_i N_i$, where $w_i$ is the hourly wage of the $i^{\text{th}}$ skill, $N_i$ is the number of hours worked by $i$-skill workers, and $w_0$ is the hourly wage of unskilled workers. So $L = W/w_0$, where $W$ is the aggregate money wage bill. Since, as we shall see, Marx assumed that in the economy as a whole actual hours worked are equivalent to socially necessary hours, no further adjustment is needed at that level to obtain the labour-time measure of value produced.

What, in similar measure, is the aggregate value of wages? Marx's answer depended on his fifth axiom, which states that labour-power is a commodity (I, 145). Like other commodities labour-power is exchanged at its value; and its value, as with all commodities, is the labour cost of producing it. The cost of producing labour-power is the cost of subsistence of the worker and his family; and the value of aggregate wages is, therefore, the labour cost of producing the aggregate volume of goods required for the workers' subsistence. If $L(G)$ is the socially necessary labour time (in unskilled-labour-equivalents) to produce the vector, $G$, of goods and services required for workers' subsistence, aggregate surplus value is

$$S = L - L(G)$$

and the economy-wide rate of surplus value is

$$s = S/L(G) = L/L(G) - 1$$

Similarly, the aggregate wage share, in terms of labour-values, is $L(G)/L$.

It is clear that the crucial assumption of this theory of income distribution is axiom no. 5, that labour-power is a commodity. The axiom implies, given the Marxian definition of a commodity, that labour-power is sold at its cost of production. But is labour-power a commodity in the sense of Marx's definition of that word? It is arguable that the worker's own daily labour-power is 'produced' with a view to exchange; but this cannot be said of the production and rearing of children. The question is important, because the supply of each commodity, in Marx's theory, is infinitely elastic at a fixed value. If this is also true of the supply of labour-power, it must mean that any increase in the real wage will induce an increase in population until the wage returns to subsistence level—a conclusion reached previously by a different route by Malthus, Ricardo, and others. Despite Marx's rejection of the Malthus–Ricardo population supply mechanism, his own model of long-run labour supply is effectively the same. And it is subject to precisely the same objection, namely, that it assumes an inflexibility in human behaviour patterns which is out of keeping with historical experience—and with Marx's own views about the determinants of social behaviour. Moreover, if one had to choose between the Malthusian and the Marxian theories of labour supply, there is surely more plausibility in the former. Under primitive conditions, a rise in the real wage is likely to reduce mortality rates, especially the mortality rates of children, and hence eventually increase the labour supply. But this is quite different from producing labour-power as a saleable 'commodity'.

## Marx's alternative theory of wages

In addition to his axiomatic theory of the value of labour-power, Marx offered an alternative theory, which is inherently more interesting. The alternative model is independent of the labour theory of value; it could, in fact, be included in any economic theory. The problem is, as before, to prove that in the long run the real wage cannot rise above subsistence.[7] Marx's alternative answer, which is in effect a renunciation of the axiomatic argument, is that capitalism continuously creates and recreates an 'industrial reserve army' of unemployed. The number of unemployed varies with the state of trade, but there are always enough, even during 'the periods of over-production and paroxysm', to hold the 'pretensions of the employed workers in check' (I, 653). Marx rejected the argument of bourgeois economists that an increase in the supply of capital always increases the demand for labour. 'The demand for labour is not identical with increase of capital, nor supply of labour with increase of the working class. It is not a case of two independent forces working on one another. Les dés sont pipés. Capital works on both sides at the same time. If its accumulation, on the one hand, increases the demand for labour, it increases on the other the supply of labourers by the "setting free" of them, whilst at the same time the pressure of the unemployed compels those that are employed to furnish more labour, and therefore makes the supply of labour, to a certain extent, independent of the supply of labourers' (I, 654–5).

This remark is an example of Marx's appreciation of aspects of capitalism which are not usually explained in orthodox theory. In modern terms, what he seems to be saying is that capital may be a substitute for labour as well as its complement. Since capital goods are designed and produced by men for specific purposes, an increase in their supply does not have the same kind of effects as an increase in the supply of agricultural land. Some machines employ more labour, others less. If machinery is predominantly labour-saving, the net demand for labour—representing the balance of the effects of expansion and displacement—may be negative.

Marx did not argue the point in precisely these terms. Instead, he concentrated on the tendency for the capi-

[7] Although some Marxists may dispute this, I do not think that there can be any doubt that this was Marx's view. See, for example, Chapter XXV of Vol. I, especially the resounding conclusion on p. 661: 'Accumulation of wealth at one pole is, therefore, at the same time accumulation of misery, agony of toil, slavery, ignorance, brutality, mental degradation, at the opposite pole.' See also the second major conclusion of Marx's 1865 report to the General Council of the First International, entitled *Wages, Price and Profit*: 'Secondly. The general tendency of capitalist production is not to raise, but to sink the average standard of wages' (Marx and Engels, *Selected Works*, 226).

tal–labour ratio (or in his terms the 'organic composition of capital') to increase (I, 625–6 and 635 ff).[8] But an increasing capital-labour ratio is not a sufficient condition for net labour displacement, especially when allowance is made for the accompanying increase in the number of workers employed in the capital goods industries. The problem is more subtle than this and requires fuller discussion. But Marx at least knew that there was a problem; and he insisted on drawing attention to the effects of labour displacement, resulting for example from the destruction of traditional and artisan industries. In practice, Marx turned out to be wrong when he predicted a long-term upward trend in the industrial reserve army. Despite a very large increase during the past century in the capital–labour ratio, the percentage rate of unemployment has fluctuated but not increased steadily.

Our conclusion must be that neither Marx's axiomatic model nor his alternative model proved that the real wage under capitalism cannot rise permanently above subsistence. Of course, as Marx accepted, the subsistence level itself is not a fixed point. It varies across countries and it contains a significant customary element (I, 150). But Marx certainly did not expect the real wage in capitalist countries to rise persistently over time. In this respect, his predictions, like those of many other economists, have been completely falsified. During the century which has elapsed since Volume I of *Capital* was published real wages in the advanced countries of Western Europe and North America have increased by several hundred per cent; and their rate of growth has accelerated.[9]

[8] If capital $(K)$ is measured at constant prices, net of linear depreciation, and labour $(L)$ is measured in unskilled-equivalents, the capital–labour ratio is $K/L$. On the other hand, the organic composition of capital (OCC) is the ratio of the labour-value of capital to the labour-value of wage-goods, or $L(K)/L(G)$. If labour productivity in producing capital goods changes in the same proportion as labour productivity in producing wage-goods, the OCC varies in proportion to variations in $K/G$. If, in addition, as Marx assumed, the subsistence wage of an unskilled worker is a fixed basket of goods, $g$, $G = gL$ and the OCC varies in proportion to $K/(gL)$. On these assumptions, therefore, the organic composition of capital varies in proportion to the capital–labour ratio.

[9] Phelps Brown and Browne (1968, 31) estimated that between 1860 and 1960 real wages per head were multiplied by a factor of 4–4½ in France, Germany, and the United Kingdom, and by a factor of about 6½ in Sweden and the United States.

It now seems that it would be more sensible to divide the industrialization process into two phases. During the first phase there are 'unlimited supplies of labour' from agriculture and other traditional occupations, while, in the second, this source of cheap labour disappears.[10] Consequently, although in the first phase the real wage of unskilled labour may be held close to subsistence, in the second it tends to rise in line with productivity. Marx was writing at a time when the first phase in Britain had already come to an end and the real wage was rising. He must have seen some evidence of this; but presumably he thought that it was only a temporary phenomenon.

During the past three decades the situation has changed in other respects also. Unemployment insurance and the pressure of working-class parties for policies of full employment have strengthened the hands of the trade unions. In so far as the level of unemployment still affects wage settlements it seems mainly to influence money wages and prices rather than real wages. The problems of modern capitalism are caused not so much by its inability to provide an increasing standard of living as by its inability to satisfy rapidly rising expectations. The consequence has been an upward trend in the rate of inflation. It is this factor, not a rising capital–labour ratio, which is mainly responsible for the growth in unemployment in the industrialized countries in recent years.

## Marx's microeconomic theory further considered

We have seen that Marx's macroeconomic model can be reduced to a single ratio: the ratio between total labour employed and total 'paid' labour or, in terms of our earlier notation, $L/L(G)$.[11] But, although this formula conveys the central message of Marx's theory, Marx was firmly of the opinion that these macroeconomic results arise from microeconomic relations. For a full appreciation of Marx's method, therefore, it is necessary to give some further consideration to his microeconomic theory.

[10] See Lewis (1954).

[11] This is strictly true only if the number of hours of work per worker is constant. To allow for this factor, we can multiply the ratio by $h$, the average number of hours, provided that, as Marx usually assumed, output increases in proportion to the number of hours worked, and that $h$ has no effect on $G$, the total subsistence cost of employed labour.

Marx did not have a theory of the firm but rather of the industry.[12] He assumed perfect competition, and he often spoke as if each industry produces a single homogeneous product. Each industry buys raw materials, uses plant and machinery, and hires labour-power. The value of the raw materials consumed and the wear and tear of machinery is equal to the socially necessary labour embodied in them, while, according to Marx's theory, the use of labour-power is the sole source of new value, or value added. The value of the output of industry $i$, therefore, is

$$L(Q_i) = L(M_i) + L(A_i)$$

where $L(\ )$ means the socially necessary labour needed—directly or indirectly—to produce whatever is in the parentheses, $Q_i$ is a vector of the industry's output (a unit vector in the one-good case), $M_i$ is a vector of material inputs (including using up of fixed capital), and $A_i$ is value added in $i$.

The industry's costs—in terms of value—are

$$C(Q_i) = L(M_i) + L(G_i)$$

where $G_i$ is a vector of the goods which are necessary to provide subsistence for the unskilled-labour-equivalent workers *actually employed* in industry $i$.

Then the industry's surplus value is

$$S_i = L(Q_i) - C(Q_i) = L(A_i) - L(G_i)$$

and its rate of surplus value is

$$s_i = \frac{L(A_i)}{L(G_i)} - 1$$

In all his examples Marx assumed that $s_i = s$, i.e. that the rate of surplus value is the same in all industries within a given economy in a given period of time. There is one passage where he remarks that 'the division of the day's work into necessary and surplus-labour differs in different countries, and even in the same country at different periods, or in different branches of industry' (I, 389). This seems to imply that $s_i = s$ is not always

---

[12] He did not use the word 'industry' in the modern (Marshallian) sense but rather phrases such as 'branch of industry' or 'line of production'. But he clearly had the same concept in mind.

true. But the passage is not unambiguous. In any case, the whole drift of Marx's argument is based on the assumption that $s_i = s$.

It is, in fact, easy to show that this condition must be satisfied if two assumptions hold: (1) that the unskilled-labour-equivalent wage is the same in every industry, and (2) that, at the level of the industry, *socially necessary* labour is the same as the *actual labour* employed.

Let

$$L(G_i) = L(g_i L_i) = L_i L(g_i)$$

where $g_i$ is the vector of wage-goods provided to each unskilled-labour-equivalent (ULE) in $i$, and $L_i$ is the number of ULEs *actually* employed in $i$. Assumption (1) above is that $g_i = g$, constant over all industries. Assumption (2) is that $L_i = L(A_i)$. With these two assumptions

$$L(G_i) = L(g). L(A_i)$$

and
$$s_i = \frac{1}{L(g)} - 1, \text{ independent of } i.$$

Marx did not give a clear and comprehensive definition of what he meant by 'socially necessary' labour. There are several partial definitions and some examples of cases where actual labour (AL) employed differs from socially necessary labour (SNL).[13] These examples show that there can be no presumption that AL= SNL at all times within a single firm. A firm which introduces a new technique will initially have AL < SNL. As the technique spreads, SNL falls and eventually, when all firms in the industry use the new technique, AL = SNL in every firm in the industry once more. In his partial definitions of the phrase 'socially necessary' Marx usually made it synonymous with 'normal' or 'average'. Although he did not say so explicitly, the most plausible interpretation is that he equated 'socially necessary' labour with 'average amount of labour actually used in the given industry'. SNL per unit of output is, consequently, the average AL per unit of output for the industry as a whole.[14]

[13] See especially the example discussed at length in (I, 306–8).
[14] Marx mentioned one exception to this. If supply exceeds demand at the

It seems safe to assume, therefore, that Marx regarded it as normal for the rate of surplus value to be equal in all industries (but not in all firms within industries) in a given period of time. He did not, however, assume that the rate of surplus value is the same in all countries, nor that it is constant within the same country over time.[15]

The difficulty with the assumption that $s_i = s$ is, as Marx admitted, that 'This law contradicts all experience based on appearance' (I, 293). Since Marx implicitly assumed that there is a perfect capital market, he believed that the rate of profit tends towards equality in all industries. But, for this to be so, the ratio of surplus value to capital employed in each industry must be the same. According to Marx, capital employed consists of two parts: the value of materials used, $L(M_i)$, which Marx called 'constant' capital, and the value of labour-power, $L(G_i)$, which Marx called 'variable' capital.[16] Then the rate of profit in industry $i$ is, in terms of values,

$$r_i = \frac{S_i}{L(M_i) + L(G_i)} = \frac{L(A_i) - L(G_i)}{L(M_i) + L(G_i)}$$

while the rate of surplus value is

$$s_i = \frac{S_i}{L(G_i)} = \frac{L(A_i) - L(G_i)}{L(G_i)}$$

It follows that $s_i/r_i = L(M_i)/L(G_i) + 1$ or, if we write $\gamma_i = L(M_i)/L(G_i)$,

$$s_i/r_i = 1 + \gamma_i.$$

The term $\gamma_i$ is Marx's 'organic composition of capital', the ratio

---

SNL value, the price falls temporarily, and this proves that during that period in that industry AL > SNL (III, 221). However, this case can be excluded by amending Marx's assumption to read: At the level of the industry *and in equilibrium* AL = SNL (see also III, 213).

[15] Modern neoclassical theory usually reverses two of these assumptions. It does not assume that the wage share in value added is the same in every industry, but it does very often assume that the aggregate wage share is constant over time.

[16] Marx usually assumed that the stock of capital is equal to the flow of inputs into production, i.e. that the rate of turnover of capital is the same for all varieties of capital and across all industries. The relaxation of this assumption would complicate the problem, but it would not affect the major issues under discussion.

of the labour-value of constant capital to the labour-value of variable capital.

It is clear, then, that if $s_i = s$, it is not possible *also* to have $r_i = r$ unless $\gamma_i = \gamma$, all $i$. But there is no empirical basis for assuming that $\gamma_i$ is constant across $i$. If $\gamma_i \neq \gamma$ while competition ensures that $r_i = r$, we must have $s_i \neq s$; and a basic assumption of Volume I is shown to be false.[17]

Although Marx did not enter into any further discussion about this problem in Volume I, he put forward a suggested solution in Volume III. The solution which he proposed (Volume III, Chapter IX) was as follows. Take from the value system—which is the underlying reality—the aggregate values of output, capital, and surplus value (measured in labour time). Divide aggregate surplus value by the aggregate value of capital to obtain an average rate of profit. Then adjust the values produced in each industry by replacing each surplus value component by a figure for profit, calculated by multiplying the value of capital in that industry by the uniform rate of profit. The adjusted values, called 'prices of production', which sum to the same aggregate of value and of surplus value, are now consistent with the assumption of a uniform rate of profit, but are no longer consistent with a uniform rate of surplus value. This is Marx's so-called 'transformation' from values into prices of production.

As many people have pointed out, this solution is not satisfactory. Bortkiewicz showed that Marx's solution fails to allow for changes in the values of constant and variable capital as values are transformed into prices; and that, when allowance is made for this, the rate of profit in terms of prices is not the same as the initial rate of profit in terms of values.[18] Seton (1957) has discussed alternative solutions to the transformation problem in which various different aggregates are kept constant. Samuelson (1971) has pointed out that, in order to make a transformation from values into prices, it is necessary to have an input–output table. For example, it is impossible to estimate $L(G)$, the amount of labour required—directly and indi-

[17] Although stated in different words, this Marxian dilemma corresponds to the problem which Ricardo faced in Chapter 1 of his *Principles*, when he showed that a rise in wages will push relative prices away from their labour-values whenever capital–labour ratios differ.

[18] See the translation of Bortkiewicz's paper in Sweezy (1975).

rectly—to produce the workers' subsistence, without such a table. But, if one has an input–output table, it is not necessary *first* to estimate the value-system and *then* to transform values into prices. If the real wage is given, e.g. at subsistence, prices can be derived directly from the input–output table. Hence the value-system is a 'détour'.

It may also be remarked that there is no reason to assume that the input–output structure of a value-system would be the same as the input–output structure of a price-system. This brings us to a major puzzle in the Marxian theory. According to Marx, material inputs produce no value, while direct labour produces the entire surplus. Thus the rate of return to a capitalist on capital invested in materials—the employment of indirect labour—is zero, while the rate of return on 'variable' capital—the employment of direct labour—is the rate of surplus value. Since Marx assumed that competition operates within the value-system, and that capitalists can change the organic composition of capital to suit their objective of maximizing surplus value (for example, when they substitute machinery for labour), it must follow logically that, within a value-system, each capitalist would have an incentive to replace indirect labour—yielding no surplus value—by direct labour. Since a given sum of money-capital produces more surplus value if used to hire direct labour than if used to buy the materials producible by such labour, there would be an advantage to the capitalist in producing as much as possible of his own requirements of materials, and even of machinery. In other words, in a value-system there would be a powerful stimulus towards vertical integration; industry boundaries would crumble; and in ultimate equilibrium the whole economy would be integrated into a single firm, or into a parallel group of integrated firms. In such a situation, there would be no input–output matrix, no constant capital, and all capital would be variable. There would be no data for a transformation algorithm to work on.

In the light of this consideration, one may say that the problem of reconciling a value-system with a price-system goes deeper than the problem of adjusting values in order to achieve a uniform rate of profit. The fundamental difficulty is that in a value-system the industrial structure as we know it would not exist. A transformation from values to prices involves the *creation* of a disintegrated input–output structure out of a fully integrated structure. There is no guidance in the value-system about how we should set about doing this. In practice, the so-called transformations from values to prices simply take the input–output structure existing in the price-system and assume that it would also exist in the value-system. But the input–output structure is not determined solely by technical considerations; it is also a reflection of the economic system in operation, and in particular of the system of economic incentives.

*Conclusions*

The above discussion has been concerned only with those parts of Marx's work which are relevant to the theory of income distribution. Marx's economic studies covered a wide range of other topics, including economic history, industrial cycles, and models of economic growth. But the aspects which concern us—the theory of value, the determination of the real wage, and the transformation from values to prices—are central to Marx's theory.

We have found that Marx's axiomatic derivation of the labour theory of value is unsatisfactory—especially the crucial axiom that labour-power is a commodity which, on Marx's definition, is therefore available in infinitely elastic supply in the long run at its cost of production. Marx's alternative theory that the wage tends towards subsistence is economically more interesting and contains an element of truth. That truth is that capital is a substitute for labour as well as its complement. But historical experience has not confirmed Marx's prediction that an increasing organic composition of capital would necessarily result in an increasing industrial reserve army of unemployed. The laws of motion of capitalism are not immutable and cannot be captured in any simple formula. Marx the dialectical materialist would surely have agreed with that.

As is well known, Marx's solution to the transformation problem is unsatisfactory. In addition, any solution which assumes the existence of a fixed input–output structure is invalid. In a value-system firms would have an incentive to replace indirect by direct labour, and hence to integrate backwards. Thus a value-system in equilibrium would have no inter-industry input–output structure. Since the observed input–output matrix, which is a product of the price-system, would not exist in a value-system, a transformation from values to prices is impossible: one must choose one world or the other.

Despite the objections which can be raised to Marx's theory as an immutable theory of capitalism, his central assumption that the supply of labour-power is infinitely elastic at the subsistence wage, which he shared with the classical economists, may have been approximately correct in the early stages of industrialization. But in later stages of capitalist development the real wage has risen in line with productivity—or even faster. Real wages in advanced capitalist countries have increased several fold since Marx published Volume I of *Capital*, and the wage share seems to have risen significantly, especially during the past few decades.

Marx's description of the horrors of early industrialization in Britain, together with his forecast of even worse things to come, has had an important influence on world history. It was influential in diverting the Russian Bolsheviks from their original view that a period of free capitalist development was desirable in Russia; and it has encouraged some other underdeveloped countries to try to jump over the capitalist stage.

In terms of analytical technique, Marx's method was a retreat from the advances made by Ricardo. Marx had no time for diminishing returns or marginal concepts. He failed to understand the stability properties of supply and demand functions, claiming that in equilibrium, when supply and demand are equal, they 'cease to explain anything' (I, 548).[19] He believed profoundly that exchange creates no surplus value, although he admitted that it makes each participant better off (I, 135). It never seems to have occurred to him that an individual who is better off as a result of exchange can convert part of his gains into money, i.e. into surplus value. He believed

[19] See also the more detailed elaboration of the point in (III, 223): 'If demand and supply balance, then they cease to have any effect . . . If two forces exert themselves equally in opposite directions, they balance one another, they have no influence at all on the outside, and any phenomenon taking place at the same time must be explained by other causes than the influence of these forces. If demand and supply balance one another, they cease to explain anything, they do not affect market-values . . .'.

that the doctrine that labour-power is the sole commodity which, when used, creates value was the solution to the great riddle of the generation of surplus value. But the riddle was one which he himself constructed.

Along with most other economists, both before and since his time, Marx accepted the assumptions of perfect competition, including a perfect capital market, and hence a uniform rate of profit. Despite some suggestive remarks about the role of the capitalist in promoting technical progress and growth in productivity, Marx was so hostile to capitalists that he underestimated the role of enterprise and initiative. Hence he tended to assume that the problem of production was already solved and that a socialist government would be able to take over a smoothly functioning industrial machine, whose further progress could easily be planned from a single centre.

Like most economists, Marx frequently resorted to 'implicit theorizing'. For example, from the identity $S/(C + V) \equiv S/V.V/(C + V)$ he deduced that, if $S/V$ is constant and $V/(C + V)$ is falling, $S/(C + V)$ must be falling. In terms of our earlier notation, $S/(C + V) = r$, $S/V = s$, and $(C + V)/V = 1 + \gamma$. The corresponding expression for Marx's identity is therefore $r \equiv s/(1 + \gamma)$. From this identity Marx argued that, if $s$ is constant and $\gamma$ is increasing, $r$ must be falling. This was the basis for his alleged law of the falling rate of profit. But the 'law' is in direct conflict with Marx's prior assumption that wages are held at subsistence, which implies that, as the organic composition of capital increases, the accompanying rise in real productivity must also lead to an increase in the rate of surplus value. Unless it could be shown that $s$ invariably increases less rapidly than $1 + \gamma$, Marx's method provides no proof that the rate of profit must fall.

Despite these weaknesses in Marx's theory, his insights into some important aspects of the capitalist economy are impressive. These include: the weak bargaining position of the proletariat *vis-à-vis* the capitalists of his day; the tendency of machinery to make labour redundant and hence further to weaken labour's position; the importance of economies of scale and technical progress and the resulting tendency towards industrial concentration; the role of self-finance through the reinvestment of profits (not, however, consistent with his assumption of a uniform rate of profit); and the inherent cyclical instability of capitalism.

It was this last point, in particular, which powerfully reinforced Marx's intellectual objection to the 'anarchy' of capitalism, and strengthened his attachment to the idea of centralized planning. He gave little weight to the value of individual freedom or the desire of people to participate in making economic decisions. 'Freedom', in the Hegelian phrase, 'is the appreciation of necessity'.[20] During the past two generations we have learnt how easy it is to use this dogma to destroy human freedom.

[20] Quoted with approval by Engels in *Anti-Dühring*, p. 128.

# 4

## *Neoclassical Distribution Theory*

I use the term neoclassical theory to refer to the dominant stream of economics during the past century. Starting with the marginal utility theorists of the 1870s—especially Jevons, Menger, and Walras—the technique of marginalism was applied to ever-widening areas of economic theory until it encompassed the whole subject. Ricardo, of course, had used a marginal method in his analysis of rent; but the full development of marginalism had to await the arrival of mathematical economists. Several early mathematical economists, including Cournot and Gossen, had already used the marginal method—which is no more than the method of the differential calculus—without having any immediate impact on economic theory. There was, however, from the beginning a strong connection between neoclassical theory and the mathematical method, even though this connection was not revealed in all its fullness until the present generation.

Initially, neoclassical theory achieved striking success in explaining the old paradox of the apparent conflict between use-value and price. Why are useful things often sold at a low price, while 'useless' things fetch a high price? The concept of marginal utility solved this problem by focusing attention on equalization at the margin. What was in some ways more important was that it made clear that marginal utility varies with the quantity consumed. Exchange value, therefore, depends on both the utility function and scarcity. Economics began to be seen as the theory of the allocation of scarce resources. Indeed, if one treated factor supply decisions as simply another instance of the equalization of marginal utility—or marginal disutility—the whole economy could be envisioned as a careful balancing of utilities and disutilities at the margins of decision-making. The concept of opportunity cost was born.

Later, neoclassical theory extended into the field of production. Early theories had been concerned essentially with a pure exchange situation, where the problem was how given supplies of goods and services could be exchanged so as to maximize the utility levels of their owners. This analysis is usually demonstrated today by means of the Edgeworth box diagram. But when factor supplies are brought into the picture there is another area of decision-making which needs analysis. Walras assumed, almost until the end, that production occurred with fixed coefficients. In that case there were no production decisions to be made, and Walras was able to skirt a difficult problem with which his system was unable to cope, namely, the role of time in economics.

Although Marshall developed a hesitant theory of marginal productivity in his *Principles*, Wicksteed was the first to make systematic use of the concept of variable proportions, and hence of marginal productivity.[1] The concept itself was clearly implicit in Ricardo's model. But hitherto economic theory had tended to follow Ricardo in treating land as a special case. Labour and capital could be applied in varying quantities to land; but labour and capital were essentially complements. This was a natural view to take so long as most capital was thought to be circulating capital, ultimately 'advances to labour' of a constant real wage. But as the role of fixed capital became more prominent, capital could be seen as a possible substitute for labour. If labour and capital could be combined in variable proportions, could not the Ricardian theory of rent be extended to *all* the factors of production? This was what Wicksteed did, with striking results.

### The production function

Wicksteed used a continuously differentiable production function with *n* factor arguments. He argued that under competitive conditions each factor is paid the value of its marginal product and that, if the function is linear homogeneous, these payments will exactly exhaust the value of the product.[2] This is the point

---

[1] Marshall's *Principles of Economics* was first published in 1890. Wicksteed's approach was outlined in his *Coordination of the Laws of Distribution* (1894). For further discussion of the origin of the marginal productivity theory see Stigler (1941).

[2] This proposition is Euler's Theorem, although Wicksteed did not use that term.

from which modern textbooks of micro-economics take their origin.

A formal representation of the production function is

$$Q = F(a,b,c, \dots )$$

where $Q$ is output, $a,b,c, \dots$ are inputs, and $F$ is a function given by 'technology'.[3] But two major problems arise in interpreting this concept. First, we need to be informed about the nature of the production unit to which this function applies. Since $Q$ is a single output, measured in physical units, the function should strictly relate to a one-product firm, or to a one-product plant with a separate operating account and under instructions to maximize its profits. The function cannot be applied to a multi-product firm, still less to the economy as a whole, unless all goods are produced in fixed proportions, as if they were a single good. Unless we are prepared to make such an assumption, the use of any degree of aggregation is strictly illegitimate. At best, such aggregate production functions are 'parables'.

The second problem arises on the input side. As the function is written, it clearly implies that the quantities of the different inputs are freely and instantaneously variable—at least over a non-negative range. For the mathematician, this presents no problem: the whole operation is formal, or in the imagination. But for the economist there is no escape from the fact that some decisions are irreversible. If all factor services could be rented for the day—or by the week—the problem of irreversibility would not exist for the individual employer, provided that his own services were also hired on the same basis. But in the economy at large the problem does not disappear: it is simply shifted back to the suppliers of factor services. The fundamental difficulty is that capital goods, and to some extent labour itself, must first be created before their services can be used. The decision to create capital goods or skilled labour is largely irreversible. When we apply the production function at the micro level to the decision-making of the individual firm, we may pretend that the firm is unconstrained by such irreversible decisions. But, if we do so, we are discarding a crucial element in the real decision-making problem. This is why Marshall

[3] The function is a maximum of all known technology, such that it is never possible to produce the same output with a smaller vector of inputs.

made his well-known distinction between the short period and the long period: in the short period some previous decisions about the availability of factor services are irreversible, while in the long period all factor costs can be freely varied.

In practice, even in the long period, there is always a residue of irreversible decisions. No man can jump into the same river twice. Past history creates unalterable preconditions of the present. A firm, or an economy, which has once made and implemented a certain decision can never completely reverse it. The effects of previous investments, previous outputs, previous experience leave permanent residues. A formal solution to this problem would be to allow the function $F$ to incorporate these effects, leaving the 'reversible' factors in the arguments. But this would mean abandoning the assumption that the production function is 'given' by science or technology, independent of the previous experience of the firm.

The problem of irreversibility, or non-malleability, is especially acute when decisions are aggregated over an entire economy. A single firm can sell its old equipment and replace it by new or different equipment. But, at a given moment of time, the economy as a whole cannot change its stock of equipment. The composition of the stock can be changed gradually over time, by investment and scrapping; but the production function does not contain information about the conditions for making such changes.

It is clear, therefore, that the production function has many different meanings, depending on whether it refers to a single firm, an industry, or a whole economy, and whether it refers to changes which can be made freely and instantaneously or only after some delay. It is these considerations which bring us to the Great Divide in the neoclassical theory of distribution. On one side of the Divide lies Walras and those of his followers who insist on the non-aggregative nature of the production function. This school accepts that each firm—or each competitive industry—has a separate production function. Under conditions of general competitive equilibrium, each firm will be using a quantity of each factor's services which is such as to make the value of its marginal product equal to its cost, and the total demand for each factor's services will be equal to the total supply available at the common competitive price. In principle, therefore, factor incomes are determined in the same general equilibrium which determines everything else; so this is also a theory of distribution. The defect of the theory from our point of view, however, is that it yields no specific predictions about the distribution of income.

## *The aggregate production function*

On the other side of the Divide are those who wish to construct a model of distribution which yields predictions about aggregate factor shares. Following the example of J. B. Clark they postulate the existence of an aggregate production function for the whole competitive economy. $Q$ is now an index of aggregate output; and the factors, if they are to represent aggregate factors such as 'labour' and 'capital', must also be index-numbers. The function $F$, in its aggregative form, is assumed to be continuous and twice differentiable. $F_x = \delta F/\delta x$ is the marginal product of factor $x$, and $F_{xx} < 0$ for all factors. Under competitive conditions each unit of factor service is assumed to receive its marginal product. If the function is linear homogeneous, aggregate income shares, equal to the amount of each factor multiplied by its marginal product, will exhaust the total product. If, in addition, the function is Cobb–Douglas, income shares will be constant, irrespective of factor supplies, and equal to the exponents of the respective factors.[4]

The concept of an aggregate production function is highly abstract and its use raises a number of difficult theoretical issues. I shall postpone a consideration of these issues for the moment and proceed to consider the uses of the aggregate production function in income distribution theory. This can be illustrated with the help of two very striking diagrams.[5]

In the first diagram (Fig. 4.1), $Q_1$ is an isoquant representing the minimum combinations of capital $(K)$ and labour $(L)$ required to produce the output $Q_1$. It is implicitly assumed that each unit of capital provides a constant flow of capital service and each unit of labour a constant flow of labour service. The isoquant is shown as convex from below because it is assumed

---

[4] The Cobb–Douglas function is of the form $Q = Aa^{\alpha}b^{\beta}c^{\gamma}\ldots$ where $\alpha + \beta + \gamma + \ldots = 1$.

[5] See, for example, Johnson (1973).

that there are diminishing returns to each factor. If the production function is linear homogeneous there are constant returns to scale, and $Q_1$ can represent any level of output by a scalar adjustment of the units in which $K$ and $L$ are measured.

The point $C$ on $Q_1$ represents the available supplies of capital and labour in the whole economy—assumed to be given

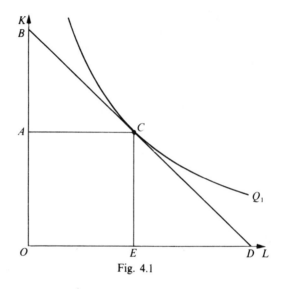

Fig. 4.1

exogenously. Under perfect competition—it is argued—the wage will be made equal to the marginal product of labour and the rental per unit of capital service will be made equal to the marginal product of capital service. Both marginal products are measured in terms of the output index. Then the line $BD$, a tangent to $Q_1$ at $C$, represents the cost of the output $Q_1$ in terms of any combination of labour and capital services at the given prices. Consequently, $OB$ represents the cost—and hence the value—of $Q_1$ in terms of $K$-units and $OD$ represents the cost in terms of $L$-units. Since $OA$ units of $K$ are employed and $OE$ units of $L$, the distribution of the product to $K$ and $L$ respectively can be represented by any one of the ratios $OA/AB$, $CD/BC$, or $ED/OE$.

The implication of this diagram is that, with given supplies of two factors and in a perfectly competitive market, the distribution of income between the two factors depends entirely on the shape of the aggregate production function. For example, if the slope of $Q_1$ at point $C$ were smaller, the share of profits in total income would be greater; and vice versa. Thus a change of technique which altered the shape of the production function in either of these ways would have a profound influence on the distribution of income. In some classifications an increase in the slope of $Q_1$ at point $C$ is called capital-saving and a decrease in the slope labour-saving.

The second diagram (Fig. 4.2) can be derived from the first by mapping points taken from a vertical section through the first diagram. Each point on such a line represents a different capital–labour ratio, and also a different level of output. In the second diagram output per worker is plotted against capital per worker. On the assumption already made that the production function is linear homogeneous, there is an alternative version of the function which relates output per worker to capital per

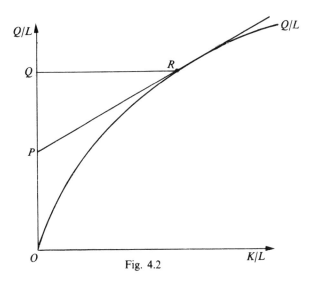

Fig. 4.2

worker, and this can be represented by a single curve as in Fig. 4.2. This curve is drawn concave downwards on the assumption of diminishing returns.

As before, when the capital–labour ratio is, say, $QR$, competition is assumed to make the capital service rental equal to the marginal product of capital. The straight line $PR$, tangential to the production function at $R$, has a slope equal to this equilibrium capital service rental. Since each unit of capital receives the same rental, total profit per worker is represented by $PQ$. With output per worker equal to $OQ$, the profit share—in terms of the product—is $PQ/OQ$ and the wage share is $OP/OQ$. In this diagram the distribution of income is shown in terms of the product, not in terms of factor inputs, but on the given assumptions about the nature of the production function the income shares are the same in all cases.

   In both diagrams, an increase in the aggregate capital–labour ratio reduces the capital service rental and increases the real wage. This is simply a reflection of the assumption of diminishing returns. But the second diagram allows a more vivid representation of the effects of technical progress. In Fig. 4.3, $(Q/L)_1$ and $(Q/L)_2$ represent the production function before

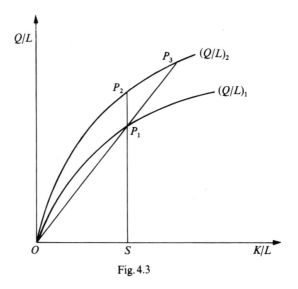

Fig. 4.3

and after a change in technique, which shifts the whole function upwards. In comparison with $(Q/L)_1$ the function $(Q/L)_2$ yields more output per worker at each level of capital per worker. If we knew the shape of the production function before and after such a change, we could predict the effect of such a change on income distribution for any given capital–labour ratio. For example if $K/L$ remained constant at $OS$, the distribution of income would depend on the heights and slopes of the two production functions at points $P_1$ and $P_2$ respectively. If the distribution of income is constant—in terms of income shares—at points such as $P_1$ and $P_2$ all along the function, the change in technique is Hicks-neutral. Alternatively, if the change in technique is accompanied by an increase in the $K/L$ ratio such as to keep the $Q/K$ ratio constant, the new equilibrium point on $(Q/L)_2$ will be $P_3$. If income shares at $P_3$ are the same as at $P_1$, the change in technique is Harrod-neutral. Under these conditions, the capital-service rental at $P_3$ is the same as at $P_1$, i.e. the slope of the tangent at $P_3$ is the same as the slope of the tangent at $P_1$. Clearly, Harrod-neutral technical progress requires an unusual coincidence of changes. As it happens, a Cobb–Douglas production function which shifts in a Hicks-neutral manner is also Harrod-neutral, because income shares with a Cobb–Douglas production function are always the same, irrespective of the factor input ratio.

These neoclassical diagrams are superficially very impressive, for they seem to provide clear and precise predictions about income distribution, factor service rentals, and much else. The effect has been reinforced by the results of empirical estimates of the aggregate production·function, starting with those of Cobb and Douglas in 1928.[6] Early estimates seemed to show a remarkably close relation between $Q$, $K$, and $L$ in a Cobb–Douglas function, and that the exponents of $K$ and $L$ were approximately equal to the factor income shares. This implied not only that the aggregate production function is linear homogeneous with diminishing returns to each factor, but that perfect competition makes the reward of each factor equal to its marginal product. In addition, the Cobb–Douglas function implies that the elasticity of substitution between capital and labour is constant and equal to unity.[7] But this is merely another way of saying that the profit share is invariant

[6] See also Douglas (1934) and (1948).

[7] The elasticity of substitution, first proposed by Hicks (1932) and Joan Robinson (1933), is defined as the proportionate change in the ratio of the marginal products of the factors divided by the proportionate change in the ratio of the quantities of the factors employed. The algebra of the elasticity of substitution and related formulae is clearly set forth in Ferguson (1971).

to changes in the capital–labour ratio, a fact—or alleged fact—which was already in the data used for these calculations.

The original estimates of Cobb and Douglas made no allowance for shifts in the production function over time, although it is obvious that technical knowledge in United States manufacturing—to which their estimates referred—was changing significantly during the period covered. Subsequent investigators have attempted to allow for this factor; but no one has yet discovered a method of measuring technical change and the shape of the production function independently of each other. In some well-known estimates Solow (1957) assumed that the aggregate production function is linear homogeneous in only two factors (capital and labour), that perfect competition makes the factor rentals equal to their marginal products, and that technical change over the period 1909–49 in the United States was Hicks-neutral. He then estimated technical change in each year on the assumption that capital's measured income-share in that year corresponded to an equilibrium point on the aggregate production function, so defined. The method clearly assumes in advance all the important relations which are required to be justified.

Fig. 4.4 illustrates the problem and Solow's proposed solu-

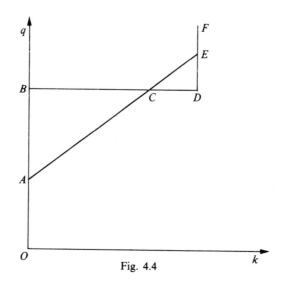

Fig. 4.4

tion. Point $C$ represents a given combination of output per man and capital per man in a given year (year 1), where $q = Q/L$ and $k = K/L$. $OA$ is the wage in year 1 and hence $AB$ is the profit per man in that year. $F$ is the combination of $q$ and $k$ in year 2. The increase in capital per man ($\Delta k$) from year 1 to year 2 is $CD$, and the corresponding increase in output per man is $DF$. The problem is to divide $DF$ into the part contributed by $\Delta k$ and the remainder, assumed to be due to technical progress. Solow assumed that between neighbouring years the marginal product of capital is approximately constant. The average capital rental in year 1 is given by the ratio $AB/BC$, and under perfect competition this would be equal to the marginal product of capital. Hence, on Solow's assumption, the contribution to total output in year 2 which is attributable to the extra capital available in that year, $CD$, is equal to $DE$. Then $EF$ is the contribution of technical progress.[8]

The neoclassical basis of this method is summarized in two assumptions: (1) the line $CE$ represents approximately the curvature of the aggregate production function as $k$ increases from $BC$ to $BD$; (2) the average capital rental is made equal by perfect competition to the marginal product of capital, approximately represented by the slope of $CE$. In effect, the aggregate production function is assumed to pass through the points $C$ and $E$. Obviously, this method of measuring the contribution of technical progress contains no independent information about either the shape of the production function or of the effects of technical progress. Technical progress is simply the difference between the measured increase in output and the increase which would have occurred if the assumptions of neoclassical theory were valid. The estimates provide no empirical proof or disproof of the latter proposition.[9]

A major problem with all empirical estimates of the aggregate production function is that in the real economy incomes do not divide neatly into profits and wages. The assumption that there are only two factors of production, with no mixed

---

[8] Since technical knowledge cannot, short of a catastrophe, be reduced, one would expect $EF$ to be positive. Solow's estimates contain a number of negative shifts in technique, which are of doubtful significance and are presumably due to errors either in his data or in his method.

[9] The same estimation formula can, however, be justified without relying on neoclassical assumptions. See Lydall (1968a).

incomes, is an abstraction which creates severe empirical problems. What is to be done about incomes of farmers and other unincorporated businesses? What is to be done about incomes of government employees? The answers are inevitably arbitrary, since these categories have no place in the standard model. For many years economists believed that the share of wages in national income was approximately constant, and theories were designed to account for this 'stylized fact'. Functions fitted by regression methods to data which were consistent with this 'fact' almost inevitably predicted that income shares would continue to be constant in the future. So long as the data showed constant shares the Cobb–Douglas function, which predicts constant shares, was bound to be a good fit.[10] But estimates for recent years, and revised estimates for earlier years, suggest that the original assumption of constant shares was not correct. If wages include salaries, the share of wages in national income, or even in private non-farm income, has grown appreciably in a number of industrialized countries over the past half-century or more.[11] Cross-section studies of income shares in manufacturing industry in countries at different levels of industrialization are consistent with the same conclusion.[12]

As it began to become clear that factor shares are not constant, the Cobb–Douglas function lost some of its popularity in empirical work, although not so far to the same extent in theoretical expositions. An alternative function, which is linear homogeneous, has diminishing returns and a constant elasticity of substitution, but which does not necessarily predict constant shares, is the constant elasticity of substitution (CES) function.[13] Empirical estimates with this function have usually found an elasticity of substitution of less than unity, which implies that as the capital–labour ratio rises the share of profits falls. These are the latest 'stylized facts', at least for the richer countries.

*Critique of the aggregate production function*

I shall undertake in the next chapter a more general critique of neoclassical theory. But it is appropriate at this point to discuss

---

[10] See Fisher (1971). [11] The evidence is summarized in Chapter 8 below.
[12] See Minhas (1963) and Lydall (1975).
[13] See Arrow, Chenery, Minhas, and Solow (1961).

the objections to the theory which have been raised by Joan Robinson, and the attempts of Samuelson and others to counter them. These objections relate primarily to the aggregate production function version of neoclassical theory. Some adherents of neoclassical theory are happy to abandon the aggregate production function, while maintaining the validity of a Walrasian-type model of general equilibrium.[14] But there can be no doubt that it is the aggregate production function which dominates neoclassical theory, especially in modern textbooks.

In our outline of the aggregate production function model it was assumed that the variables $Q$, $K$, and $L$ were index-numbers of physical quantities of output, capital, and labour respectively. Then the partial derivatives of $Q$ with respect to $K$ and $L$ measure the marginal products of capital and labour in terms of these index-numbers; and under perfect competition the reward per unit of each factor is equal to its marginal product. But this conclusion would follow only if there were a high degree of substitution—ideally perfect substitution—between different units of labour and different units of capital, and if output consisted of a fixed basket of goods, equivalent to a single good.

There is, in practice, some degree of substitution between different units of labour and, in a rough way, the skill composition of the labour force adjusts fairly quickly to changes in the skill composition of the demand for labour. The adjustment is not perfect, nor smooth, and if the change in the skill composition is substantial, wage differentials may be permanently affected. An exact analysis of this problem would show that, after allowing for the human capital component of labour earnings, differences in tastes, and differences in abilities, any large change in the structure of the labour force would be likely to produce a change in average labour earnings somewhat different from that which would be predicted by an index number of labour earnings with fixed weights.

So far as output is concerned, the assumption of a fixed basket of consumer goods will usually not lead to seriously erroneous conclusions when the changes in the economy are fairly small, for example, an increase in aggregate output per

[14] See, for example, Bliss (1975).

worker of 10 per cent. But, if the changes are large, the structure of final demand will be considerably affected, and the fixed basket of goods assumption will give misleading results. The trouble is that the marginal product which is payable, under perfect competition, to each unit of labour is a money product; and when the structure of demand for goods is changing, the average money value of the marginal products of labour over the whole economy does not necessarily move in proportion to the average money wage.

When the determination of capital rentals is considered these problems are multiplied, and others are added. A distinction must first be made between short-period and long-period equilibrium. In the short period, the vector of capital goods is given, and there is virtually no scope for substitution between them. A plough cannot do the work of a sewing-machine (even though the ploughman can if necessary work in a clothing factory). In the short period, therefore, on the usual assumptions of perfect competition, each capital good earns a rent, as if it were a piece of land. There is no such thing as a marginal product of capital in general, and the aggregate production function has no relevance.

In the long period, on the other hand, a new set of considerations comes into play. It is now assumed that capital goods are fully substitutable for one another, because eventually they can be scrapped and replaced by different goods. The ploughs can be converted into sewing-machines. In some neoclassical models it is assumed that capital is instantaneously malleable in this sense, as in Swan's assumption (1956) that capital consists of Meccano. But even without going so far as to assume instantaneous malleability, the stock of capital is assumed to be malleable in the long run. Hence, the aggregate production function is regarded as a description of alternative points of long-period equilibrium.

The question which now arises is: what is the reward to capital which is equalized by competition in the long run? Since capital is assumed to be ultimately malleable, the reward cannot be expressed as a physical unit of output per physical unit of capital—the 'marginal product' of the aggregate production function. Investors are not interested in physical rewards as such, but seek rather to maximize the money rate of return on the money value of investment. Here 'money' simply stands for general purchasing power. Investors may make adjustments for expected changes in the value of money when considering alternative earnings profiles; but the profit-maximizing objective of investment is to maximize the number of pounds received per pound invested.[15] When risk and uncertainty are absent, as in the standard neoclassical model, the long-period equilibrium position is one in which it is the *rate of interest* which is equalized across the whole economy. This is the fundamental objection to the aggregate production function.

Let us suppose that we could estimate an aggregate production function for a particular economy. Under what conditions would the marginal product of capital—the partial derivative of output with respect to capital—derived from that function be equal to the rate of interest? Let us accept the usual neoclassical assumptions of perfect competition, given technique, a closed economy, and homogeneous labour. Let us also assume a single consumption good and a single capital good and that the economy is in a stationary state. Gross output consists of a mixture of consumption goods and capital goods, while capital is a stock of capital goods. But the net output is only consumption goods, since capital goods are produced only for replacement. Imagine further that there is an indefinitely large number of economies of this sort, each in a stationary state with a different capital–labour ratio. If these capital–labour ratios vary continuously, the partial derivative of output of consumption goods with respect to capital goods across economies will measure the marginal product of capital in this sense.

It is clear that the marginal product of capital under these conditions will be equal to the rate of interest if and only if the price of capital goods in terms of consumption goods is constant over the relevant stationary states. But the neoclassical model implies that the rate of interest changes as the capital–labour ratio changes. And the rate of interest is a component of the cost of production of goods. Hence, the consumption good–capital good price ratio would remain constant over alternative stationary states only if the capital–labour ratio were the same in the

[15] I am not suggesting that, in fact, the only motive for investment is to maximize profits. At this point, I am merely following the logic of neoclassical theory.

production of both types of goods.[16] In the absence of this very special assumption, therefore, the derivative of output with respect to capital from an aggregate production function would not yield the rate of interest. Nor could one 'transform' the marginal product of capital into the rate of interest by making an adjustment for any change in the consumption good–capital good price ratio. For investors, as I have said, are not interested directly in the marginal product of capital. Perfect competition will drive them to equalize the rate of interest, and hence to make the rate of interest equal to the marginal rate of return on financial investment in all industries. The aggregate production function whose derivative with respect to capital would be equal to this uniform rate of return would be one which related the *value* of output to the *value* of capital.

### The pseudo-production function

This is the point at which Joan Robinson entered the discussion.[17] She assumed that there is available at any given time a spectrum of alternative techniques, each of which is, in effect, an input–output system for the whole economy. At any given wage, the optimal technique is that which yields the highest rate of interest, and from any set of techniques there can be derived a frontier of maximum wage–interest combinations. Different economies will be at different positions on this frontier; and Joan Robinson assumed that a single economy could be employing two different techniques at the same time if they both produced the same rate of interest for the same wage. From this set of assumptions she constructed her 'pseudo-production function' relating output per worker to capital per worker. But she chose to measure capital in wage units, with the consequence that a rise in the real wage, with a given technique, must reduce the value of capital. Hence her production function was a strange kind of zig-zag.

Samuelson (1962b) proposed an alternative method of measuring capital, within the same framework of assumptions,

---

[16] In this case, the Marxian labour-value system would be a valid theory of prices, since the organic composition of capital would be the same for both types of good. Of course, a capital-value system, or a labour-and-capital-value system, would work equally well.

[17] First outlined in Robinson (1953) and revised in Robinson (1956).

by expressing it in terms of consumption units. This generated a production function more like the textbook model, but with a series of linear links in place of a smooth curve. The Keynesian counter-attack was to insist on the theoretical possibility of 'double-switching' and 'capital-reversing'.

The problem of double-switching can be illustrated by means of a simple example.[18] Suppose that an economy consists of two industries. Industry 1 produces a consumption good and industry 2 produces a capital good which is supplied as an input to both industries. It is assumed that capital goods are fully used up within the production period, and that in equilibrium they earn a uniform rate of interest based on the value of capital goods consumed during that period.[19] Labour is homogeneous and earns the same wage in each industry. No interest is earned on advances of wages.

Let $p_1$ and $p_2$ be the money prices of consumption goods and capital goods respectively; let $a_1$ and $a_2$ be fixed coefficients relating inputs of capital goods per unit of consumption goods and capital goods, and $b_1$ and $b_2$ be the corresponding coefficients of labour input; let $r$ be the rate of interest and $w$ be the wage. Then, in equilibrium,

$$(1 + r)a_1 p_2 + b_1 w = p_1$$

$$\text{and} \quad (1 + r)a_2 p_2 + b_2 w = p_2$$

If we set $p_1 = 1$ and eliminate $p_2$ by substitution, we obtain

$$(1+r)a_2 + b_1 w + w(1+r)(a_1 b_2 - a_2 b_1) = 1 \tag{4.1}$$

In the special case where $a_1/b_1 = a_2/b_2$, (4.1) reduces to

$$r = \frac{1 - a_2}{a_2} - \frac{b_1}{a_2} w \tag{4.2}$$

which can be represented geometrically by a negatively sloping straight line in the positive $(w,r)$ quadrant.

In his (1962b) paper Samuelson assumed that alternative

[18] The subject is well treated by Harcourt (1972), who gives also a full list of references.

[19] A similar assumption was made by Ricardo in much of his analysis, by Marx, and more recently by Sraffa (1960). But both Ricardo and Marx included 'advances to labour' as part of the total capital on which interest must be earned.

technologies have such characteristics, namely, that the capital–labour coefficients are the same in both the consumption goods industry and the capital goods industry. On this assumption, the frontier of $(w,r)$ combinations for different technologies will be described by a series of intersecting straight lines such as those shown in Fig. 4.5. It follows that, if there is perfect knowledge of 'given' technologies, any economy in a

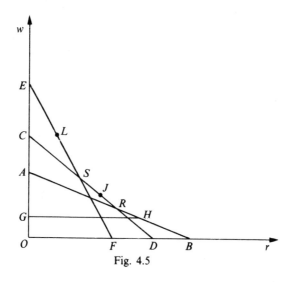

Fig. 4.5

stationary state will be somewhere on the $(w,r)$ frontier. In the case illustrated, where there are only three alternative technologies, represented by the lines $AB$, $CD$, and $EF$, any economy would be located on the frontier described by the segments $BR$, $RS$, and $SE$. Under these conditions, it is easy to show that an economy with a lower value of $r$ will always have a higher value of $k$, where $k$ is the value of capital goods per unit of labour, measured in terms of consumption goods.

For example, an economy at point $H$ on $AB$ has a wage equal to $OG$ (measured in consumption goods) and a rate of interest equal to $GH$. Output per worker in such an economy (also in consumption goods) is equal to $OA$ (the wage which would be paid if $r = 0$) and hence profit per worker is $GA$. It follows that the value of capital per worker is $GA/GH$, the profit per worker divided by the rate of interest. And in general, for any point such as $H$ on a $(w,r)$ function the value of capital per worker in terms of consumption goods is given by the tangent of the angle $GHA$, where $OG$ is the wage and $OA$ is output per worker. It follows that, when the $(w,r)$ functions are linear, an economy which is at point $J$ on $CD$ has a lower value of $r$ and a higher value of $k$ than an economy at $H$; and similarly for point $L$ on $EF$. A set of linear $(w,r)$ functions is, therefore, a sufficient condition for the existence of a 'well-behaved' production function, in which the wage rises and the rate of interest falls as the real value of capital per worker increases.

But there is no guarantee that the $(w,r)$ functions are linear. If the capital–labour ratio in the capital goods industry $(a_2/b_2)$ is different from the capital–labour ratio in the consumption goods industry $(a_1/b_1)$ the $(w,r)$ function will be non-linear. By differentiation of $(4.1)$ it can be shown that, when $a_2/b_2 > a_1/b_1$, the $(w,r)$ function is concave downwards; and, when $a_2/b_2 < a_1/b_1$, the $(w,r)$ function is convex. Convex $(w,r)$ functions create no problem; but concave functions may generate a 'badly behaved' production function.

An example which is often used to demonstrate the problem of double-switching and capital-reversal is illustrated in Fig. 4.6. Suppose that there are two alternative techniques, represented by $AB$ and $CD$ respectively. $AB$ has equal $a/b$ coefficients in each sector, but $CD$ has a more capital-intensive capital-goods sector $(a_2/b_2 > a_1/b_1)$. An economy at point $J$ now has a higher wage and a lower rate of interest than an economy at point $H$, but, because $OC < OA$, its value of capital per worker (in terms of consumption goods) is lower. This represents a 'capital-reversal'; and it is clear that it can occur only if the $(w,r)$ lines intersect each other twice, as at $S$ and $T$, with a 'double-switch'.

It is sometimes suggested that the possibility of capital-reversals is very damaging to the neoclassical aggregate production function model. But this is a misconception. All that it shows is that the pseudo-production function is sometimes 'badly-behaved'. But even if the pseudo-production function were always 'well-behaved' and had no capital-reversals, it would not answer the questions which it is supposed to answer. The aggregate production function is supposed to be a method of informing us what will be the marginal products of the factors when they are employed in various proportions, from which could be deduced the factor distribution of income under perfect competition. But the question which eventually needs to be answered is: what are the effects of *changes* in the relative supplies of the factors on the distribution of income? The

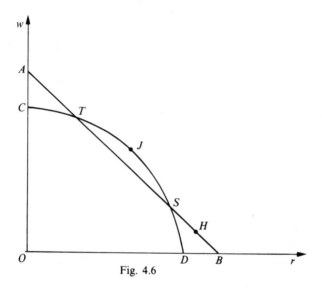

Fig. 4.6

pseudo-production function, which is a description of positions occupied in alternative stationary states, does not answer that question, since stationary states are positions reached only in very long-run equilibrium after all change has ceased. To assume that an increment in the physical capital–labour ratio, starting from stationary state *A*, will have the same effects on distribution as can be derived from a comparison of state *A* with state *B* (which has a higher physical capital–labour ratio) is no more than an act of faith.

Apart from this theoretical defect, the pseudo-production function is empirically useless. It requires us to estimate the input–output structures of a spectrum of alternative (non-inferior) techniques, assumed to be given exogenously. Each economy is assumed to be in a stationary state, employing either one technique or two neighbouring techniques with a common wage–interest combination. Before we could use this model for empirical application, even if we could make all the prior estimates, we should need (1) to find an economy in a stationary state and (2) to estimate its ratio of capital to labour, where capital is measured in consumption goods and labour is homogeneous. In practice, of course, no modern economy is in a stationary state, and we have no means of estimating what its capital–labour ratio would be if it were so.

The purpose of a positive theory of factor income distribution must surely be to answer questions such as: (1) Why is the factor income distribution in a given economy what it is—or seems to be? (2) What would be the effect on income distribution in different kinds of economy of changes in such variables as the over-all degree of capital-intensity, technique, tastes, industrial structure, the forms of competition, the distribution of education, regional policy, and the distribution of ownership of the factors? The aggregate production function sets up a model of alternative stationary states which, at best, could answer one question, namely the effect on output per worker of the amount of capital per worker, all other variables being assumed constant. But it fails even to answer that question. The fundamental reason is that the methodological assumptions of the aggregate production function—an attempt to use comparative static equilibrium analysis for an aggregate problem involving capital, and hence time—are inappropriate. The excursion into a meta-economy of alternative stationary states is a 'détour', just as Marx's world of labour-values is a 'détour'. The theoretical model makes it more difficult to answer our questions, not less.

*Alternative approaches*

One may well wonder whether it was necessary for neoclassical theory to get entangled in the concept of an aggregate production function in order to make meaningful predictions about the effects of changes in the aggregate capital–labour ratio. The classical economists solved the problem quite easily, because they assumed that capital was predominantly circulating capital—in the final analysis, advances to labour. While the long-run supply of labour was assumed to be infinitely elastic at the subsistence wage, the classical economists admitted that the short-run supply of labour is inelastic. Hence an increase in the supply of capital at a rate above the anticipated rate would, under competition, lead to a bidding up of the wage rate. But this effect could only be temporary.

Ricardo also predicted that in the long run the rate of profit would fall as the aggregate supply of capital increased. But his explanation was the scarcity of land. Since Ricardo thought of capital mainly—although not exclusively—as advances to labour, he did not conceive that there might be diminishing returns to capital in relation to labour. On the other hand, one might interpret Marx's theory of the declining rate of profit as a theory of diminishing returns to capital. Marx did not specify his theory in that way; but, without such an assumption, it is difficult to rationalize his model.

In neoclassical theory, capital ceases to be mainly advances to labour, and is thought of mainly as plant and machinery. But in long-run equilibrium, as we have seen, capital is imagined as a malleable substance—putty, jelly, butter, or Meccano; and it is assumed that the law of diminishing returns applies to this substance. But there are no grounds for such an assumption. The law of diminishing returns is a technical relation between physical inputs and physical outputs. Its logical basis is the imperfect substitutability of different physical factors of production. We cannot presume imperfect substitutability between a perfectly *malleable* factor and other factors. If capital can be transmuted costlessly into any desired shape, why should there ever be diminishing returns to capital? Capital in some form could be used to replace the services of land or of labour, so that there need never be any relative scarcity of the latter two factors.

But perhaps this is taking the concept of malleability too literally. Capital may be malleable, but there may be a limit to the number of forms which it can take. The Meccano set may come with an instruction book which contains only a few diagrams; the butter can be pressed into only a limited range of moulds. These designs or moulds are determined by the current state of technical knowledge. Let us imagine, then, that there is a given list of possible machines. We can have specified types of spades, ploughs, typewriters, steel works, cotton looms, and so forth, but nothing else. Does this help us to predict the effects of an increase in the capital–labour ratio?

It seems that the answer will depend on how many of these machines are already in use. If every gardener, or potential gardener, has a spade, there is no point in adding more spades; but if some farmers do not have ploughs, there will be a substantial return on adding to the number of ploughs. But, if we assume perfect competition and perfect knowledge of technique, it is not clear why some farmers should already have ploughs and others not. The logic of the neoclassical model is that, if one producer uses a machine, all producers of the same product use that machine. In that case, there seems to be no advantage from increasing the stock of existing types of machines. It must be presumed, therefore, that there are models of machinery which 'exist', in the sense that they can be made with existing technology, but which are not yet in use. They are not in use because the rate of return on installing them is less than the rate of interest. But, if the rate of interest were to fall, they would be installed. It follows that, if the supply of capital—strictly, the supply of finance—were to increase, the rate of interest would fall and these machines would be installed. Since there is no scope for investment in any new machine unless the rate of interest falls, we can say that an increase in the capital–labour ratio is possible only if the rate of interest falls.[20]

It seems, then, that if we choose an appropriate set of assumptions we can establish a law of diminishing returns to capital. But it is important to note how special these assumptions are. There is perfect competition; perfect knowledge of existing technique; and all producers already use the machines which yield a return equal to or exceeding the current rate of interest. It follows logically that any machines which are not in use have a rate of return below the current rate of interest. Hence there must be diminishing returns to any additions to capital (other than for general expansion).[21]

[20] There will be an increase in the capital–labour ratio if the new machines cost more than those which they replace. There is no certainty, however, that this will be so.

[21] An alternative line of argument might be that at a lower rate of interest some firms will invest in machines of types already in use elsewhere in the economy but not yet used in the given industry; for example, a farmer may buy himself a typewriter for use on the few occasions when he needs to type a letter. There is certainly some scope for investments which yield diminishing returns of this sort; but it is very limited so long as the list of available machines is strictly specified.

But this model is extremely artificial. It is true that some items of machinery, fully specified in advance, are offered by their manufacturers as standard products for general sale. But these constitute only a minor part of total fixed investment. All the rest is either construction or custom-built plant and machinery, produced to the customer's requirements. It is impossible to say how much of such investment represents the application of 'existing' techniques, and how much incorporates new techniques. In the real world, new techniques are being discovered every day and almost every new investment incorporates something new or different. There is no 'perfect knowledge' of existing techniques; new knowledge is constantly coming into existence, and it is initially the exclusive property of the first discoverer. Hence, it is impossible to draw up a list of 'existing' machines and to deduce that all machines already in use are necessarily more profitable than those which are not yet in use.

There is a further weakness in this line of argument. Because machines are so heterogeneous, an increase in the use of one type of machine frequently raises the profitability of another type of machine. Cars, for example, raise the profitability of garages. As investment edges forwards it creates new investment opportunities in complementary industries. The list of investment opportunities is not given *ab initio*, but is constantly being extended as conditions change and experience grows. The demand for investment is not like a housewife's shopping list for groceries but more like steps in solving a jig-saw puzzle, a puzzle of indefinitely large dimensions. There is no reason to presume that the productivity of time spent on a jigsaw diminishes as the number of completed pieces increases; on the contrary, it is quite likely to be increasing.[22]

*Conclusion*

We must conclude that neoclassical theory provides no clear predictions about the factor distribution of income. The Walrasian general equilibrium model is empirically empty and, as will be seen in Chapter 5, it is also theoretically unsatisfactory. The aggregate production function appears at first sight to offer

[22] Compare Scott (1976).

important insights, but it is logically insecure. Even if the marginal product of heterogeneous capital were a meaningful concept, it does not correspond to a unique rate of interest. Finally, there is no direct way of establishing that an increase in the capital–labour ratio must inevitably produce diminishing returns.

While this completes what we have to say about the neoclassical theory of distribution, we cannot simply dismiss neoclassical theory as a whole. If there is to be a better theory of distribution, it must stand on the shoulders of previous economic theory. It is necessary, therefore, to look more closely at the fundamental assumptions of neoclassical theory in order to discover which of them have been fruitful and which misleading. We proceed with this task in the following chapter.

# 5

## THE METHODOLOGY OF NEOCLASSICAL THEORY

Any theory of the behaviour of a market economy seems to require the following elements: (1) assumptions about the objectives of the decision-makers; (2) a competitive mechanism; (3) a role for time and change; and (4) some kind of equilibrium. Without the first of these, there is no means of predicting the responses of decision-makers to alternative environments; without the second, there are no market constraints on individual decisions; without the third, the economy is in a timeless vacuum; and without the fourth, it is impossible to predict the aggregate effects of individual decisions.

In classical economics the last three elements were included explicitly, but the first was largely implicit. If legal constraints were removed, it was assumed that competition would be 'free'; the economy was thought of as in a process of continual change, with powerful forces driving it forwards; and there was a tendency towards equilibrium. The sources of dynamic change were growth of population, accumulation of capital out of profits, economies of scale associated with specialization in a widening market, and technical improvement. The classical economists, however, gave little direct attention to the objectives of decision-makers. Implicitly, they seemed to assume that landlords aim to maximize their rents; capitalists have two objectives—to maximize current profits on invested capital and to accumulate more capital as rapidly as possible (presumably subject to some constraint on their minimum level of consumption); while workers were considered to be in the grip of forces outside themselves, which led them to produce at least as many children as their wages would allow to survive. Nothing much was said about the objectives of consumers: in any case, in a world where workers were assumed to buy only necessities and other classes mainly luxuries there was not much to be said.

The point of view of neoclassical theory is quite different. First, there is great emphasis on a precise specification of the objectives of decision-makers. The utility-function and the logic of rational choice are regarded as being of fundamental importance. Competition is 'perfect', and equilibrium is general. But time and expectations tend to disappear.

From the point of view of modern neoclassical theory it is easy to find fault with the classical economists. Why should workers go on producing children up to the limits of subsistence? Why should capitalists go on accumulating mechanically until the profit rate is driven to its minimum? Why does classical economics contain no explicit theory of rational choice? But neoclassical theory is very weak in its handling of time and change. It is instructive to see why this is so.

*The method of rational choice*

The root of the difficulty lies in the emphasis which neoclassical theory gives to the role of rational choice.[1] When closely examined, the economic theory of choice is a curious concept. Since economics is intended to be (at least in part) a positive science, one would have assumed that a theory of choice would start from (or at least include) a study of the actual behaviour of choosers, or decision-makers. A theory would then be developed with a view to explaining these observed patterns of behaviour. But this has not been the procedure in economics. Economists have not been primarily interested in *explaining* choice. Instead, they have made use of certain assumptions about the objects and methods of economic choices in order to explain other phenomena. Thus it would be more correct to describe neoclassical theory as the *method* of rational choice.

A typical problem which neoclassical theory is designed to solve is as follows: Suppose that a group of independent utility-maximizing people have the opportunity to trade in a free market. What will be the outcome? In order to solve this problem it is necessary to specify more clearly what is meant by 'utility-maximizing people' and a 'free market'. A good deal of attention has been given to the latter concept; and it is not too difficult to define it in a meaningful way, i.e. in a manner which

---

[1] In recent years, some economists have gone so far as to assert that economics *is* a theory of choice, and nothing more. This was, of course, the central concept in Robbins's influential essay on economic methodology, *The Nature and Significance of Economic Science* (1932).

permits the making of falsifiable predictions. But less attention has been given to defining the meaning of utility-maximization. The general tendency has been to assume that the concept is intuitively self-evident. But a little thought will show that this concept conceals a number of important assumptions, which play a crucial role in determining the effects of employing the method of rational choice. The elucidation of these assumptions is the task to which we must now address ourselves.

It is assumed, in the first place, that a utility-maximizer is *rational*. If utility-maximizing meant no more than 'choosing', the use of the term would add nothing, since the statement that people 'choose' gives no guidance about either (a) the objectives of their choices or (b) their methods of choice; and without these we cannot make any prediction about the outcome of their decisions. It is possible, however, to infer what economists mean by rational choice from the more fundamental concept of utility-maximization. To say that a person is a utility-maximizer implies (1) that he is interested in maximizing his satisfaction from 'economic', or scarce, goods and services; (2) that he takes account of relevant alternative ways of achieving this objective; and (3) that he uses reason, or good sense, in weighing one alternative line of conduct against another. The first characteristic is necessary to make him a *utility*-maximizer; the second and third characteristics make him a utility-*maximizer*. It is the latter two characteristics which permit us to describe him as *rational*.

There is nothing more that need be said from a methodological point of view about the first characteristic. As a statement about people's objectives it is perhaps neither perfect nor complete; but it is a plausible assumption, and it has proved to have great explanatory power. Indeed, without an assumption of this sort there could be no theory of economics. But both the second and the third characteristics raise some difficult problems, which require further discussion.

The difficulties arise because the above descriptions of these characteristics lack precision. In particular, we are not told, in the case of the second characteristic, what is the range of relevant alternatives which should be taken into account by a utility-maximizer, nor, in the case of the third characteristic, what is the degree of reason or good sense which he is expected to use. It is a known fact that people vary considerably both in the amount of information available to them and in their reasoning ability. Something must, therefore, be specified about assumed levels of information and ability if the theory of utility-maximization is to produce definite results.

Neoclassical theory has dealt with these problems by adding a further—often implicit—assumption. That assumption is that all decision-makers are equal in both their information and their reasoning, or decision-making, ability. It is easy to see why the theory has chosen this assumption. The alternative would be to embark on a complex study of the reasons why people differ in these two respects. Moreover, if the theory of choice is confined to simple cases, it is not unreasonable, as an approximation, to assume that everyone has equal information and ability. And the bulk of textbook examples of market equilibrium are simple.

The assumption of equal information and ability is not implausible in cases where both the amount of information required for a rational decision and the degree of required reasoning ability are limited. In the theory of consumer choice, for example, potential consumers are required to know only the qualities of different goods and services (i.e. their capacities to provide satisfaction) and the prices at which they are available; while the required level of reasoning ability amounts to no more than an ability to imagine potential satisfactions from different goods, to compare them, and to do simple arithmetic. It may be presumed that knowledge of the qualities of goods and services comes from previous experience, knowledge of prices comes from the market, imagination and the ability to compare are given by nature, and a knowledge of arithmetic is learnt in school.

Production decisions, however, are not quite so easy. In this case the standard decision-maker is assumed to know (1) the qualities of alternative goods, (2) the qualities of alternative factors of production, (3) the range of alternative production techniques, and (4) the current prices of goods and factors. His reasoning ability must also extend beyond simple arithmetic. He must have an elementary knowledge of accounting and he is usually assumed to be able to think in marginal terms. Finally, investment decisions are not at all easy. They require estimates of future events, an ability to calculate either internal rates of return or present discounted values, and an ability to estimate the present and future cost of capital.

So long as neoclassical theory is confined to problems of consumer choice and pure exchange equilibrium the required levels of information and ability are sufficiently limited to be compatible with the assumption that everyone is equal in these respects.[2] But to make a similar assumption about production and investment decisions is inherently implausible, unless one is dealing with very simple techniques or very short-lived investments. Yet this is precisely the assumption on which neoclassical theory has so far been based.

I shall not pursue at this point further discussion of the effects of differences in abilities. They will be given much emphasis in subsequent chapters in which I present my positive theory of income distribution. But the problem of information is one which needs to be examined more fully at this stage, since it is of central importance for neoclassical theory.

If, as has been said, everyone is assumed to take account of relevant alternatives before making his choices, the range of alternatives about which he is informed must be specified. If that information is limited to the immediate qualities and prices of goods and services, it seems reasonable to assume that in a developed market everyone can easily obtain equal information about all relevant alternatives. In other words, everyone has 'perfect' information about relevant alternatives. This will be called the 'perfect knowledge' assumption.[3] Although it is a strong assumption, it must not be confused with the assumption of 'infinite' knowledge, or omniscience, which goes much further.

If all decisions in a competitive market economy were taken simultaneously, and the effects of those decisions occurred in the same instant of time, all relevant facts could in principle be known by all decision-makers at that moment of time. This being so, each decision-maker would not only *think* that he was

---

[2] Even in this case it would be easy to raise objections. Knowledge of the qualities of durable and luxury goods, i.e. goods purchased infrequently, is usually very unequal; and rational decisions about purchases of durables require abilities of a type similar to those required for investment decisions.

[3] See also Hutchinson's discussion (1960, Chap. IV) of the 'perfect expectation' assumption.

maximizing his utility but would *in fact* be maximizing his utility, subject to the constraints of his resources and the market environment in which he was operating. The position of general equilibrium which would be reached (with the help of an 'auctioneer', no doubt) could then be described as an 'optimum' in the Pareto sense, i.e. in the sense that no person could by revising his decisions make himself better off without making at least one person worse off.[4] And this optimum would at the same time be both an *ex ante* optimum, i.e. one chosen by each person with the expectation that it would give the most utility, and an *ex post* optimum, i.e. one which did in fact yield the most utility to each person (subject as before to the constraints of resources and the market).

It follows that, in these circumstances, a state of general equilibrium is both a positive prediction of the theory and a normative condition. An 'equilibrium' becomes an 'optimum', not only in the *ex ante* sense but also in the *ex post* sense. A competitive market is shown to produce certain definite results; and in addition, those results are the *best possible* results.

This is the fundamental theorem of neoclassical economics: the theorem of Walrasian general equilibrium. Because it is such a striking theorem, and apparently corresponds so closely to the intuitive conclusions of Adam Smith and those of his followers who accepted his faith in the wisdom of the 'invisible hand', there has been a tendency for the theorem to be generalized far beyond the restrictive assumptions on which it is based. In particular, there has been a tendency to believe that rational choice *plus* a competitive market *equals* an *ex post* optimum. The point at which this logical chain is most insecure is the point at which an *ex ante* optimum is equated with an *ex post* optimum. This weakness is usually concealed by using the word 'optimum' to cover both conditions, without clearly recognizing that this is only true if every decision-maker has perfect knowledge.

But when time exists there cannot be perfect knowledge. Time means lack of simultaneity between decisions and the outcome of those decisions. And time means change and the

---

[4] Since the job of the auctioneer is to ensure that everyone is satisfied with his own decisions, given everyone else's decisions, it necessarily follows that the general equilibrium is Pareto-optimal.

expectation of change. Expectations of change and of the outcome of current decisions are inescapably uncertain. Hence, in all cases where a decision is likely to have future consequences which are relevant to that decision, it is logically impossible to assume that decision-makers have perfect knowledge of all relevant facts. It follows that, wherever decisions have relevant future consequences, the fundamental theorem of neoclassical theory is invalid. There is no method of demonstrating that, in such a case, a competitive market will necessarily produce an *ex post* optimum. This is the great dilemma of neoclassical theory: how to reconcile rational choice (leading to an *ex post* optimum) and time.[5]

*Attempts to avoid the dilemma*

As we have seen, the fundamental cause of this dilemma is the desire to combine a normative objective with the existence of time. It would be easy to escape the dilemma if the normative aim were abandoned. There is no incompatibility between choice, as such, and uncertainty. On the contrary, if there were certainty, there would be no choice. Nor is there any necessary inconsistency between uncertainty and *rational* choice, provided that rational choice is not defined to include perfect knowledge. A man may behave more or less rationally in the face of uncertainty. While there is no unique definition of perfectly rational behaviour in such circumstances, there are some actions which can be shown to be less-than-rational.[6]

But neoclassical theory is loath to abandon its normative aim. The fundamental theorem is too good to let slip. Hence, the suggested ways out of the dilemma have concentrated on the other alternative: how to eliminate the disturbing influence of time. Three ways of escape have been suggested. The first is static analysis; the second is the stationary state assumption; and the third is the Arrow–Debreu model. I shall consider these in turn.

[5] Among those who have given emphasis to this conclusion special mention should be made of Shackle. Out of many possible citations from his work see, for example, (1970, 20–1).

[6] For example, although future net cash flows resulting from an investment cannot be reduced to certainty by any purely rational process, it would be less-than-rational to refuse to estimate them or to refrain from calculating the net present value of those estimates.

The static method is the most simple; and it has also proved to be the most fruitful in practice. In this case, the dilemma of rational optimizing choice *versus* time and uncertainty is avoided by assuming that at the moment of decision the future is irrelevant. The data which are relevant to an optimal decision are allowed to include past events and current events, but not future events. In such circumstances, there is no logical obstacle to the assumption of perfect knowledge of all relevant facts. The method can be applied without gross implausibility to decisions about consumption of non-durable goods and services, and to the achievement of general equilibrium in a 'pure exchange' economy in which there are no durable goods. But it is clearly inapplicable to decisions about saving and investment, including investment in human capital, as well as to most production decisions. Attempts have been made to overcome this difficulty by assuming, either explicitly or implicitly, the existence of 'static expectations', which means that people always expect the future to be exactly like the present. But this method creates more problems than it solves. If, for example, people expected future prices to be the same as current prices, those expectations themselves would cause shifts in market supply and demand curves, and hence lead to changes in current prices. Analysis of the interactions between present and expected future prices would require a complex model going far beyond the usual assumptions that supply and demand curves are determined by tastes, techniques, and resources.[7]

It must be admitted, however, that the static method, with all its defects, has proved a powerful tool of economic analysis. Without comparative statics, there would be little to show for economic theory, whether neoclassical or not. All economic models are about the interacting forces of supply and demand (even the models of Ricardo and Marx, despite their protestations to the contrary). In the absence of empirical estimates of dynamic adjustment functions, the static method of solving by simultaneous equations gives at least a first approximation. Yet it is clear that static analysis is no solution to the problem of optimal choice in a world of time.

---

[7] Hicks's concept (1946, 205) of an elasticity of expectations, although more general than the concept of static expectations, runs into the same difficulties.

The second method of avoiding the dilemma is to limit the analysis to stationary states. While in static analysis the future is irrelevant, in a stationary state the future exists and is relevant. But the stationary state is one in which nothing has changed for as long as anyone can remember, with the consequence that no one expects any change in the future. Everyone is currently in equilibrium, i.e. satisfied with his past decisions, and, because everything is expected to remain unchanged in the future, no new decisions are ever made. Hence everything in fact remains unchanged; and so the system perpetuates itself. Thus the future has been allowed to exist without abandoning the assumption of perfect knowledge and without destroying equilibrium. But the price which is paid for this result is excessive, since the stationary state assumption rules out change. It allows perfect freedom of choice, but only on condition that no new choices are ever made.[8] Whereas the method of comparative statics is illuminating in many contexts, the comparison of alternative stationary states has no conceivable operational significance. In statics, new decisions can be made and the economy can move; in stationary states, no new decisions can be made, and the economy cannot move from one stationary state to another.[9]

In the third proposal—the Arrow–Debreu model—it is assumed that on some initial date everyone enters into conditional contracts for deliveries of goods and services at all possible future dates.[10] The contracts are conditional on the development of the physical environment up to each specified date. It is sometimes said that they are conditional on the 'state of the world'; but the 'state of the world' is defined as a scenario of the evolution of the physical environment at all future dates until the end of time. Hence the true 'state of the world' can never be known at any finite point in time. All that can be known at a given date is the history of the environment up to that date. Consequently, at every date there will be continuing uncertainty about future changes in the environment beyond that date. The most that could be achieved by the proposed sets

[8] In this respect it is reminiscent of the Hegelian conception of freedom as 'the appreciation of necessity'.

[9] See the discussion in Hicks (1946, 117–19).

[10] The principal references are Arrow (1964), Debreu (1959), Radner (1968), and Arrow and Hahn (1971).

of conditional contracts, therefore, would be a consistent set of deliveries at each future date. To this extent they would reduce uncertainty; but uncertainty would never be completely eliminated, since contracts conditional on a given history of the environment up to a specified date would still be subject to uncertainty about the future beyond that date.

There appear to be two major logical objections to the Arrow–Debreu model. The first arises from the fact that the environment includes not only natural conditions, such as the weather, but also the state of technical knowledge. Even if it were possible to describe other aspects of the environment in the detail necessary for a valid contract, it is logically impossible to describe today every kind of technical knowledge which might exist in the future. We cannot *describe* technical knowledge which we do not already *know*. The second logical problem is how to make choices today on behalf of people who may have different tastes in the future. New generations may well have different tastes; indeed, the person who chooses today may himself have different tastes in the future. Even if one could describe all possible changes in taste in advance—which is doubtful—there is no method by which the preferences of those signing contracts today could be balanced against the different preferences of those who would be implementing those contracts in the future.[11]

Apart from the practical obstacles to making millions, or possibly an infinite number, of conditional contracts, given the costs of information, decision-making, and transactions (e.g. drawing up the contracts), together with the super-*tâtonnement* process which would be required to reach equilibrium, it is probable that uncertainty about future changes in tastes and techniques would raise an absolute barrier to the proposal. Because of these uncertainties, people prefer to retain freedom of choice. Indeed, freedom of choice is a condition which yields a utility in its own right, independent of the fruits of choice. One of the principal virtues of the market is that it permits freedom of choice and decentralized decision-making. It is a paradox that a theory designed to prove the virtues of a market system should generate a model in which freedom of choice for all subsequent generations would disappear.

[11] See also Kurz (1974).

*The perfect knowledge assumption*

We have seen that the root of the problem of reconciling rational choice with time is the assumption of perfect knowledge. A partial solution to the problem is to employ the static method, which excludes the relevance of the future. But economic theory is thereby debarred from studying saving and investment decisions, and also the majority of production decisions. It is clear, therefore, that the knowledge assumptions of economic theory need to be reconsidered. But, before proceeding with this task, it will be useful to review some of the other unsatisfactory consequences of the perfect knowledge assumption. By 'unsatisfactory consequences' of an assumption I mean empirical predictions, flowing from the assumption, which are inconsistent with known facts.

Consider first the area of consumption behaviour. If all consumers had perfect *ex ante* knowledge of the qualities and prices of products, there would be no advertising. Marketing costs would be zero; product differentiation, no matter how elaborate, would not create significant market imperfections; and there would be no need for the existence of consumer advice organizations. In recognition of these facts, the theory of imperfect competition is based on the abandonment of the assumption of perfect knowledge of the qualities and prices of products.

Much more serious difficulties arise from the use of the perfect knowledge assumption in the theory of the firm, especially in relation to decisions about production and investment. Leaving aside for the moment the assumption of perfect knowledge of the *future*, let us consider some implications of perfect knowledge of the *present*. If every firm had complete knowledge of existing techniques, and all had equal ability to choose the most appropriate technique, there would be no differences between any two firms making the same products in their efficiency, their size, or their profitability. Nor would there be such a phenomenon as learning-by-doing. If the equal technical knowledge assumption were extended across regions and national boundaries (as it sometimes is), a large part of existing trade between regions and countries would be inexplicable; and there would be no demand from the less developed countries for improvements in the arrangements for 'transfer of technology'.[12]

Perfect knowledge of the qualities of the managements of firms by potential lenders would greatly reduce the imperfections of the capital market. If extended to include perfect knowledge of the future, it would entirely remove the risk element in lending or investing in equity, and there would indeed be a uniform rate of profit equal to the rate of interest. Despite the fact that almost every economic theory has predicted that under competitive conditions there will be a uniform rate of profit, the prediction is clearly inconsistent with empirical observations.

When perfect knowledge of existing techniques is combined with a perfect capital market and free entry (an essential element in the definition of a competitive market), but without perfect knowledge of the future, the results are likely to be explosive. In these circumstances, an increase in demand for a product would attract an indefinitely large inflow of new entrants which, together with some expansion of the capacity of existing producers, would cause the price of the product to collapse in the future.[13] While there is some tendency for such market behaviour to occur, it is never as serious as it would be under the assumed conditions of perfect knowledge, and in most industries it is of slight importance. While this is partly due to the fact that most markets are not perfectly competitive (although there is usually free entry), the main reasons are that knowledge of techniques is unequally distributed and the capital market is imperfect.

It should be noted that one of the implications of the instability of the combination of perfect competition with perfect knowledge of techniques and a perfect capital market is that a steady state of positive growth is impossible under such conditions. Indeed, it is doubtful whether a stationary state (a steady state with zero growth) is possible, since a stationary state can be maintained only by a positive amount of *gross* investment, and there is no mechanism under these conditions for ensuring that

---

[12] Legal patent rights are, of course, always treated as an exception to the perfect technical knowledge assumption. But they constitute only a minor obstacle to the equalization of technical knowledge.

[13] See Richardson (1960).

the correct amount of gross investment is undertaken in each industry.[14]

As mentioned earlier, a consequence of combining perfect knowledge of techniques with a perfect capital market would be that no firm in a competitive industry would operate in the long run at a scale below the optimum. Hence, except in the unlikely event of constant long-run costs, all firms making a given product, or combination of products, would be of the same size. Although it is difficult to find an industry which precisely matches the requirements of perfect competition, in those in which the conditions are approximately satisfied there is no convincing evidence that firms tend to be of equal optimum size. Indeed, the main lesson of the statistics is that the distribution of firm sizes in *any* industry is very unequal and positively skew.

On similar assumptions, there would be no tendency for firms to grow in size over time, except as a consequence of changes in technique or in relative factor prices; and the well-known phenomenon of persistent reinvestment of a considerable part of net profits would be inexplicable. Finally, with perfect knowledge of the present, information costs would be zero and no resources would be devoted to 'search'; and with perfect knowledge of the future, there would be no need for money or for other liquid assets.

*Possible alternative assumptions*

If it is agreed, as I believe that it must be agreed, that the perfect knowledge assumption is often an absurd assumption, and destructive of economic theory, we need to ask what assumption, or set of assumptions, should be used in its place. The question seems to be a very open one. Once we have thrown over the simple extreme assumption, almost anything is possible. Clearly we must assume some degree of knowledge, or decision-making would be entirely random. The problem is to suggest some intermediate position which is both realistic and helpful.

There are five major types of information which are needed

---

[14] Such a mechanism would exist if there were no gestation lag in investment. But that assumption is an arbitrary addition to the stationary state.

by decision-makers in a market economy, and each of these can refer either to the date of the decision or to various future dates. Information is required about (1) the qualities of goods and factors, (2) their prices, (3) techniques, (4) the natural enviroment, and (5) the resources of goods and factors at the disposal of each decision-maker. As regards *present* knowledge, it is not unreasonable to assume that each decision-maker has a good knowledge of the natural environment and of his own resources, and a fairly good, although approximate, knowledge of prices. Prices are not freely available even in the most competitive economy; but they are for the most part public information, or information which can be obtained at a low cost. Similar considerations apply to the qualities of *products* but not to the qualities of *factors*. Knowledge of product quality in a market economy is a public good. But knowledge of factor qualities is largely private. The qualities of employees, for example, cannot be discovered except by actual experience (or from the experience of previous employers), and the qualities of entrepreneurs and management groups are even less easy to assess with accuracy.

The type of current information which is most imperfectly distributed is knowledge of techniques. Broadly, information about techniques can be divided into that which is public and that which is private. Public techniques include those which are (1) taught in schools and other institutions, (2) described in books and journals, and (3) widely diffused through the movement of employees from firm to firm. Private techniques are techniques which are known only to the firm in which they are used. As time passes, private techniques gradually become public; but the rate at which this change takes place may be slow, especially for the more complex techniques. In general, physical techniques can be made public fairly easily, since an examination of the product will often provide essential clues about its method of production. But techniques of organization and management are much more difficult to discover and to imitate. These are the kinds of assumptions which, it is suggested, should replace the usual assumption of 'given' technique. We shall see what effects they produce when my model of income distribution is described in Chapter 9 below.

As regards knowledge of the future, the degree of certainty

will vary both with the decision-maker and with the type of information. In no case, of course, can knowledge of the future be absolutely certain. Even with a futures market, there is no guarantee that contracts will be honoured. In general, knowledge of the future trend of the natural environment over a fairly short period is regarded as fairly certain. Knowledge of other matters, however, is usually very uncertain, especially knowledge of the more distant future. No system of economic organization can, therefore, guarantee the *ex post* optimality of decisions.

*Conclusion*

In this chapter we have examined some of the fundamental assumptions of neoclassical theory. A major difference between neoclassical theory and previous economic theories is the emphasis placed on the role of rational choice by the utility-maximizing decision-maker. But the concept of rational choice cannot be defined clearly without specifying (1) the amount of information available to the chooser and (2) his ability to take a rational decision. In neoclassical theory it is normally assumed that all decision-makers are equal, both in their range of information and in their reasoning abilities. The influence of differences in abilities on the distribution of income is an important matter for discussion in subsequent chapters, where my theory of income distribution will be described. In this chapter I have given further consideration to the role of information.

If the effects of decisions are assumed to occur without any time-lag—as in the Walrasian system—the assumption of *equal* information is equivalent to an assumption of *perfect* information about all relevant facts. This is the implicit assumption which underlies the neoclassical model of general competitive equilibrium, and which yields the striking theorem that an equilibrium is also an *ex post* optimum (in the Pareto sense). Thus a positive theory appears to lead directly to normative conclusions.

But perfect knowledge of the future is logically impossible. Attempts to avoid the dilemma of choosing between the model of optimal choice and the effects of time and uncertainty have taken three forms: the static method, the stationary state assumption, and the Arrow–Debreu model. In static analysis, the future is assumed to be irrelevant; in the stationary state, the future is assumed to be exactly like the (unchanging) present; and in the Arrow–Debreu model part of the problem of future uncertainty is assumed to be removed by a comprehensive system of futures contracts. The defects of these models have been examined, and the conclusion has been drawn that in a realistic model of an economy developing in time the perfect knowledge assumption must be abandoned. Some of the other undesirable consequences of the perfect knowledge assumption—including perfect knowledge of conditions existing in the present—have also been discussed.

If perfect knowledge is dropped, it becomes necessary to make alternative assumptions about the extent of knowledge available to decision-makers. No great objection can be taken to assuming a fairly good knowledge *in the present* of product qualities and prices, the resources available to the decision-maker, and the natural environment. But, even in the present, it is unrealistic to assume that there is equal knowledge of the qualities of the factors of production or of techniques. In particular, it is necessary to relinquish the assumptions of a perfect capital market and 'given' technique. As regards the future, nothing can be known for certain; and the aim of demonstrating that a general equilibrium is also an *ex post* optimum must be abandoned.

These conclusions will play an important role in the model of income distribution which will be presented in Chapter 9. But before we proceed with that task there are three more topics to be discussed. The first is the work of Marshall, whose approach was different from that of modern neoclassical theory based on Walras; the second is the group of theories associated with Keynes and some of his followers; and the third is a survey of the known facts about income distribution, which should be a prerequisite for constructing an explanatory theory. We shall discuss these three topics in the next three chapters.

# 6

## MARSHALL

Modern economic theory is essentially Walrasian. As Professor Samuelson (1962, 3) has said, 'Today, there can be little doubt that most of the literary and mathematical economic theory appearing in our professional journals is more an offspring of Walras than of anyone else'. The attraction of the Walrasian approach is that it permits the construction of a general equilibrium model without abandoning the simplicity and power of the static method. But the price which must be paid is very large: there is no time, no uncertainty, no expectations, no time-lags, no unexploited economies of scale, no learning-by-doing, no cobwebs, no business cycles, no involuntary unemployment, and no logical place for money. The Walrasian world is a world of simultaneous equations.

By comparison, Marshall has an earthy quality. Above all, he was impressed by the importance of time in economics, 'the centre of the chief difficulty of almost every economic problem' (1920, vii). This preoccupation is shown by Marshall's emphasis on the role of expectations, by his distinction between market-day, short-period, and long-period equilibria, by his recognition of the continuing importance of internal economies of scale, and by his theory of the growth and decline of firms. The conversion of modern economics in the English-speaking countries from a Marshallian to a Walrasian basis has produced some striking technical results but has been accompanied by a growing superficiality of economic analysis.

In this chapter we shall first discuss two aspects of Marshall's work, which are especially relevant to the theory of income distribution which will be outlined in Chapter 9. These are his theory of market equilibrium and his theory of the growth of firms. At the end of the chapter I shall briefly review Marshall's views on the theory of distribution as a whole.

*Walrasian equilibrium*

Before we turn directly to Marshall's concept of equilibrium it
will be useful to say something about the alternative Walrasian
concept. In this way we shall be able to appreciate more clearly
the essential contribution which Marshall made in this area.

In the Walrasian model, market equilibrium is a condition
where prices—and hence incomes—are such as to make supply
equal to demand for every product and factor service; or, in
other words, where the vector of excess demands is zero. Since
this is a timeless equilibrium, Walras was obliged to assume
that production is timeless, which is clearly absurd. If production is left out, the Walrasian model is a model of a pure
exchange economy, corresponding approximately to Marshall's concept of market-day equilibrium. It may be supposed,
for example, that producers bring their goods to market on a
certain day and offer them in exchange for other goods, *nothing
being withheld with a view to future sale*. In these circumstances, we
can imagine prices as being determined by the balancing of
consumer preferences, as in an Edgeworth box diagram. If
equilibrium is reached on that day, there is nothing more to be
said. No consequences follow.

But what would happen if equilibrium were not achieved? It
is necessary first to clarify what is meant by saying that equilibrium is not achieved. According to Walras's definitions, there is
disequilibrium when excess demands are not all equal to zero.
As applied to our market day, this presumably means that
when trading ends (at the end of the day) there are suppliers
who would have liked to have exchanged their goods for other
goods but who have—at least partly—failed to do so. Some
suppliers are obliged to take home goods which they had hoped
to sell. If this is called excess supply, there will be an exactly
equal value—at some notional prices—of excess demand, the
demand which would have existed if the suppliers had been
able to sell their goods at those prices.

But we need to go more deeply into the question. Why, we
may ask, did some suppliers fail to sell all the goods which they
had hoped to sell? The Walrasian answer is that at the prices
'ruling' in the market there were not enough buyers for those
goods. But what is a 'ruling' price? Walras suggested a model in

which, after a random start, an auctioneer proclaims a set of suggested prices. After each such proclamation, these are the prices which are 'ruling'. But, of course, they are quite hypothetical, as indeed is the auctioneer himself. In a real competitive market (for example, in stocks and shares or in commodities) no one proclaims prices at which everyone can expect to trade. The only prices which exist are *ex post* prices, records of the terms on which previous bargains have been made. But in a free market no one buys or sells except to suit himself. Hence every actual sale is an equilibrium transaction for the actual buyer and seller at that instant of time. If it is agreed that all actual sales in a market are equilibrium transactions, the only remaining source of disequilibrium will be 'frustrated' sales—the sales which would have occurred if prices had been different.

But why should there be such a phenomenon as 'frustrated' sales? Except in the case where sellers are unable to dispose of their goods at a positive price, the only free-market explanation of the sellers' frustration is that they were unwilling to sell at the price which buyers were willing to offer; and hence they *voluntarily* withheld their goods from the market. But this contradicts the original assumption that no goods were voluntarily withheld for future sale. Hence, a disequilibrium can exist, in practice, only if sellers set reserve prices on their goods. And these reserve prices arise because sellers have expectations that if they withhold their goods today they will be able to sell them at a better price in the future. A Walrasian disequilibrium can occur, then, only if sellers have expectations about future prices, which prevent them from selling today at whatever price they can get today. But this conflicts with the whole basis of the Walrasian model, which rules out time and expectations. The Walrasian definition of disequilibrium appears, therefore, to be internally inconsistent.

## Marshall's equilibrium

Marshall's views about the nature of market-day equilibrium are best understood by a consideration of the example which he gave of a corn market in a country town. Each farmer is assumed to bring to market corn of identical quality. The

amount which he offers for sale 'is governed by his own need for
money in hand, and by his calculation of the present *and future*
conditions of the market' (1920, 332, italics added). 'Everyone
will try to guess the state of the market and govern his actions
accordingly.' Each farmer is assumed to have a minimum
reserve price, below which he would rather leave the market
without selling. If the amounts available at each price are
arranged in order of price and the amounts which buyers are
willing to buy at each price are arranged similarly, it becomes
clear to an outside observer that at one particular price (36s in
his example) supply and demand will be equal. Through 'higgl-
ing and bargaining' the price gets 'tossed hither and thither like
a shuttlecock' but, unless either the buyers or the sellers are
'very simple or unfortunate in failing to gauge the strength of
the other side, the price is likely to be never far from 36s; and it
is nearly sure to be pretty close to 36s at the end of the market'
(p. 333).

From Marshall's description of how his corn market behaves
it is clear that expectations play a very important role. Both
buyers and sellers are influenced on the given day by their
expectations of the price at which corn will be sold on subsequent days. 'Even in the corn-exchange of a country town on a
market-day the equilibrium price is affected by calculations of
the future relations of production and consumption' (p. 337).
Within the day, also, the prices quoted are influenced by dealers' expectations about the prices likely to be quoted later in the
day. Thus Marshall's analysis, even of market-day equilibrium, is never strictly static, but always takes account of the
influence of the future on the present. In such a context it
is impossible to argue that the sole determinants of market
price are the immediate marginal utilities of the goods to the
transactors.

### Short-period and long-period equilibria

On market day the maximum possible supply of goods—but
not of services—is the stock on hand, which has been created as
a result of previous production decisions. For the reasons given
above, there is no guarantee that the whole of this available
stock will be sold, or, if sold to dealers, that it will be taken off

the market. Part of it may be on offer again on the next market day. But the prices at which sales are made on market day—there is no guarantee that they will converge to a single price—give producers important information. These prices help producers to formulate their expectations about future market prices—the prices which will exist at the time when future supplies of their products are put on the market. These expected future prices are the prices which are relevant for current decisions about (a) production with existing plant and equipment, and (b) expansion or contraction of existing plant and equipment. These are, approximately, what Marshall meant by short-period and long-period supply decisions.

It is unfortunate that Marshall did not always make it absolutely clear that short-period and long-period supply decisions are dependent on *expected* prices. He did so in some verbal passages (e.g. pp. 372–3), but in his diagrams (e.g. pp. 344 and 346) he slurred over the distinction between current and expected future prices—a practice which has become standard in all subsequent textbooks to this day. It makes no sense, of course, to put 'price' on one axis of a two-dimensional diagram if the demand price is today's price and the supply price is the price which is expected to exist in, say, 12 months from now. The practice can be excused if it is clearly stated that the diagram refers either to a world in which prices never change, so that next year's expected price is the same as today's price (the stationary state assumption), or to a world in which there is no future (the static assumption).[1] But a clear statement of these limitations would rob the diagram of most of its apparent significance. These supply and demand diagrams are, therefore, an illogical cross between statics and dynamics, logically static (or stationary) but interpreted in practice dynamically (or in terms of changes in conditions).

Nevertheless, the very fact that Marshall drew his distinctions between market-day supply, short-period supply, and long-period supply means that he was forcing attention on the problem of time-lags, and on the effects of expectations on

[1] As explained in the previous chapter, there is no way out of this dilemma by making the 'static expectations' assumption that future prices are always equal to current prices. For in that case both the positions and shapes of the supply and demand curves are indeterminate.

decisions about activities which have a gestation lag. There is none of this in Walras and—despite verbal acknowledgements—it plays very little part in modern treatments of economics. Yet the fact that most production and all investment decisions have to be taken in a state of uncertainty about the prices and other conditions (e.g. incomes, technique, natural conditions, and sources of competitive supply) which will exist in the future has profound importance for economic theory. Uncertainty is a main cause of market imperfection, of fixed prices, of industrial concentration, and of the size of measured profits. If expectations and uncertainty are excluded, it is impossible to make sense of most of the central problems of economics.

Because Marshall ultimately slurred over the distinction between current prices and expected future prices, his analysis of the stability of short-period and long-period equilibria is unsatisfactory. What he seems to say is that, when the price (or, more realistically, the range of prices) on market day is expected to be the same on certain future dates, producers make current production and investment decisions which will result in particular supplies being forthcoming on these future dates; and that these decisions will tend to reduce the discrepancy between today's market price and the price which would have corresponded to the expectations of the producers of the current supply. Unfortunately, however, this theorem cannot be proved without additional assumptions. Either there must be differences in the response rates of different firms, or the expectations of firms must be 'adaptive', i.e. adjusted only partially in the direction of the difference between current prices and those which were expected earlier. In any case, there is very likely to be a cobweb pattern of adjustment in a perfectly competitive market. These additional assumptions merely ensure that the cobweb is convergent.

In modern textbook expositions of economic theory the cobweb model is sometimes mentioned, but only as an exception, a special case. The general case is the instantaneous static model where, even in the long period, equilibrium is somehow achieved without any awkward oscillations. But this is an evasion. The more closely a market approximates to the perfect competition model the more likely it is to follow the cobweb pattern of adjustment.[2] Thus the cobweb, instead of being the exception, should be the typical model of perfect competition. The fact that most markets for manufactures and services do not follow this pattern does not prove that such markets are perfectly competitive, but precisely the opposite. Any market which has stable prices is an imperfectly competitive market; and we need a theory other than the perfect competition model of supply and demand to account for such stability.

## The growth of firms

Marshall was a firm believer in the importance of persistent internal economies of scale in manufacturing.[3] Yet he also employed the method of competitive equilibrium analysis. On strictly static assumptions, these components of Marshall's theory are inconsistent with one another. Hence modern Walrasian theory, which adheres to the static method, rejects persistent economies of scale. If the economy is in a static (or stationary) equilibrium with perfect competition, all firms must be operating at a point where long-period marginal cost is rising and is equal to average cost; and there will be no remaining unutilized internal economies of scale. Hicks (1946) and Samuelson (1947) argued that this theorem proves the validity of the law of diminishing returns and the absence of unutilized internal economies of scale. But they failed to justify two important prerequisite assumptions: first, that the real economy is a perfectly competitive economy; and second, that the real economy is in a static or stationary equilibrium.[4]

How did Marshall reconcile his belief in continuing internal economies of scale in most non-primary industries with his use of the apparatus of competitive equilibrium? The first part of

[2] Recent examples are the international markets for wool and sugar. Coffee prices will probably follow a similar pattern as the market adjusts to the recent scarcity.

[3] Summarizing his views on this matter, he wrote: 'In other words, we may say broadly that while the part which nature plays in production shows a tendency to diminishing return, the part which man plays shows a tendency to increasing return. . . . Therefore in those industries which are not engaged in raising raw produce an increase of labour and capital generally gives a return increased more than in proportion' (1920, 318).

[4] Samuelson's rhetorical question (1947, 5) 'How many times has the reader seen an egg standing upon its end?' is hardly a sufficient proof that the economy is in static equilibrium.

the answer to this question is that, at least in Books IV and V, Marshall did not assume *perfect* competition, as it is defined in modern usage. He did not consider that all firms have equal technical knowledge, nor equal access to the capital market; he did not assume perfect competition in the market for entrepreneurs; and he argued that for many commodities in whose production economies of scale are important there are limits to the size of the market, implying that the firms in question face an inelastic market demand.[5]

By contrast with the static model of perfect competition, according to which new entrants to an industry are instantaneously established at an optimum size, Marshall described the process of new entry in historical terms. An aspiring entrepreneur starts in a small way; if he is successful, he attracts credit and builds up wider trade connections; and so his business continues to grow.[6] He is not necessarily producing a commodity which is the same as that produced by hundreds of others; indeed his product may be in some respects unique. Thus, on the one hand, Marshall assumed that there are usually indefinitely continuing opportunities for scale economies, which give a steady incentive to grow. On the other hand, there are obstacles to growth: the time needed to learn new techniques, the time needed to create a larger organization, the time needed to accumulate capital, and the time needed to widen the market. So the process of growth takes time. This brings us to the other part of Marshall's answer.

Marshall did not take the view that a large firm with economies of scale has a permanent advantage over smaller firms. In his vision of an economy, there is a steady turnover of firms. Young and vigorous entrepreneurs start small enterprises which, with luck, become larger, more efficient and more profitable. The process continues, but eventually the business man grows old and tired. His successors are usually not as

---

[5] His general comments on these matters will be found in Book IV, Chapter XI of the *Principles*. On the problem of limited demand see also p. 458.

[6] Note also Marshall's assertion that 'every step in the advance of an able and enterprising manufacturer makes the succeeding step easier and more rapid; so that his progress upwards is likely to continue so long as he has fairly good fortune, and retains his full energy and elasticity and his liking for hard work' (1920, 457).

efficient as he, especially those of the second succeeding generation, and the firm begins to decline. Its decline may be temporarily arrested by converting it into a joint-stock company,
but such companies usually stagnate. Marshall supported his
view of the business life-cycle with his famous analogy of the
trees of the forest (pp. 315–16). Hence he drew the conclusion
that 'in almost every trade there is a constant rise and fall of
large businesses, at any one moment some firms being in the
ascending phase and others in the descending' (p. 316).

This model has two important implications: first that, since
each individual firm can continue to expand only for a limited
period of time, there is usually no risk that competition will be
completely eliminated; secondly that, since size and profitability are positively associated, the variation in firm sizes within a
single industry entails also a variation in profit rates within the
same industry. The outcome is, therefore, a coexistence of
competition and positive profits, with differential rates of profit
in different firms—a conclusion which is completely at variance
with the conclusions which would be drawn from static
assumptions.

Marshall tried to formalize his model by introducing the
concept of the 'representative firm'. The representative firm is a
kind of average firm for a given industry: it is 'one which has
had a fairly long life, and fair success, which is managed with
normal ability, and which has normal access to the economies,
external and internal, which belong to that aggregate volume of
production' (p. 317). It is the expenses of the representative
firm which determine the 'normal cost' of producing a commodity. But this is really a tautology, if 'normal' means 'average'. The concept is reminiscent of Marx's 'socially necessary
labour cost', which, as we have seen, is implicitly defined as the
average actual labour cost in a given industry. It is curious that
Marshall failed to use at this point of his analysis the marginal
concept which he employed so effectively elsewhere.

It is important to notice the difference between Marshall's
conception of the equilibrium of an industry and the modern
textbook conception. In the modern textbook all firms operating in a perfectly competitive industry are assumed to be identical, except perhaps for slight differences in the efficiency of
their entrepreneurs, which are reflected in the rents paid for

their services. Under given outside conditions, therefore, every
firm is fixed in size and in the nature of its activities. It hangs
suspended in a completely static world. Changes, or strictly
speaking differences, between one static equilibrium and
another, can come only from exogenous sources. There is no
inner tendency for firms to grow and change. In Marshall's
model, on the other hand, even in a stationary state, where all
outside conditions are constant and expected to remain constant, there is continual movement within each firm and within
the industry. The industry is not a fixed collection of machines
but more like a population of living creatures, whose equilibrium is the consequence of a continual balancing of births and
deaths, of growth and decay. It is an equilibrium in motion;
and such an equilibrium does not necessarily respond to outside stimuli in the same manner as a mechanical equilibrium
would do.[7]

*Theory of distribution*

Marshall devoted the whole of Book VI of his *Principles* (more
than a quarter of the whole volume) to the theory of distribution. But he eventually failed to produce a coherent theory of
his own. As he warned the reader in advance (p. 510), 'It has
now become certain that the problem of distribution is much
more difficult than it was thought to be by earlier economists,
and that no solution of it which claims to be simple can be true.'
Implicitly, Marshall made use of the concept of a micro-
production function, but he did not endow it with fully differentiable properties. Although he assumed that, within certain
limits, the factors of production could usually be combined in
variable proportions, Marshall emphasized that in most cases
it was not possible to vary one factor while keeping all other
factors strictly constant. An extra man, for example, requires

[7] For Marshall's concept of the stationary state see (1920, 367). In other
passages he used mechanical analogies, such as that of a stone on an elastic
string, but these were only provisional simplifications (p. 323). Summarizing
his attitude, he wrote (p. 461): 'economic problems are imperfectly presented
when they are treated as problems of statical equilibrium, and not of organic
growth . . . The statical theory of equilibrium is only an introduction to
economic studies; and it is barely even an introduction to the study of the
progress and development of industries which show a tendency to increasing
return.'

more working capital for materials (and also, although Marshall did not say so explicitly, for his wages). Hence the employment of labour will proceed up to the point at which the value of its marginal *net* product—after subtracting incidental expenses—is equal to the wage. The value of the net product of one factor depends, therefore, on the earnings of the other factors; and it is not possible to arrive at a theory of factor earnings by this route 'without reasoning in a circle' (p. 519). A Walrasian might well reply that the technique of general equilibrium analysis is precisely the appropriate method for solving the problem of 'reasoning in a circle'. But Marshall refused to be drawn into general equilibrium analysis. He did not give clearly stated reasons for his attitude, but from a number of hints one can guess that his main objection was to the static implications of the general equilibrium approach.

Marshall was cautious and somewhat evasive in his discussion of marginal productivity theory. For example, in illustrating the manner in which the investment of capital in a business is pushed to the point at which 'the margin of profitableness is reached' he considered the hat-making industry, and he assumed that 'competition prevents anything more than the ordinary trade profit being got' from investment in that industry (p. 520). Naturally, it follows inevitably from that assumption that investment in the industry will be pushed to the point at which each firm expects to receive the market rate of interest on the final instalment of its investment. But this assumption is inconsistent with Marshall's previous discussion of the pervasive role of internal economies of scale. Curiously, he noticed this inconsistency when commenting on the work of von Thünen,[8] but he failed to notice it in his own discussion.

As we shall see, the reconciliation of internal scale economies with competition depends on the explicit introduction of *time* into the model. A project which is expected to return a rate of profit in excess of the current (and expected) rate of interest

[8] 'With characteristic breadth of view, von Thünen enunciated a general law of diminishing return for successive doses of capital in any branch of production; and what he said on this subject has even now much interest, though it does not show how to reconcile the fact that an increase in the capital employed in an industry may increase the output more than in proportion, with the fact that a continued influx of capital into an industry must ultimately lower the rate of profits earned in it.' (p. 522, fn).

cannot usually, for technical reasons, be implemented instantaneously; and there are other even more cogent reasons why profitable investment projects are spread out over time. These include management bottlenecks, labour-training problems, the desire to provide a sufficient part of the capital out of internal sources, and the time needed to widen the market. All of these obstacles can, if desired, be boiled down into a marginal cost of investment; but their effect is to invalidate the proposition that the marginal expected product of investment is equal to the rate of interest. Marshall had at his disposal all the ingredients of a theory along these lines, but when it came to the point he forgot about them.

There is a strange contrast in Marshall's work between the insight which he revealed in his detailed analysis, as shown by many original and unorthodox ideas which he proposed, and the very conventional conclusions which he reached in the end. Despite all the early emphasis on the role of economies of scale Marshall concluded in Book VI that, other things being equal, 'an increase in the supply of an agent will generally lower its price' (p. 678); and, more specifically, that 'if . . . capital increases much faster than labour, the rate of interest is likely to fall' (p. 670). On the basis of such quotations it is easy for modern economists to regard him as a true member of the neoclassical school, while quietly suppressing the memory of his idiosyncrasies.

# 7

## KEYNESIAN THEORIES

Under this heading I include the theories of the modern Cambridge school of post-Keynesians, in particular Joan Robinson, Kaldor, and Pasinetti; and also Kalecki who, although not a member of the same group, proposed a theory of distribution to which some members of the group are sympathetic. How far Keynes himself would have agreed with these theories is a debatable question, just as it is doubtful whether Marx would have approved of neo-Marxists, or Ricardo of neo-Ricardians. But that is not really of any importance. It will be convenient to start with the theory of distribution proposed by Kaldor and later elaborated by Pasinetti; then to consider the views of Joan Robinson; and finally to examine Kalecki's theory.

*Kaldor*

Kaldor's original theory (1955) was apparently rather simple.[1] Assume that the population is divided permanently into two classes: capitalists and workers. Capitalists have incomes from capital—called profits—and workers have income from work—called wages. Each class has a constant average (and hence marginal) propensity to save. Then, if the ratio of aggregate investment to aggregate income is given exogenously, the distribution of income between profits and wages is determined.

Let $Y = Y_1 + Y_2$, where $Y$ is total income, $Y_1$ is the income of workers, and $Y_2$ the income of capitalists. Let $S = S_1 + S_2$ be the corresponding amounts of saving. Now assume that $S_1 = s_1Y_1$ and $S_2 = s_2Y_2$, where $s_1$ and $s_2$ are constants. Then

$$S = s_1Y_1 + s_2(Y-Y_1) \quad \text{or} \quad S/Y = s_2 + (s_1-s_2)Y_1/Y$$

If we write $s = S/Y$, $y_1 = Y_1/Y$ and $y_2 = Y_2/Y$, where each of these is a dependent variable, we have

---

[1] As Kaldor makes clear, his theory was much influenced by Keynes's theory of the 'widow's cruse', described in *A Treatise on Money* (1930, I, 139), by Kalecki's theory of profits (1942), and by discussions with Joan Robinson.

$$y_1 = \frac{s_2-s}{s_2-s_1} \; , \qquad y_2 = \frac{s-s_1}{s_2-s_1}.$$

$$(7.1)$$

and $y_1 + y_2 = 1$.

Since $s$ is a weighted average of $s_1$ and $s_2$, it is clear that either $s_2 > s > s_1$, or $s_2 = s = s_1$, or $s_2 < s < s_1$. In practice, Kaldor assumes that the first set of inequalities holds: saving out of profits is greater than saving out of wages.

Equations (7.1) cannot be solved without further information about either $y_1$, $y_2$ or $s$. Kaldor chose the last alternative by assuming that the aggregate investment–income ratio, $I/Y$, is given exogenously. Since in a closed economy $s = I/Y$, we can replace $s$ in (7.1) by $I/Y$, which we shall write for convenience as $i$. Then the solution to (7.1) becomes

$$y_1 = \frac{s_1-i}{s_2-s_1} \text{ and } y_2 = \frac{i-s_1}{s_2-s_1} \qquad (7.2)$$

There are several difficulties in the way of accepting this theory as it stands, two of which are of major importance. The first major objection was raised by Pasinetti (1962) when he pointed out that if $Y_1$ = wages, as Kaldor assumed, it is not possible to have $s_1 > 0$. For if $s_1 > 0$, $Y_1$ is not entirely wages but is the income of a class of persons with mixed incomes. I shall consider Pasinetti's further development of this argument below.

The second major difficulty arises from Kaldor's assumption that $I/Y$ is given exogenously. In fact, Kaldor assumes in a surprisingly un-Keynesian manner that $I/Y = I^*/Y^* = i^*$, where $i^*$ is the 'full employment' investment ratio. But how is $i^*$ determined? Since, by Kaldor's own model,

$$I/Y = s_2 + (s_1-s_2)y_1,$$

then $\quad I^* = Y^*\{s_2 + (s_1-s_2)y_1\}$ $\qquad (7.3)$

where $I^*$ is a variable and $Y^*$ is a parameter. But this shows that we cannot determine the full employment level of investment unless we *first* know $y_1$, the distribution of income between the classes. Hence, if we wish to use $i^*$ in order to determine $y_1$, we cannot derive $i^*$ in the manner suggested by Kaldor. Kaldor's theory of distribution appears, therefore, to be inconsistent with Keynes's theory of employment. The decision to split the propensity to save into two 'class' propensities means that Keynes's model no longer works unless the distribution of income is given exogenously. The Keynesian system can be used to solve for the employment level or for income distribution, but not for both.

There are also other difficulties about Kaldor's theory. Firstly, it is not clear how the variables $Y$, $S$, etc. are defined. Since this is a Keynesian model, they must be monetary variables. But in that case something has to be said about prices. Saving propensities are real relations and if prices change—as they are assumed to do by Kaldor in order to produce the right amount of profit—we have to ask what effect this will have on the saving propensities. Given the existence of money, even if there are no fixed-interest assets, a rise in prices will be likely to affect the saving propensities, which can no longer be taken as predetermined constants. Secondly, as has frequently been pointed out, Kaldor's model has no solution if there are more than two classes. Thirdly, there is no convincing reason why saving propensities should be held to differ for different *sources* of income rather than for different *levels* of income, which is the usual Keynesian assumption.

## Pasinetti

Pasinetti's well-known contribution arose from the defect which he discovered in Kaldor's model. Pasinetti redefined $Y_1$ as a mixed income from wages and profits (although the people who receive this income are still described as 'workers'). Now $Y_1 = W + P_1$ and $Y_2 = P_2$, where $W$ is wage income and $P_1$ and $P_2$ are profit incomes received by 'workers' and 'capitalists' respectively.

Following Kaldor, Pasinetti assumed that 'workers' have a fixed saving ratio, $s_1$; but this is now a 'class' propensity to save, not a propensity to save out of wages. The capitalist saving ratio, out of profits, is $s_2$, and $s_2 > s_1$. But Pasinetti introduced at this point a completely new assumption: that the economy is in a state of 'dynamic equilibrium', i.e. in a steady state of growth.

This implies that, since the beginning of time, all inputs and outputs have been growing at a steady rate, with prices and the rate of interest constant. It also implies that the factor distribution of income is constant over time, i.e. that both wages and profits are growing at the same rate as the national income.

Pasinetti deduced from these assumptions that the shares of 'workers' and 'capitalists' in total capital, total profit, and total savings must also have been constant over all time. This conclusion does in fact follow if, but only if, it is assumed that $s_1$ and $s_2$ have always been constant. Consider, for example, what happens if $S_1/P_1 > S_2/P_2$. Then the capital owned by 'workers' is growing faster than the capital owned by 'capitalists' (on the assumption that both classes receive the same rate of interest on their savings). Hence the profits of 'workers' are growing faster than the profits of 'capitalists' and, since in the steady state total wages and profits must be growing at the same rate, the incomes of 'workers' are growing faster than the incomes of 'capitalists'. But in the steady state $I/Y$, which is determined by the general rate of growth, is also a constant. Hence $S/Y$, which is the income-weighted average of $s_1$ and $s_2$, is a constant and, if $s_1$ and $s_2$ are assumed to be constants, the income-weights must also be constants. So the incomes of 'workers' and 'capitalists' must be growing at the same rate. But this is impossible if $S_1/P_2 > S_2/P_2$. And the same conclusion applies if $S_1/P_1 < S_2/P_2$. Hence the maintenance of the steady state of growth, with $s_1$ and $s_2$ constant, is possible only if $S_1/P_1 = S_2/P_2$. Workers' saving must have the same proportion to their profit income as capitalists' saving has to their profit income, which is their *total* income.

By definition $S_2/P_2 = s_2$; and hence in the steady state $S_1/P_1 = s_2$. So $S = S_1 + S_2 = s_2 P$, $P = S/s_2$ and

$$P/Y = i/s_2 \tag{7.4}$$

Furthermore, in a steady state of growth,

$$r = P/K \equiv P/Y.Y/I.I/K$$

where $K$ is total capital. Then, by substitution from (7.4) we have

$$r = g/s_2 \tag{7.5}$$

where $g = I/K$, the steady rate of growth.

Pasinetti considered that (7.4) and (7.5) are remarkable results. Equation (7.4) seems to imply that the profit share is determined only by the aggregate investment ratio and the propensity to save of the 'capitalists'; while equation (7.5) seems to imply that the rate of interest is independent of 'technology', i.e. of any kind of production function. Let us look a little more closely at these claims.

The first equation certainly has a paradoxical appearance, for it would be equally true if the 'capitalist' class consisted of a large number of people receiving most of total profits or, at the other extreme, of only a single small *rentier* who received an infinitesimal share of total profits. How can it be that the saving propensity of this one small *rentier* 'determines' the share of profits in the whole economy? The answer is, of course, that his saving propensity does not 'determine' anything of the sort. It is Pasinetti's set of assumptions which ensures that (7.4) is a correct statement of equality between two ratios. The most important of these assumptions are (1) the steady growth and (2) the constancy of $s_1$ and $s_2$.

The second equation follows immediately from the first, again on the assumption of a steady state of growth. This is really the 'trick' assumption. A steady state of growth sounds an innocuous sort of assumption; but it carries all sorts of hidden implications.

What justification is there for Pasinetti's two key assumptions? The steady state assumption is the same as that which is often made by neoclassical theory. It is a mathematically convenient assumption, and it seems to take care of the problem of expectations; but it is an assumption which kills the very subject it is supposed to sustain. For it rules out all change, other than the uniform rate of growth. It is a very strange assumption for a Keynesian to make. As for the assumption that 'class' saving propensities are constant over time, this is, if possible, an even more extraordinary assumption. Why should the class of persons with mixed incomes have a different saving propensity from the class of persons with only profit incomes? Is saving related to the *source* of income rather than to its level? If so, why is the saving propensity of persons with mixed incomes given exogenously, independently of the proportions of wages and profits in those incomes? Finally, who are these 'classes' which have existed for all time? In particular, who are the 'pure capitalists', whose incomes have never had any element of labour income as one generation succeeds another?

## *Joan Robinson*

Joan Robinson has never committed herself fully to the Kaldor–Pasinetti model, and her own theory of income distribution has a somewhat eclectic character.[2] She appears to accept the 'ancient and respectable' proposition that 'relative shares of wages and profits are governed by the supplies of factors and the elasticity of substitution between them' (1960, 145); but she adds three other ingredients. The first two are derived wholly or partly from Kalecki while the third seems to have a different origin. It is that 'relative shares depend on the relative bargaining strength of workers and employers' (p. 146). The first Kalecki ingredient is the doctrine that under imperfect competition 'gross profit margins . . . are governed by the price-policy of firms'. The second Kalecki ingredient may be summarized in Kalecki's aphorism that 'workers spend what they earn and capitalists earn what they spend'.[3]

Unlike Kaldor, Joan Robinson employs the original Kalecki assumption that workers' savings are always zero, which, as we have seen, is the only assumption which is really consistent with Kaldor's model. It follows that gross profits are equal to gross investment plus *rentiers'* expenditure. When output is at 'capacity', prices are determined by supply and demand, as under perfect competition. But this is a rare event, which 'is found only in extreme conditions of a seller's market' (p. 148). Normally, firms work below capacity and their prices depend on their price policies, i.e. their gross profit margins, which Kalecki attributed to their 'degree of monopoly'. When profit margins are high, a given amount of capitalist spending (on gross investment plus consumption) will generate a smaller amount of employment than if profit margins are low. As so often in modern Keynesian theories, it appears to be assumed

---

[2] The following summary is based on Joan Robinson's (1960) article entitled 'The Distribution of Income'. She has touched on the subject in more recent writings, and added some details, but the main structure of her thinking does not seem to have changed.

[3] Kalecki's formal model is described in Kalecki (1942).

that investment decisions are made independently of the level of profit margins—an assumption which Keynes would surely not have made, since it is inconsistent with his analysis of the determinants of investment.

In effect, Joan Robinson now assumes that *rentier* expenditure is zero. In that case, total profit in a closed economy is equal to gross investment. When the economy is operating at full capacity, 'the share of wages in national income is determined by the ratio of investment to income' (p. 149); but when the economy is operating below capacity, the wage share is determined by the pricing policies of firms, and it is the level of employment which is determined by the level of investment.

The model can be formalized if a number of simplifying assumptions are made. Assume a closed economy consisting entirely of imperfectly competitive firms, and that the current input of these firms consists only of homogeneous labour. Let every firm have the same profit mark-up on wage costs, $m$, so long as it is operating below 'full capacity'. Then aggregate national income is $Y = (1+m)W$, where $Y$ is money national income and $W$ is the total wage bill. Clearly, total profit, $P$, is given by $P = Y - W = mW$. But, on the assumptions made previously, total profit is equal to gross investment expenditure, $I$. If the profit margin in making investment goods is the same as elsewhere, $I = (1+m)W_1$, where $W_1$ is the wage bill in the investment-goods industry. So $mW = (1+m)W_1$. Since the wage per man is the same in all industries, this implies that $mL = (1+m)L_1$, where $L$ is total employment and $L_1$ is employment in the investment-goods industry. Hence

$$L = \frac{1+m}{m} L_1 \qquad (7.6)$$

But equation (7.6) is valid only when $L$ is freely variable, i.e. when the economy is operating below full employment. When full employment is reached, $L = L^*$ and $L$ ceases to be a variable. If $L_1$ is still regarded as being given exogenously, (7.6) becomes overdetermined, unless $m$ ceases to be a constant and becomes a variable. In that case, with $L = L^*$, (7.6) becomes $mL^* = (1+m)L_1$, and

$$m = \frac{L_1}{L^* - L_1} = \frac{\eta}{1-\eta}, \text{ where } \eta = L_1/L^* \qquad (7.7)$$

This corresponds to Joan Robinson's first case, where the wage (or profit) share depends on the investment–income ratio.

The difficulty about this theory, apart from its many simplifying assumptions, is that no explanation is given for the sudden conversion of price-making firms into price-taking firms when they reach full employment. If profit margins are rigid below full employment, why do they suddenly become infinitely flexible at full employment? Alternatively, if they are infinitely flexible at full employment, why do they suddenly become rigid at less than full employment? (The same questions can be raised about Kaldor's model also.)

Is it not more probable that, when full employment is reached in an economy of price-making firms, it will be the level of investment which becomes an endogenous variable rather than the profit margin? Investment orders will pile up, but profit margins will be more or less steady. Instead of (7.7) therefore, we have

$$L_1 = \frac{m}{1+m} L^* \tag{7.8}$$

There is a limit, after all, to the power of the 'widow's cruse'.

Joan Robinson suggests, finally, that trade union bargaining power can be used to reduce $m$, and hence to raise the level of employment (when it is not yet at full employment). This argument is clearly inconsistent with the previous assumption that $m$ is constant below full employment, unless $m$ is made a function of *both* the 'degree of monopoly' (which was Kalecki's assumption, discussed below) *and* trade union bargaining power. No evidence is produced in support of the latter assumption. We are simply asked to suppose that there are initially industries which are operating below capacity and in which profit margins are 'fairly high'. Then, if the trade unions succeed in raising money wages in one such industry, the industry will not raise its prices in the same proportion. 'The workers then attack somewhere else, and the story repeats itself' (p. 150). 'Thus the exercise of bargaining strength playing against monopolistic power raises real wages and increases employment'.

What is lacking from this theory is an explanation of the initial 'monopolistic' factors which determine profit margins. Joan Robinson limits herself to quoting a statement by Kaldor that 'profit margins are what they are because the forces of competition prevent them from being higher than they are and are not powerful enough to make them lower than they are' (p. 148). This does not give us much help, but it at least suggests that the 'forces of competition' are at the bottom of the matter. If this is so, it is difficult to see how profit margins can be squeezed by trade union bargaining power. Trade unions, as Keynes emphasized, can bargain about money, not real, wages. In a money economy prices can be adjusted to keep profit margins steady, unless the money supply is constant and one accepts monetarism (which is hardly a Keynesian argument). The only alternative explanation for a profit squeeze in a closed economy would be some form of price control. Clearly, if wages rise and prices are held down, the profit margin falls. But one cannot assume that in such conditions the level of investment will be unaffected. In the end, Joan Robinson admits that 'raising money wages in the face of unemployment is very difficult' (p. 151), and this seems to undermine her argument.

Of the four ingredients in Joan Robinson's model of income distribution, there is only one which seems to have any force, namely, the assumption that profit margins are more or less constant under conditions of imperfect competition. But the crucial question is: what determines these profit margins? Joan Robinson did not answer that question, although she repeated Kalecki's phrase 'the degree of monopoly'. I turn now to consider how Kalecki developed his argument.

### Kalecki

Kalecki's original (1939) statement of his theory may be summarized as follows. He assumed a closed economy of universal imperfect competition without a government sector. In the short run all firms have inelastic demand curves for their products and, as is usual in such discussions, each firm is assumed to sell only one homogeneous product. Firms follow a profit-maximizing policy of making short-run marginal cost equal to estimated marginal revenue. If each demand curve has a constant elasticity, firms will fix their selling prices in accordance with the formula:

$$p = m/ \left\{ 1 - \frac{1}{e} \right\} \tag{7.9}$$

where $p$ is the price, $e$ is the (negative of the) elasticity of demand and $m$ is the marginal cost.[4]

Kalecki took over Lerner's definition of the 'degree of monopoly', $\mu$, as the ratio of the gross profit margin to the price. Then it follows from (7.9) that

$$\mu = \frac{p-m}{p} = \frac{1}{e}$$

The 'degree of monopoly' varies inversely with the elasticity of demand.

Kalecki next assumed that all firms normally operate below full capacity, in a region where their short-run marginal cost is approximately equal to their average cost of manual labour and materials per unit of output. Hence each firm fixes its price by adding a percentage mark-up to this average unit cost equal to $(p-m)/m = 1/(e-1)$.[5] Since all firms follow the same policy, there emerges an economy-wide average mark-up or, in Kalecki's words, an 'average degree of monopoly'.[6]

It is obvious that, with a given percentage mark-up for a given firm, the share of wages in its value added will vary directly with the proportion of its wage costs to its material costs. Kalecki transfers this idea directly to the aggregate level, arguing that the share of wages in national income depends on the prices of 'basic raw materials', which are already given exogenously. However, if we adhere to Kalecki's original

---

[4] Although Kalecki does not use this formula explicitly, it is implicit in his argument and in his reference to Lerner's concept of the 'degree of monopoly'. The formula, discovered by Joan Robinson (1933, 54), applies only to a monopolist who maximizes his immediate profits, regardless of the threat of new entry.

[5] Clearly, the formula is unworkable if $e < 1$. I return to this point later.

[6] Since firms sell intermediate goods to one another, the average mark-up on labour costs for the whole economy must depend on its input–output structure.

assumptions, the raw materials industries are part of the closed economy, and raw materials must be produced by imperfectly competitive firms. In that case, the effects of an increase in the price of such materials are no different in principle from the effects of an increase in the price of any other product which is used as an input by other firms. The effects of a price increase by any firm on the rest of the economy can be measured only by a general equilibrium input–output method.

In the revised formulation of his theory (1954) Kalecki attempted to avoid this latter difficulty by treating industries producing raw materials as a separate sector, in which prices are determined by demand and supply in perfectly competitive markets. But if raw materials industries are part of a closed economy it is not possible to assume that their prices are independent of the price and output policies of other industries. In this later formulation Kalecki also revised his definition of the 'degree of monopoly' so as to remove all reference, open or implied, to the elasticity of demand. The degree of monopoly is now defined as $p/u$, where $p$ is price and $u$ is average prime cost per unit; and it is suggested that this ratio depends on the degree to which price is adjusted when (a) the firm's own level of $u$ changes and (b) there are changes in the average prices of 'other firms producing similar products' (1954, 12). But this is too vague to be regarded as a theory of the determination of mark-up policy. The words 'degree of monopoly' no longer have any distinct meaning and the theory says no more than that prices under imperfect competition are fixed by firms according to their standard mark-up policies.

Kalecki believed that, in practice, the 'average degree of monopoly' is fairly stable, although it may increase in periods of recession and it may have a long-term upward trend. He presented data for the estimated wage share in private GDP for Great Britain and the United States, which suggested considerable stability in that share over periods as long as 1880 to 1935 in Great Britain and 1919 to 1934 in the United States; and he argued that this stability was largely the result of mutually offsetting changes in the 'degree of monopoly' and the price of raw materials. But this argument was supported by a very brief and inadequate statistical analysis.

The principal weakness in Kalecki's theory is that no satisfactory explanation is given for the size of individual mark-ups. His only coherent explanation was his first model, based on orthodox monopoly pricing theory. But he later abandoned this and offered nothing substantial in its place. As he may have realized, the orthodox model implies that every firm is a myopic short-term profit-maximizer, exploiting to the maximum the elasticity of demand for its own product. Apart from the practical difficulty that firms have only the vaguest notion of the elasticity of demand for their products, this theory implies the possibility of mark-ups much larger than those which are actually used. For firms with demand elasticities equal to or less than unity, for example, the mark-up predicted by the theory would be either infinite or indeterminate.[7] If, however, the model is interpreted as referring to the 'long-period' elasticity of demand, it becomes necessary to explain precisely what this means and why it should be less than infinite. Long-period demand, even more than short-period demand, is simply a description of the state of expectations of the firms concerned, and if this concept is to be used we need a theory to account for such expectations.

By attributing differences in profit margins entirely to the 'degree of monopoly' Kalecki was implicitly denying that firms can vary in their efficiency. This is, of course, a very common assumption; but it has not the slightest factual justification, and it is inconsistent with Kalecki's own belief in the importance of economies of scale. The key to the explanation of inter-firm variations in mark-ups can more usefully be found in this direction than in the grossly overworked theory of static monopoly.

Nevertheless, Kalecki was right, in my opinion, to focus on the problem of mark-ups and to reject the perfect competition model as an explanation of prices and profits over the greater part of a modern industrialized economy. The theory of income distribution which will be outlined below owes a good deal to these ideas of Kalecki, even if it is not formulated in precisely the way in which he formulated his own theory.

[7] As shown above, the mark-up, according to the theory, is equal to $1/(e - 1)$, where $e$ is (the negative of) the elasticity of demand.

# 8

## SOME STATISTICAL EVIDENCE

There is always a tendency in economics for empirical facts to be squeezed into a framework of preconceived ideas. But nowhere, to my knowledge, has this tendency been greater than in the field of income distribution. In this chapter we shall start by considering statistics of factor shares, and then proceed to examine available data on the distribution of personal incomes. In neither case shall we find a close correspondence between the usually quoted facts and the theoretical concepts which have been created to explain the facts.

*Factor shares*

The first thing to notice about this part of our discussion is the bias introduced by the very title. Although 'factor shares' could, in principle, mean anything, in practice it implies that all incomes are attributable to a limited number of 'factors'—land, labour, and capital in some versions, even just labour and capital in others. In the standard classification there are no factors called entrepreneurship, organization, or technical knowledge. Technical knowledge is assumed to be a free good, and factors like entrepreneurship and organization are simply forgotten. The implication is that land, labour, and capital combine spontaneously to produce output. There must be few doctrines so widely accepted which are so completely false.

The traditional division of income into three factor shares goes back to Adam Smith, and it was firmly fixed by Ricardo. Marx consolidated the division into two 'class' shares, with rent, interest, profit, and managerial salaries on one side and wages and junior salaries on the other. Marshall insisted on the role of organization, or entrepreneurship, and discussed its net earnings; but few of his successors paid any attention to this part of the Marshallian apparatus. Schumpeter (1934) made a valiant effort to demonstrate the crucial role of the entrepreneur, and Knight (1921) emphasized that measured profits include a large component rewarding risk and uncertainty. These important contributions to the theory of income distribution have never been refuted: they have been almost entirely ignored. In all recent discussions of neoclassical and neo-Keynesian theories of income distribution it has been tacitly agreed by all parties that there are only two factors of production—labour and capital, pure and unadulterated.

It is implicit in any listing of factors that each factor contributes a reasonably homogeneous factor service, or a fixed basket of factor services. Unskilled labour, and land of a specified quality and location, approximately meet these requirements. Labour of varying skill and efficiency, and land of varying quality and location, do not. However, if it can be assumed that the quality compositions of labour and land are fairly constant, it may be legitimate to treat all labour and all land as single factors. But these assumptions cannot easily be justified, especially the assumption about labour. It is obvious, for example, that the skill composition of the labour force in an advanced industrialized country is incomparable with the skill composition of the labour force in a country which has just started to industrialize.

When we turn to the factor 'capital' we are faced by all manner of confusions. If a factor service is normally hired, there is a reasonable presumption that its earnings correspond to the flow of services for which it is hired. While this rule clearly applies to hired labour, rented land, and interest on loans, it gives us no guidance about the nature of the services provided by persons or organizations whose income is classified as 'profits'. In order to earn profits it is normally necessary to provide some equity capital; but the provision of such capital is not a sufficient condition. This is obvious in the case of unincorporated businesses and farms, where the proprietor, and often also members of his family, contribute labour, organization, and technical knowledge. In corporate enterprises there appears to be a clear separation between the earnings of labour and the earnings of capital; but this is largely a legal fiction. In practice, no company earns profits unless some person or group of persons takes responsibility for ensuring that the organization works efficiently. To a large extent this work is now done in large firms by hired managers. But it does not follow that their salaries reflect their full contribution to the success of the business. For if managers' services were worth no more than the amount which they are paid, organizations would invariably be badly managed. Good managers contribute much more to the success of their enterprises than the value of their salaries, just as good workers do. Their reward is partly the satisfaction of a job well done; but it is also the prospect of promotion, of higher income in the future, and of more scope for the exercise of authority. These services, which are made in return for future expectations, are essentially entrepreneurial services. To the extent to which they are productive they are a major contribution to the success of the business and hence to its current profits.

We may conclude that all measured profits reflect contributions of labour, organization, and technical knowledge as well as of capital. Moreover, since profits are inevitably uncertain, the average expectation of profit includes some reward for willingness to take risks. All of this becomes abundantly clear as soon as we examine actual statistics of income shares. In countries at an early stage of economic development usually at least one-third of national income represents the profits of unincorporated businesses and farms;[1] and even in the industrialized countries of Western Europe as recently as 1960 the share of such profits in national income was between 20 and 30 per cent for all countries except the United Kingdom.[2]

Thus, even if one decides—illegitimately—to ignore entrepreneurial inputs in the case of companies, there is a major problem in trying to allocate profits to labour and capital over the economy as a whole. This problem is, indeed, insoluble in principle because (1) there is no means of estimating the quality of the labour contribution in unincorporated businesses, and (2) there is equally no means of estimating the productivity of the capital employed by unincorporated businesses. The universal finding of empirical studies is that, if labour and capital employed in unincorporated businesses are given imputed earnings equal to the average earnings of labour and capital in corporate businesses, there is not enough profit to go round. In the case of farms in the United States, for example, the measured profit is usually less than half the required

[1] See, for example, Kuznets (1959).    [2] See Denison (1967, 353).

amount.[3] Hence the allocations which are actually made by statisticians who attempt to squeeze all income into the required categories of land, labour, and capital are arbitrary.[4]

The first major attempt to compile a long time-series of estimates of labour's share in national income was made by Bowley (1937) for the United Kingdom.[5] He concentrated on the share of wages received by manual workers; and his estimates of the aggregate wage-bill for the United Kingdom covered the years from 1880 to 1914, and from 1924 to 1936. When these figures (which include the earnings of shop assistants) were related to estimates of national income for the earlier period, they turned out to move closely around an average figure of 40 per cent. Phelps Brown and Hart (1952) revised and extended Bowley's figures, and their results showed that the share of wages (excluding shop assistants) in national income over the periods 1870 to 1913, and 1924 to 1950, was never less than 36·6 per cent and never more than 42·6 per cent. In 35 out of 71 years this share was between 39 and 41 per cent. Bowley's results were considered so impressive that they led Keynes (1939, 48) to conclude that 'The stability of the proportion of the national dividend accruing to labour . . . is one of the most surprising, yet best established facts in the whole range of economic statistics'. More recently, Kaldor (1955, 84) expressed the opinion that: 'No hypothesis as regards the forces determining distributive shares could be intellectually satisfying unless it succeeds in accounting for the relative stability of these shares in the advanced economies over the last 100 years or so, despite the phenomenal changes in the techniques of production, in the accumulation of capital relative to labour and in real income per head.'

Unfortunately, these opinions can now be seen to be incorrect. While the share of *wages* in national income was fairly stable between 1870 and 1950, the proportion of wage-earners

[3] Denison (1974, 261).

[4] Denison (1967), for example, assumed that in all the Western European countries covered by his study unincorporated profits could be divided into 63 per cent for labour and 37 per cent for capital.

[5] Bowley's book largely summarized his earlier estimates in various publications going back over the previous forty years. Early estimates of factor shares in the United States were prepared by W. I. King, for a summary of which see Lebergott (1964).

to the whole occupied population fell from 84 per cent to 66 per cent.[6] Over the same period, according to the estimates of Phelps Brown and Hart, the share of salaries rose from 16 per cent to 23 per cent; and the combined share of wages and salaries rose from 55 per cent to 65 per cent. According to Feinstein (1968) the share of wages and salaries in the gross national product of the United Kingdom rose from 45 per cent in 1860–9 to 66 per cent in 1950–9.[7] Most of this increase took place after 1914: in 1910–14 the wage and salary share of GNP was still only 48 per cent. From that period onwards Feinstein made estimates of the total labour share of GNP by allocating self-employment income between labour and capital, and his results show the labour share rising from 55 per cent in 1910–14 to 73 per cent in 1950–9, with the main increases occurring during the two world wars.[8]

The share of labour in national income has increased during the past one or two generations in most other developed countries. In the United States the wage and salary share rose from 55 per cent in 1900–9 to 71 per cent in 1960–5, and the share of labour—after allocating self-employment income in the same proportion as in the rest of the economy—from 72 per cent to 80 per cent.[9] From 1938 to 1968 the wage and salary share rose from 45 to 62 per cent in Belgium, 63 to 71 per cent in Canada, 50 to 63 per cent in France, 54 to 64 per cent in the Federal Republic of Germany, 39 to 54 per cent in Japan, and 52 to 72 per cent in Sweden.[10] According to Denison's (1967, 38) estimates for the United States and eight countries of Europe, the shares of labour income (after allocating self-employment income) in national income in the period 1960–2 ranged from 72 per cent (for Italy) to 79·9 per cent (for the United States). The average for the eight European countries was 76·5 per cent. In 1950–4 the United States figure had been 77·3 per cent

[6] See Phelps Brown and Hart (1952, 276–7).
[7] These figures are taken from Atkinson's (1975, 162) summary of Feinstein's estimates. See also Feinstein (1976).
[8] These figures are again taken from Atkinson's summary (1975, 162).
[9] Atkinson (1975, 163) based mainly on Kravis (1959).
[10] Atkinson (1975, 167) based mainly on Heidensohn (1969). Other countries covered by Atkinson's table include Ireland, Norway, United Kingdom, and United States. The German share is expressed as a percentage of net domestic product and the Swedish share as a percentage of gross national product. The remaining figures are percentages of national income.

and the European figure 75·4 per cent, but in 1924–8 the United States figure was only 69·7 per cent.

Of course, none of these estimates is strictly relevant to the theories which we have considered in earlier chapters. Those theories relate to an abstract world: a closed economy, with no government and with only two or three factors. All workers are homogeneous; there are no entrepreneurs; and no mixed incomes. All capital receives the same uniform rate of profit and all such profits (including interest) are paid to *rentiers*, whose only function is, like that of landlords, to hire out their property to the highest bidder. There is no simple way in which statistical data could be assembled to correspond with the categories used in these theories. Presumably the government sector would need to be excluded, on the ground that both the powers and motives of governments are different from those of commercial enterprises; and preferably also the unincorporated business sector, on the ground that the labour and capital shares of self-employment profits are indeterminate. We should be left with the corporate sector, in which the division of incomes between labour and capital is at least legally specified. In practice, estimates of income shares in the corporate sector are not available for any substantial series of years except for the United States, and to a more limited extent for the United Kingdom.

Even if we had such estimates for a number of countries, extending back for 50 or 100 years, it is doubtful whether they would give us the data which are relevant for testing the theories. During the past two generations the corporate sector has grown in importance in every market-economy country and swallowed up large sections of the economy previously served by unincorporated enterprises. With such changes in the boundaries and composition of the corporate sector it would be difficult to draw unambiguous conclusions about underlying changes in the shares of labour and capital in the whole business sector of the economy. Moreover, there is no certainty that, if an economy existed which corresponded to the theories, it would behave like the corporate sector of actual economies. In the actual world companies are subject to many pressures from governments, especially through taxation, and it would be a heroic assumption to believe that these pressures have no effects on the division of factor shares in the corporate product.

Nevertheless, it is of some interest to study such estimates of corporate shares as are available. According to Alterman (1964, 93) the labour share in United States corporate *net* product (i.e. the contribution of the corporate sector to national income) was, on the average, 77·0 per cent in 1922–9 and 76·8 per cent in 1947–59.[11] Estimates for individual years, however, are less stable than this: for example, in 1929 the labour share was 74·6 per cent and in 1957 78·5 per cent. Glyn and Sutcliffe (1972, 264) give estimates for more recent years of the labour share in corporate *gross* domestic product (net of stock appreciation) in the United States and the United Kingdom. For the period 1950–4 to 1969 there seems to have been no trend in the United States figures, which fluctuated closely around 71 per cent. In 1970, however, Glyn and Sutcliffe's figure rose to 73·3 per cent, and subsequent estimates derived from the *Survey of Current Business* suggest even further increases. For the United Kingdom, Glyn and Sutcliffe show that the labour share in corporate gross domestic product rose from 68·5 per cent in 1950–4 to 78·4 per cent in 1970; and subsequent estimates from *National Income and Expenditure* again show further increases. The years since 1973 have, of course, been years of exceptionally rapid inflation, followed by severe recession. As is well known, the labour share in corporate product rises in recession and falls in boom periods. Long-term comparisons should, therefore, be based on approximately comparable levels of capacity utilization.[12]

The general conclusion from available evidence is that there is no really long-term constancy in labour's share on any definition.[13] The share of wages of manual workers in British gross national product was remarkably stable for more than 70

[11] The post-war data have been adjusted to add back to both profits and net product the accelerated amortization allowances which started in 1950. The depreciation allowances actually deducted are straight-line and at historical cost.

[12] Estimates of the labour share in the Indian private 'organized' sector (approximately the same as the corporate sector) show an upward trend from about 55 per cent in the early 1960s to about 59 per cent in the early 1970s (with an exceptional temporary peak of 61–63 per cent in 1968–70). See government of India, *National Accounts Statistics, 1960–61 to 1973–74.*

[13] See also King and Regan (1976, Chap. 2).

years—from 1860–9 to 1930–9—and the total imputed labour share in United States national income was, on certain assumptions, fairly steady from 1930–9 to 1960–5 (Atkinson, 1975, 162–3). In addition, the labour share in United States corporate income seems to have had no significant upward trend from the 1920s to the early 1960s. Other examples of at least temporary stability in the labour share—on various definitions—in different countres are given in Glyn and Sutcliffe (1972, 264).

It is apparent, therefore, that if one wishes to believe in the constancy of labour's share it is necessary to choose special definitions and special periods in each country. In every country which has followed the path of industrialization there has been a fall in the share of land rent, a decline in the proportion of self-employed in the work-force, a rise in the proportion of government employees, and an increase in the proportion of salaried workers. During the early stages of industrialization the proportion of wage-earners usually increases, as labour moves off the farms into industry; and this is likely to increase the share of wages in national income. Later, however, the proportion of wage-earners begins to fall as the rise in the number of salaried workers becomes sufficient to offset the continuing decline in the number of self-employed. Constancy of the wage share during this period can only be a reflection of balancing movements in the proportion of wage-earners and in their earnings relative to other income receivers. None of the economic theories discussed earlier gives reasons for expecting such an exact balance to occur, and it must be regarded as an example of a number of temporarily stable ratios in economics which are the outcome of differing movements and pressures.

*The size distribution of personal incomes*

Although economists have been discussing the distribution of income by factor shares for more than two centuries, the problem of the size distribution of personal incomes has not become a major interest of economics until recently.[14] Part of the reason may be that only fragmentary statistics of size distributions

[14] The great exception was the work of Pareto (1897, 1927). Notable contributions to early British studies were also made by Bowley (1914), Cannan (1914), Dalton (1920), and Stamp (1920).

existed, even in most industrialized countries, until the past thirty or forty years. But this is scarcely an adequate explanation. The discussion of the determinants of factor shares was never inhibited by lack of factual information. Most probably, those who discussed factor shares thought that they were also—indirectly—discussing size distributions. Rent went to rich landlords, wages to poor workers, and profits were received by the 'middle' classes. This assumption may have been reasonable in eighteenth-century and early nineteenth-century Britain, but it became increasingly inappropriate as the nineteenth century moved towards its close; and it is obviously quite invalid in the latter part of the twentieth century.

It remains true that in most countries the ownership of land is unequally distributed—often very unequally; and that personal incomes from interest, dividends, and profits are also highly unequal. But in industrialized countries there is now a considerable overlap in personal incomes from different sources. House ownership is widespread; large proportions of employed workers have significant amounts of savings, especially in insurance policies and pension funds; and many self-employed workers and *rentiers* have lower personal incomes than those in employment. For both welfare and other reasons, it is now necessary to go beyond factor shares and to examine the distribution of personal incomes by size.

What do we mean by a size distribution of personal incomes? Many difficulties arise in trying to give a precise and logically defensible answer to that question. It is necessary, first, to decide what we mean by a person. Do we include all the men, women, and children in a given country at a given moment of time? But most women and children, and many men, receive no primary income: they are supported by their families. Should we, then, seek a distribution of family—or perhaps household—incomes? This is the usual solution; but it overlooks many problems. The most obvious problem—yet the one which is rarely faced—is that households vary in size and composition. Does it make sense to count a household of husband, wife, and three teenage children as the equivalent of a household consisting of one pensioner living alone? Most published statistics of household incomes tacitly make such an assumption. A second problem is that changes in demographic patterns and social customs cause changes in the size and composition of households. For example, in industrialized countries there are increasing proportions of single-person and two-person households, especially in younger and older age groups. This trend inevitably has effects on the measured distribution of personal incomes, particularly so if every household is counted as an equal unit in the distribution. Some of these problems can be overcome if every member of a household is assumed to have an equal share in the household income; better still, if some kind of 'equivalence scale' is used to weight household members and to impute to each member a share in household income in proportion to his or her share of the household total of such weights. Some experiments have been made in the use of these techniques, but they are not yet accepted as standard practice.[15]

Another matter requiring decision is the definition of income. Should it include income in kind and fringe benefits? Should it be before or after direct taxes and compulsory contributions? Should it be adjusted for differences in prices affecting different parts of the country, or affecting different social or economic classes? Should income be measured for a week, for a month, for a year, or for a 'lifetime'? Would it be better to measure consumption expenditure rather than income? All these questions raise fundamental, and usually extremely difficult, questions. Very little systematic work has been done so far in trying to find optimal answers to them, i.e. answers which strike the best compromise between what is theoretically desirable and empirically practicable. For the most part, we simply have to take what we are given by the statisticians, who have usually collected the data for other reasons.

In the light of these many problems of definition and measurement it seems probable that very few valid inter-country comparisons can be made from existing data; and there is no

---

[15] Some countries, such as India, Pakistan, and Indonesia, publish their household survey results in ranges of *per capita* household income or expenditure. Recent examples of the use of equivalence scales for the analysis of income distribution in the United Kingdom and the United States can be found in Stark (1972), Taussig (1973), Smeeding (1976), Fiegehen and Lansley (1976), and Das (1977). For a general discussion of the problem of allowing for demographic aspects of the measurement of income inequality see Kuznets (1976).

guarantee that comparisons for a single country over time are reliable, even when the data have been collected and processed by a constant method. Nevertheless, with due recognition of all the difficulties, let us consider what available data appear to show. We shall start by considering the inter-country pattern of inequality and then examine evidence on changes in the degree of inequality in individual countries over time.

Most of the early inter-country comparisons of income inequality were confined to a few advanced countries of North America and north-western Europe. These were, until about thirty years ago, the only countries for which sufficient data existed to make even the roughest comparisons. But since the end of the Second World War there has been a rapid growth in the number of income censuses and household sample surveys of either income or expenditure, and at least one such census or survey has now been made for over 80 countries. The World Bank has recently published a compendium of estimates derived from these sources (Jain, 1975). There are wide differences in the definitions and methods used in preparing the underlying statistics for each of these countries, but some comparisons can be made. For this purpose Das (1977) selected 118 distributions from 71 countries. Two major criteria were employed in the selection process: (1) in each country, only distributions for one year—the latest available year—were included; (2) only those distributions were included in which the income unit was either a 'household', an 'income recipient', or an 'economically active person'.[16] (In some countries the distributions relate only to employed workers' earnings; in others households are classified by *per capita* income or expenditure.) Most of the chosen distributions cover the whole non-institutional population but some relate to rural or urban areas, others to agricultural or non-agricultural populations.

When the countries in this sample were classified by their *per capita* income (*per capita* GNP at factor cost in the year of the survey, converted to U.S. dollars at 1971 dollar prices) all standard measures of inequality of the distributions were found to exhibit a similar pattern. On the average, the degree of inequality is fairly low in the poorest countries, increases with

---

[16] Distributions for Rhodesia and South Africa were excluded because of the exceptionally large racial heterogeneity of incomes in those countries.

*per capita* income up to a certain level, and thereafter follows a continuous downward trend. A more precise estimate of this pattern can be made by regressing the degree of inequality (measured in alternative ways) on various functions of *per capita* income, with the inclusion in the regression equation of dummy variables to take account of differences in the definitions of the income unit and the area coverage. An example of such regression results, taken from Das's study (1977), is as follows:

$$G = 0.784 - 0.050 \log X - 12.184 X^{-1} + 0.051 D_1 + 0.129 D_2 -$$
$$(0.106) \quad (0.015) \qquad\qquad\qquad (0.016) \qquad (0.021)$$
$$0.033 D_3 - 0.007 D_4$$
$$(0.018) \qquad (0.016)$$
$$n = 118 \quad R^2 = 0.38$$

where $G$ is the Gini coefficient, $X$ is per capita income (the logarithm is exponential), $D_1$ is a dummy variable which takes a value of 1 for income recipients and 0 otherwise, $D_2$ is a dummy variable which takes a value of 1 for economically active persons and 0 otherwise, $D_3$ is a dummy variable which takes a value of 1 for the rural or agricultural sector and 0 otherwise, and $D_4$ is a dummy variable which takes a value of 1 for the urban or non-agricultural sector and 0 otherwise. Although the value of $R^2$ for this equation is not very large, it is highly significant, and all the estimated regression coefficients except that for $D_4$ are significant at the 95 per cent level.[17]

This equation gives us some interesting information. It says that, on the average, when the distribution refers to income recipients the Gini coefficient is 0.051 higher than when the distribution refers to households; and when the distribution refers to economically active persons it is 0.129 higher. Since a change in the Gini coefficient from, say, 0.45 to 0.40 can usually be regarded as a sign of a significant change in the degree of inequality, these regression results warn us that differences in the definition of the income unit in two distributions can produce misleading conclusions from comparisons of those distributions. The estimated coefficient of $D_3$ also shows that, on the average, rural or agricultural distributions are more equal

---

[17] The figures in parentheses are standard errors. An alternative equation, where $X^{-1}$ was replaced by $(\log X)^2$, proved to be slightly less satisfactory on the usual statistical criteria (value of $R^2$ and *t*-statistics).

than national distributions. But the coefficient of $D_4$ is both small and statistically insignificant.

When all the dummy variables are equal to zero, the equation yields estimates of the Gini coefficient of a national household distribution at different levels of *per capita* income. On the average, the Gini coefficient for such a distribution rises with *per capita* income until the latter reaches a level of $243 (in 1971 prices), and thereafter declines. Table 8.1 presents estimates of

TABLE 8.1

*Regression estimates of inequality measures at selected levels of* per capita *GNP (national household distributions)*

| | | Percentage income share of: | | |
|---|---|---|---|---|
| *Per capita* GNP (1971 U.S. dollars) | Gini coefficient | Bottom 20 per cent | Top 20 per cent | Top 5 per cent |
| 100 | 0·43 | 6·1 | 49·5 | 23·6 |
| 200 | 0·46 | 5·5 | 51·9 | 25·0 |
| 300 | 0·46 | 5·4 | 51·8 | 24·6 |
| 500 | 0·45 | 5·3 | 50·8 | 23·5 |
| 1,000 | 0·43 | 5·4 | 48·4 | 21·5 |
| 2,000 | 0·40 | 5·5 | 45·5 | 18·5 |
| 3,000 | 0·38 | 5·6 | 43·6 | 16·8 |

*Source*: Regression equations in Das (1977) based on data in Jain (1975).

the Gini coefficient and of a selection of income shares (estimated by the same method) at given levels of *per capita* income.[18] These figures probably understate the differences in the degree of inequality between the rich countries and those in the region of $200–300 *per capita*, for the following reasons: (1) direct taxes are normally more progressive in richer countries, so that post-tax incomes in such countries are less unequal than the pre-tax incomes on which the table is based; (2) families are more fragmented in richer countries, and there are more single-person and two-person households in such countries; (3) the degree of under-reporting of higher incomes is likely to be smaller in the richer countries. Some other features of this table will be discussed in Chapter 12, where possible reasons for the

[18] Broadly similar results can be found in Paukert (1973) and in Ahluwalia (1974 and 1976), but without adjustments for the effects of differences in the income unit definitions.

differences in inequality between rich and poor countries are considered in detail.

Cross-section data about countries which are at different levels of *per capita* income at the present time do not necessarily describe the pattern of changes in inequality which countries experience as they industrialize. Unfortunately, we do not have reliable long time-series of size distribution data for any country, and the short or medium series which we do have relate only to countries which were already fairly highly industrialized at the beginning of each series. Hence, it cannot at present be confirmed that inequality increases in the early stages of development, although some studies claim that there has been an increase in inequality—especially at the bottom of the distribution—in certain developing countries during the past two decades.[19]

We can, however, state with confidence that the degree of inequality of income fell in the United States between 1929 and 1948, and that it fell in the United Kingdom between 1938 and 1954. For example, Williamson (1977) concluded, on the basis of trends in a number of measures of inequality in the United States between 1929 and 1948, that 'The historical documentation that does exist confirms without doubt a marked leveling of earned incomes . . . quite independent of government transfers. The income share of Kuznets's top 5 per cent declined by one-third, while the percent in poverty very nearly halved'.[20] In the United Kingdom, estimates derived from distributions of tax units have shown that between 1938 and 1954 the income share of the top 5 per cent fell from 29·0 per cent to 20·5 per cent before tax, and from 24·1 per cent to 15·4 per cent after tax.[21]

Evidence on changes in income inequality in the same two countries in more recent years is consistent with two possible interpretations. Some series suggest a continued slow decline in inequality, while others suggest that the level of inequality has been approximately constant. The results depend on the

---

[19] See, for example, Weisskoff (1970).

[20] See also the estimates of income shares of pre-tax 'family personal income' in Radner and Hinrichs (1974, Table 10), which show the share of the top 5 per cent falling from 30·0 in 1929 to 20·9 in 1947, while the share of the bottom 20 per cent rose from 3·5 per cent to 5·0 per cent.

[21] See Lydall (1959). The estimates given in that paper for 1957 were probably too low in the light of the figures now available for subsequent years.

definitions of income coverage and of the income unit. In the United States, for example, the Gini coefficient of inequality of pre-tax money incomes of a pooled sample of families and unrelated individuals has followed an almost horizontal trend between 1947 and 1972.[22] But over this period there was a considerable increase in the proportion of unrelated individuals in the total of consumer units, and this suggests that there may be a case for regarding the distribution of income between families as being a better indicator of underlying trends in inequality. The Gini coefficient for this latter series shows a definite downward trend over this period, with trend estimates running from 0·373 in 1947 to 0·350 in 1972.[23] Although neither of these series has been adjusted for taxes, income in kind, changing composition of families, or other variables, it seems doubtful whether these adjustments could produce an *upward* trend in income inequality in the United States over this period.

In the United Kingdom, the evidence from distributions of tax units suggests a continued declining trend in inequality since 1954, both before and after tax. According to recent official estimates, the share of the top 5 per cent of tax units in pre-tax income fell from 20·8 per cent in 1954 to 16·8 per cent in 1974/75 and from 15·9 per cent to 13·7 per cent after tax.[24] The Gini coefficients for the same two series also show downward trends: the pre-tax coefficient fell from 0·403 in 1954 to 0·371 in 1974/75, while the post-tax coefficient fell from 0·358 to 0·324. There is, however, an alternative series of estimates of the incomes of households, derived from the Family Expenditure Surveys, which have been adjusted for all taxes and benefits; and this series shows no significant trend in over-all

[22] A regression line fitted to the annual series given in Danziger and Smolensky (1976) yields trend estimates of the Gini coefficients of 0·411 for 1947 and 0·410 for 1972. Budd's estimates (1970) for the period 1947 to 1968 (excluding 1953), which are on the average about 0·01 higher, suggest a very slightly steeper downward trend.

[23] These estimates are based on a linear regression fitted to the time-series of Gini coefficients for families published by Paglin (1975).

[24] United Kingdom, Royal Commission on the Distribution of Income and Wealth, *Report No. 5*, 1977, Tables D1 and D3. In 1970/71 and 1971/72 there was a slight and temporary rise in the post-tax share of the top 5 per cent of tax units, and this was reflected in the movements of the Gini coefficient in those years.

inequality—as measured, for example, by the Gini coefficient—between 1961 and 1975.[25] Nevertheless, there is a slight upward trend in the share of the bottom 10 per cent of households in this series, rising from 1·7 per cent in 1961 to 2·9 per cent in 1975. The effect of making a further adjustment to an 'equivalent adult' basis would be to reduce the general level of the Gini coefficients derived from this series, but it would probably not significantly affect their estimated trend.[26] As in the United States, therefore, the balance of evidence suggest that the trend of inequality in the United Kingdom during the post-war years has continued to be slightly downwards.

If we look back over the experience of the past 40–50 years in these two countries, the general pattern is broadly the same: a marked reduction in inequality during the earlier part of the period, especially during the Second World War, and a gradual flattening out in the trend during the latter part of the period. Undoubtedly, an important influence was the achievement of high levels of employment during the Second World War and for most of the post-war period. But there seems also to have been a secular shift in the degree of inequality. Although the greater part of this shift occurred during the war period, when people, customs, and technology were all unusually mobile, this fact is not inconsistent with the hypothesis that the long-term trend has been in a downward direction. So far as Britain and other European countries are concerned, it is impossible to believe that relative inequality was not very much greater a century ago than it is today.[27] There is no evidence on long-term changes in inequality in the richer countries which is inconsistent with the hypothesis that the degree of inequality has been declining for at least 50 years, perhaps for 100 years, roughly in line with the pattern of differences found in current cross-sections of countries.

---

[25] *Ibid.*, Table D16.

[26] Das (1977) converted pre-tax household incomes reported in the Family Expenditure Surveys to an equivalent adult basis and found that the Gini coefficients of the latter series had a very slightly smaller upward trend between 1963 and 1975 (see Table 5.11 in his thesis).

[27] Soltow's (1968) figures give some statistical support for this statement so far as Britain is concerned.

*Conclusion*

Although statistical evidence on factor shares cannot easily—or even in principle—be adjusted to the definitions of factors used in the major theories, the best evidence now available suggests that there is no long-term constancy of the share of labour in national income. The share of the wages of manual workers in the gross national product of the United Kingdom was remarkably stable from the average of the decade 1860–9 to the average of the decade 1930–9; the share of total imputed labour income in the national income of the United States was, on certain assumptions about the method of imputation, fairly steady from 1930–9 to 1960–5; and the share of employee compensation in the corporate income of the United States had no significant upward trend from the 1920s to the early 1960s. But outside these definitions of labour's share and these periods of measurement there is no evidence of stability of labour's share. When salaries are included as well as wages, the share of employee compensation in national income has shown an upward trend in all industrialized countries over many decades—for as far back as estimates are available. This is partly the result of the steady decline in the shares of self-employment income and land rent; but it also reflects a growth in the proportion of salaried workers, especially in government employment. Against this, there has been a considerable increase in imputed income from owner-occupied housing.

When we turn to the size distribution of personal income, which is more relevant for welfare, we are confronted by other statistical problems. As before, there is a choice of alternative definitions as well as a scarcity of reliable statistics. But the evidence of recent cross-section data from a large sample of countries suggests that, after an increase in inequality during the early stages of industrialization, the degree of inequality gradually and persistently declines as *per capita* income continues to rise. And the latter part of this finding is also consistent with available evidence about changes in inequality in the richer countries over recent decades.

A useful theory of income distribution must be able to provide an explanation of the known facts, both of the present time and, so far as available, of the past. This means that it must direct attention to the major social and economic relationships which are believed to be responsible for those facts. On this basis it may be possible to generate predictions about future changes in the distribution of income, on given assumptions about likely changes in other characteristics of the economy. The task to be faced in the remaining chapters of this book is the development of a theory which will explain why the distribution of income, either by so-called factor shares or by size, has shown considerable stability over medium periods of time while changing significantly over longer periods. Suggestions for a new approach to a theory of factor shares will be outlined in Part II, and theories to account for the size distribution of personal incomes will be discussed in Part III.

# PART II

## A THEORY OF WAGES AND PROFITS

# 9

## INCOME SHARES UNDER COMPETITIVE CONDITIONS

In Chapter 5 it was concluded that the neoclassical concept of perfect competition is unsatisfactory because it requires the assumption of perfect knowledge. Perfect knowledge of the future is clearly impossible; and perfect knowledge of current techniques and of the qualities of the factors of production—especially of enterpreneurs—is unrealistic. It is necessary, therefore, to use a different concept of competition, which does not depend on these kinds of knowledge. In this concept of competition I shall allow perfect product and labour markets, and a perfect market for land, but there will be imperfect markets for knowledge, for entrepreneurial skills, and for capital. I shall retain, however, the crucial competitive condition that there is free entry into all trades and occupations, subject only to such legal constraints as are genuinely designed to safeguard the public interest. Since it is desirable to distinguish the proposed concept of competition from perfect competition, I shall call it Entry and Product Market competition, or EPM competition for short.

*Theory of the firm under EPM competition*

The change from perfect competition to EPM competition has profound effects on the theory of the firm. In the first place, when there is imperfect knowledge of the future, there is no guarantee that firms or industries will attain full stationary equilibrium. But, since we shall be concerned with an economy which is in a constant state of change, this is not a serious loss. I shall, nevertheless, assume that firms make some estimates of the future, without which they would be unable to make rational production or investment decisions.

Secondly, imperfect knowledge of technique implies that, while firms and potential firms have some knowledge of existing techniques, the range of such knowledge is limited. We may, therefore, distinguish between two kinds of technique:

*public* technique and *private* technique. Public technique may be defined as those techniques which are known to or can be learnt by anyone, without requiring experience in their actual operational use.[1] Such techniques can be learnt, for example, from books and journals, from study in educational institutions, from the instructions given by machine and industrial materials manufacturers, and from an examination of the products of existing firms. Private technique consists of techniques which are not available publicly, but which can be learnt only by actual experience in the relevant industry or firms. Private technique covers knowledge of how to do things under production conditions ('production' technique) and knowledge of how to organize production on a particular scale ('organizational' technique). An alternative name for private technique is 'know-how'. Because knowledge of private technique depends on experience, it is a form of technique which grows with experience, through learning-by-doing.[2]

A person who is considering whether to set up in business for the first time will have access to the relevant public techniques, but his knowledge of private technique will be limited to what he may have accumulated as an employee of another firm. His knowledge of both production know-how and organizational know-how (especially the latter) will usually be such that he will be reluctant to start his enterprise at a scale above the minimum, which in most cases will be as a one-man firm (OMF). Even apart from his own fears, he will usually be unable to finance investment on a larger scale, for reasons which I shall discuss below. If the owner of an OMF is above-average in his efficiency, or if he has unusual good luck, he will make a significant margin of profit above his living expenses in his first period of operation, and this will satisfy one condition for the expansion of his business. Moreover, the longer that his firm survives, and the more that it grows, the greater will be his accumulation of know-how; and this will satisfy the second condition.

[1] As will be shown in Chapter 11, the word 'anyone' in this definition really means anyone living within a given nation. Techniques which are public within one nation cannot so freely be transferred across international boundaries, because of barriers of language, custom, educational methods and standards, legal institutions, and so forth.

[2] See Penrose (1968).

The problem of finance brings us to a third form of imperfect knowledge, namely, imperfect knowledge of the qualities of the factors of production. Unlike the qualities of materials, personal productive abilities can be assessed only by extended observation of the individual at work, or in a quasi-work situation. The qualities of employed workers may be assessed from their work records; and information of this type is often passed on in some form to potential employers. In the same way, the qualities of an entrepreneur, or would-be entrepreneur, can be assessed from observation of his record of performance as an entrepreneur. But a person who has never been self-employed has no entrepreneurial record, and his entrepreneurial qualities are uncertain. He is, therefore, usually unable to raise finance from outside lenders, except perhaps from his relatives or close friends, until he has proved that he has satisfactory business abilities.[3] This is a second, and perhaps more important, reason why a person setting up in business for the first time normally starts as an OMF. But, once an entrepreneur has shown that he can make a profit, he will have two advantages in raising additional finance: first, he will have his own savings from his profits, which will increase his equity, and hence the security against which he can borrow; secondly, he will have raised his reputation as a credit-worthy borrower. Thus, success opens the door to expansion, and hence to possible further success; and so on cumulatively. The process may, however, be interrupted by bad luck, which is an ever-present risk.

We have seen that there are two compelling reasons why most new entrants to entrepreneurship should start as OMFs, namely, lack of accumulated know-how, and lack of accumulated funds. But the successful OMF will acquire both the necessary know-how and the necessary funds for the expansion of his business. The typical process of the growth of the firm under competitive conditions will, therefore, be as follows.[4] New entrants start as OMFs. Of all OMFs in existence in any year, some will be more successful than others; hence there will be a wide variation in their profitability, depending on the efficiency of the entrepreneur and on his luck. The OMFs

---

[3] He may, of course, borrow on the security of his own assets up to a certain point, especially on any non-business assets which he may happen to own.

[4] Cf. Marshall (1920, 457).

A Theory of Wages and Profits

which are successful will have profits to plough back and will have acquired a good reputation among lenders. They will also have gained useful experience, generating private technique or know-how which may be used for further expansion. Hence, so long as they have the prospect of reaping further economies of scale, they will use their accumulated know-how and funds for expansion.[5] On the other hand, OMFs which have failed to cover their costs, including the imputed wage cost of the entrepreneur, will need to borrow even to survive (or the entrepreneurs will have to reduce their living expenses). But their record will not be such as to improve their chances of obtaining additional loans; and eventually, unless they soon have better luck, they will be forced to give up and to seek paid employment.[6] Thus, out of each cohort of new OMFs entering an industry, some will prosper and grow, others will stagnate, and a third group will eventually withdraw from the industry. After a few years, the size distribution of each cohort of firms will be positively skew, since many of the original OMFs will still be of that size or only a little larger, many will have left the industry, and only a few will have grown to larger sizes. If, in each successive year, a new cohort of OMFs enters the industry, the combined size distribution of all surviving firms after a number of years will be even more positively skew than the distributions of the individual cohorts.

*Comparison of perfect competition and EPM competition*

It is a well-recognized fact that in most industries there are, over at least a certain range, economies of scale internal to the firm. If static perfect competition existed, these economies of scale would need eventually to turn into diseconomies at a size of firm which is small enough to preserve competition within the industry. Empirical studies, however, suggest that in many

[5] In some cases, firms which no longer enjoy internal economies of scale may continue to reinvest retained profits.
[6] OMFs in agriculture can survive longer than in other industries, because they can usually produce part of their food requirements, while their family members can sometimes engage in subsidiary occupations more readily than in urban areas. It is easier to be a subsistence farmer than a subsistence artisan or garage proprietor. But there is some scope for being a subsistence grocery store owner, which may partly account for the large number of OMFs surviving in this line of business.

industries, especially in certain types of manufacturing, there is no point at which diseconomies of scale become dominant, and that the long-run average cost curve is often L-shaped rather than U-shaped.[7] Nevertheless, we may start by considering the case of an industry in which the cost curve is U-shaped.

In Fig. 9.1 *LAC* is the long-run average total cost curve of firms in such an industry, assumed to be operating under conditions of perfect competition. This curve is the envelope of all possible short-run average cost curves, the costs being calculated on the assumption of perfect factor markets, i.e. that each unit of factor service receives the same payment, irrespective of the size of firm in which it is employed. The only short-run

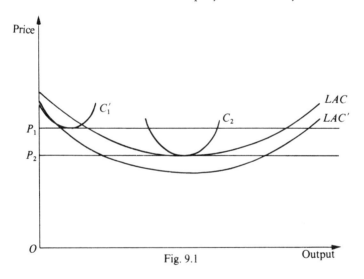

Fig. 9.1

average cost curve which is relevant under perfect competition is $C_2$, the curve which touches *LAC* at its minimum point, and which therefore describes the costs of the 'optimum' firm. For well-known reasons, the long-run equilibrium price of the product under perfect competition will be equal to the minimum

[7] Major empirical studies of this question include those by Blair (1942), Bain (1956), Moore (1959), Johnston (1960), Walters (1963), Haldi and Whitcomb (1967), and Pratten (1971). Variations in profitability with size of firm have been analysed by Hall and Weiss (1967). General surveys of the evidence have been made by Smith (1955), Wiles (1956), and Silberston (1972).

average cost per unit of the optimum firm, $OP_2$. This price will be sufficient, but no more than sufficient, to pay each unit of factor service employed in the firm its uniform reward. Under conditions of perfect knowledge, the rate of profit on capital, which is included in the price, would presumably be equal to the bond rate of interest.

Under EPM competition, however, the position is quite different. Since, by assumption, the markets for knowledge and capital are imperfect, the size of a firm in any industry will depend on its length of experience and its accumulated stock of internal funds. Hence the industry will usually contain, at any one moment of time, firms of every size ranging from the OMF up to the optimum size, or even beyond. In these circumstances, the firm with the highest costs will be, on the average, the OMF; and the equilibrium product price will be just sufficient to induce a sufficient number of OMFs to remain in the industry.

If the demand for the industry's product is growing at a rate which, after allowing for the natural rate of expansion of output from existing firms, requires a net inflow of new OMFs, it might be supposed at first sight that the equilibrium price would be equal to total cost per unit of an OMF, including the normal rate of profit on its capital. On the same line of reasoning, if the number of OMFs were falling, the equilibrium price would be equal to the variable cost per unit of an OMF. But under EPM competition OMFs entering an industry will have expectations of making higher profits in future years if they succeed in growing to a larger size. Hence, they may be prepared to accept an immediate profit rate which does not cover the opportunity cost of capital. On the other side, when OMFs are being squeezed out of an industry, many of those which remain in operation may continue for a considerable time without covering their variable costs, i.e. they may accept lower incomes than would be justified by their alternative labour earnings, if suitable work were available. Evidence cited in the previous chapter suggests that unincorporated businesses as a group do not usually earn sufficient to cover their opportunity costs of both labour and capital; and the situation of OMFs is likely to be even worse than this. We may not go far wrong, therefore, if we assume that, on the average, OMFs earn only enough to cover their variable costs.[8] I shall define the relevant variable costs of an OMF as the sum of the imputed wage of the owner, the cost of inputs purchased from other firms, land rent, and depreciation.

Thus the model implies that the equilibrium product price of an industry operating under conditions of EPM competition, and in which there are some OMFs, is equal to the unit variable costs of an OMF of average efficiency. Even if actual prices deviate from that level, it seems unlikely that the degree of deviation will be large. It may be, however, that there are some industries in which there are no OMFs. This is less likely to be the case under EPM competition than under conditions of imperfect product markets; but it might nevertheless occur. Then the firm with the highest unit costs in such an industry, say, industry $N$, will be, on the average, a firm employing $n$ workers, where $n > 1$. But the long-period supply price of output from such a firm will not be equal to its unit variable costs, but will include an allowance for the normal profit margin of an $n$-worker firm. The supply of $n$-worker firms to industry $N$ will come predominantly from industries which are closely related in technique and, if there is at least one of these closely related industries in which there are OMFs, the alternative costs of an $n$-worker firm in industry $N$ will depend on the profit margin per worker of a firm of that size in the closely related industry. We may describe this relationship by saying that the equilibrium product price in industry $N$, in which there are no *actual* OMFs, is equal to the variable cost per unit of a *hypothetical* OMF in industry $N$, where the ratio of unit variable costs of a hypothetical OMF in industry $N$ to the unit variable costs of an $n$-worker firm in industry $N$ is similar to the same ratio in a closely related industry in which both sizes of firm exist. If no closely related industry contains OMFs, the relationship becomes more indirect; but, since ultimately all industries are related to one another, there will always be a positive profit margin for $n$-worker firms so long as there is any industry in which OMFs occur.

---

[8] If it is asked whether this could be true even in highly capital-intensive industries, I would suggest that differences in capital-intensity are usually rather small at the OMF level, and that such differences as remain may be offset by the prospects of higher profits from expansion.

Thus the model implies that, in all industries operating under EPM competition, the equilibrium product price will be equal to the unit variable costs of an actual or hypothetical OMF of average efficiency. In Fig. 9.1 the curve $LAC'$ is the envelope of the short-run unit variable costs of firms of different sizes making product $X$, and $C_1'$ is the short-run unit variable cost curve of an OMF of average efficiency. Then the equilibrium price of the product under EPM competition will be $OP_1$, which may be either greater or less than $OP_2$. This illustrates one crucial difference between the predictions generated by the perfect competition model and the model of EPM competition. A second crucial difference between the models is that, whereas under perfect competition all firms are of optimum size, i.e. on curve $C_2$, under EPM competition there is a skew distribution of firms ranging from a minimum size, usually an OMF, up to the size corresponding to $C_2$, or even larger. Moreover, EPM competition, unlike perfect competition, is compatible with a long-run average cost curve which is either L-shaped or continuously declining.

With a given curve such as $LAC'$ in an industry, a given size distribution of firms along that curve, and a product price equal to the unit variable costs of an average OMF, the total profits of the industry are uniquely determined. These profits, which are the surplus of sales revenue over costs of labour, materials, land rent, and depreciation, are approximately the profits estimated by normal accounting methods, provided that in the case of unincorporated businesses an adjustment is made for the imputed labour costs of the proprietors. These profits cannot in any meaningful sense be described as a pure return to capital. Although the sum of profits may be divided by the accumulated cost of net investment to yield a so-called 'rate of profit', there is no reason to assume that this rate tends to equality with the bond rate (or rates) of interest.

Before I proceed to specify a more exact model of income shares, i.e. of the proportion of profits, as defined above, to the sum of wages and profits, it is necessary to say something about the size distribution of firms.

*The size distribution of firms*

Competitive capitalist industry using modern techniques developed historically in most countries from a situation where there was already a multitude of small enterprises—mainly OMFs—in agriculture, commerce, services, and artisan activities. These small enterprises provided the main source from which entrepreneurs were drawn into manufacturing and other industries offering opportunities of higher profits from larger-scale operation. Hence at first the great majority of firms in all industries were quite small, and the bulk of output was produced by such firms. But the invention of new techniques opened great new opportunities for large-scale operation at lower cost. These opportunities were usually more limited in agriculture than in manufacturing and transport, where the scope for economies of scale seemed to grow continuously as the sizes of firms expanded. The process of industrialization was, therefore, not only a process of applying new techniques, but also of increasing the scale of operation of the larger firms, and hence of steadily stretching out the distribution of firm sizes in an upward direction.

In modern industrialized countries the size distribution of firms is extremely dispersed and skew. If the size of the firm is measured by the number of its employees (including working proprietors), sizes of private firms vary from one worker employed to over 100,000, and the frequency density appears to decrease continuously over the whole range. Statistical data on sizes of firms (or establishments) are available in most countries only for manufacturing industries. These are always highly skew, and in their upper reaches they approximate to a Pareto distribution.[9] Scattered data for other industries, e.g. retail and wholesale trade and transport, follow a similar pattern, but in these cases the Pareto function usually provides a reasonable fit over a wide range extending down to smaller sizes of firm.[10] In no country, to my knowledge, is there a complete size distribution of firms in all industries, including

[9] The Pareto distribution is $Y = aX^{-b}$, where $Y$ is the number of units exceeding a value $X$. For example, $Y$ may be the number of firms or establishments employing $X$ persons or more.

[10] Some examples of size distributions of firms in various countries are given in Steindl (1965), pp. 187–200.

such industries as agriculture, building, and services, which usually consist to a large extent of OMFs. If such a distribution were available, it seems likely that it would approximate to a Pareto distribution over most of its range, although possibly with some deviation from the function in the lowest size classes.

The industries covered by published statistics are not, of course, exclusively—or even mainly—operating under conditions of EPM competition. But the technical and financial factors influencing the growth of firms are the same under imperfect competition as under EPM competition. The major difference is the limitation on expansion of sales of any one product, which may restrict the rate of growth of the firm to some extent. We might, therefore, expect the degree of skewness and dispersion of firm sizes to be rather less under imperfect competition than under EPM competition. But without further research it is impossible to say for certain whether this is so.

Empirical evidence, again mainly from manufacturing, suggests that the relative size distribution of firms remains comparatively stable in a given country over fairly long periods of time. For example, the slope of the Pareto section of the distribution, when the function is transformed to logarithms, remains fairly steady.[11] While there is no reason to expect this stability to persist indefinitely, since the growth of firms is continuously increasing the range of firm sizes and reducing the relative importance of the smaller firms, the empirical evidence, together with the results of simulated experiments, suggests that the relative size distribution of firms is likely to change rather slowly.[12]

*A model of aggregate income shares*

With a view to aggregating across industries, it is convenient to measure the size of the firm by its number of employees. By this method, also, we may more easily identify the OMF, which plays a crucial role in the theory.[13] I shall assume that, when indus-

---

[11] See Steindl, *loc. cit.*

[12] Results of some simulations of the growth of firms are given in Appendix C.

[13] As explained in Appendix B, the *empirical* measurement of the size of the firm by its number of employees is probably not the best method to use, since it introduces biases which are likely to be more serious than those arising from other methods of classification.

tries are aggregated, there are persistent economies of scale over the whole range of firm sizes. Thus, while economies of scale in one industry may be limited, in another they are more extensive, and in some industry they extend right up to the largest observed size of firm. I shall also assume that, when firms are classified by their number of employees, average value added per employee (at given prices) increases monotonically with size of firm.[14] Consistently with our previous discussion, I shall define value added as the sum of profits and wages, i.e. net of land rent. Both profits and value added will be taken net of depreciation.

Evidence from manufacturing censuses (of which some examples are given in Appendix B) suggests that the relation between value added per worker (on a wider definition) and size of firm approximates over a substantial range to a power function of the form

$$v = BL^{\beta-1} \qquad B > 0, \beta > 1 \qquad (9.1)$$

where $v$ is value added per worker and $L$ is the number of workers in the firm.

Similar evidence also suggests that the average wage per employee varies with size of firm according to a function of the form

$$w = AL^{\alpha-1} \qquad A > 0, \quad 1 < \alpha < \beta \qquad (9.2)$$

where $w$ is the average wage (i.e. total labour cost) per employee. A major reason for upward movement of the average wage (implied by $\alpha > 1$) is the increase in the proportion of specialized workers in larger firms, reflected in the rising proportion of administrative, technical, and clerical workers. But larger firms may also pay higher wages for other reasons.

For the purpose of this model I shall assume that the functions (9.1) and (9.2) are valid, on the average, across all sizes of firms in the whole economy. But it has been argued above that, under EPM competition, valued added in the OMF will, in equilibrium, be equal to the imputed wage of the owner. This implies that the coefficient $B$ in (9.1) is equal to the coefficient $A$

---

[14] While economies of scale do not necessarily imply increasing average productivity for each factor input, there is every reason to believe that the two relations are mutually consistent in practice.

in (9.2); or that the two functions—henceforth to be called the $v$-function and the $w$-function—intersect at the point corresponding to $L = 1$. This relationship is shown in Fig. 9.2, where the two functions commence at the same point on the ordinate corresponding to $L = 1$.

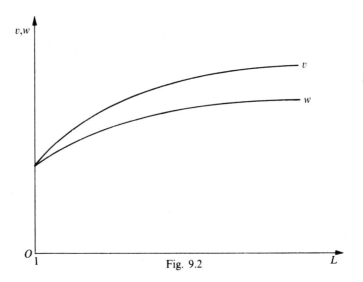

Fig. 9.2

If we write $m$ for average profit per worker in firms employing $L$ workers, we have $m = v - w$; and it is obvious that our assumptions imply that $m$ is a monotonically increasing function of $L$. It follows that, so long as the capital–value added ratio is non-increasing with size of firm, the rate of profit on capital is also monotonically increasing with $L$. I shall further assume that, under these conditions, a firm will always have an incentive to expand its operations up to the limit imposed by its internal supplies of know-how and retained profits.[15]

The final requirement for determining the aggregate wage (or profit) share is the form of the size distribution of firms. As noted above this distribution is invariably highly positively skew and approximates over a wide range to a Pareto distribu-

[15] Even if the capital–value added ratio is increasing with $L$, there may be a considerable range of sizes of firm over which the rate of profit is increasing.

tion. If we assume that the distribution is of the Pareto form over its entire range, we have

$$N = RL^{-\rho} \qquad R > 0, L \geqslant 1, \rho > 1 \qquad (9.3)$$

where $N$ is the number of firms employing $L$ workers or more. (The assumption that $\rho > 1$ is necessary if the total number of workers, and hence total output, is to be finite). When this last assumption is added to the preceding assumptions, the aggregate share of wages in value added is

$$S_w = \frac{\rho - \beta}{\rho - \alpha} \qquad (9.4)$$

provided that $\rho > \beta > \alpha$.[16]

This formula shows that, on the given assumptions, the aggregate wage share increases with $\rho$ and $\alpha$ and diminishes with $\beta$. An increase in $\rho$ represents a reduction in the proportion of large firms, and hence in the average profit margin in the whole population of firms. An increase in $\alpha$ represents an increase in the wage differential paid by large firms, and hence a reduction in their profit margins. An increase in $\beta$ represents an increase in the value added differentials of larger firms, and hence a widening of their profit margins. Even if the functions (9.1), (9.2), and (9.3) are not exactly satisfied, the aggregate wage share will clearly be influenced by parameters analogous to $\rho$, $\alpha$, and $\beta$, i.e. by the dispersion of firm sizes, and by inter-firm size differentials in wages and value added per worker.

I have already remarked that $\rho$ tends to be fairly stable over time; and it seems likely that $\alpha$ and $\beta$ (or their analogues) change rather slowly. For reasons which we shall consider below, it seems likely that $\beta$ gradually declines during the later stages of industrialization. The effect of this, unless there are offsetting changes in either $\rho$ or $\alpha$, will be to increase the wage share. It seems likely, however, that there will also be some reduction in $\rho$ (or its analogue) as the process of concentration of production in larger firms continues; and there may be, in addition, a fall in $\beta$ as firms of all sizes become more technically homogeneous.[17]

[16] For the derivation see Appendix A.
[17] See Appendix B for some empirical evidence consistent with this view.

*The effects of technical change*

An improvement in *public* technique raises the potential productivity of firms of all sizes, including OMFs. This represents
an upward shift in the function (9.1) from, say, $v_1 = B_1 L^{\beta_1 - 1}$ to
$v_2 = B_2 L^{\beta_2 - 1}$, where the subscripts refer to different public
techniques. I shall describe the case where $\beta_2 = \beta_1$ as 'neutral'
technical progress. In such circumstances, if all firms were to
shift simultaneously from $v_1$ to $v_2$, all firms would increase their
value added per worker (at constant prices) in the same proportion, namely, by $B_2/B_1 - 1$. Since the increase in real output of
the OMF would, with free entry, encourage workers to move
from paid employment into self-employment, there would be a
tendency for the real wage also to increase in the same proportion. In ultimate equilibrium, therefore, the change in $A$ in
(9.2) would be the same as the change in $B$ in (9.1), and the
imputed real wage of the OMF would be equal, as before, to its
value added. Moreover, if the parameters $\rho$ and $a$ were to be the
same after full adjustment to the new level of technique, aggregate factor shares would remain the same as before.

In practice, however, there is likely to be a substantial
time-lag in adjustment to a new technique, especially when the
new technique is significantly different from the old technique.
In these circumstances, the firms which first move to the new
technique are likely to be the most enterprising and, on average, more efficient than the firms which stick to the old technique. Since the new technique will normally require some
investment in new equipment, small firms, which usually have
limited resources, will be slower to make the change than
medium and larger firms. At the other extreme, however, very
large firms may also be slow to change, because of bureaucratic
inertia. The firms which are first to change will reap large
benefits and, out of the resulting profits, they will tend to grow
more rapidly than firms which cling to the old technique. As a
consequence of both these factors, it may be expected that, after
a certain interval of time, there will be a positive correlation
between the type of technique used and the size of firm. The
position at that time is illustrated in Fig. 9.3.

In this diagram $v_1$ is the original *v*-function and $v_2$ is the
*v*-function appropriate to the new technique. Since, after some

time there will be a larger proportion of large firms on $v_2$, the observed relation between value added per worker and size of firm at this intermediate stage will be a curve such as $v_3$. The observed pattern of wages may also be tilted upwards to a curve such as $w_3$. In this intermediate situation, then, both $\beta$ and $\alpha$

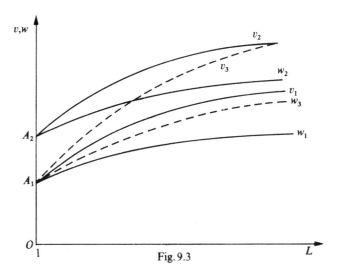

Fig. 9.3

will be greater than in either the original or the ultimate situations. At the same time, because of an increase in the dispersion of firm sizes, the value of $\rho$ is likely to be smaller.[18] On balance, it seems likely that $\beta$ will grow more than $\alpha$, while $\rho$ may slightly decline, so that the wage share will be lower than in the original situation.

At a later stage, smaller firms will also move to $v_2$; and eventually the whole economy will have adopted the new technique. The effect of this will be to reduce both $\beta$ and $\alpha$ and to shift the imputed OMF wage upwards from $OA_1$ to $OA_2$. The wage share will recover and, if $\beta_2 \approx \beta_1$, $\alpha_2 \approx \alpha_1$, and $\rho_2 \approx \rho_1$, the wage share will return to approximately the level at which it stood before the invention of the new technique. This is one

---

[18] It must be remembered, however, that, while the sizes of the firms which first move to $v_2$ will increase in terms of output, the use of the new technique will tend to reduce their size in terms of $L$. The change in $\rho$ may, therefore, be fairly small.

possible interpretation of observed changes in income distribution during the process of industrialization. The problem will be discussed further in Chapter 12 below.

Our conclusions on the effects of technical change may be summarized as follows. In the first instance, an improvement in technique will widen the differences in productivity between the firms which adopt the new technique and those which do not. The dispersion of firms will tend to grow and, although higher wages will absorb part of the higher value added (often because of the greater skills required to work the new technique), the average wage share will tend to fall. But gradually all firms which survive will move to the new technique, the OMF real wage will rise, and the wage share will start to recover towards its original level. If the size distribution of firms is permanently affected by the changes which have occurred, the wage share may not return exactly to its original level; but it will be steadily rising during the later stages of adjustment. When an economy experiences a succession of important technical changes, the wage share will be continuously depressed below its long-term equilibrium level; but, when that series of technical changes comes to an end, or slows down, the wage share will follow an upward trend. In any case, although the *wage share* will be depressed by rapid technical change, the average *real wage* will tend to rise, even in the early stages.

It is consistent with these conclusions that the wage share is higher in a country like the United States than in Japan, and higher in Japan than in countries at an earlier stage of industrialization, such as Brazil.[19]

*Inter-industry price equilibrium*

I have argued that, in equilibrium, value added in an average OMF will be equal to that OMF's imputed wage. We may write this equilibrium condition as

$$\bar{v} = \bar{w}$$

where $\bar{v}$ is value added in an average OMF and $\bar{w}$ is its imputed wage. But in the preceding section we have been taking an

---

[19] For evidence on the relation in a sample of countries between the wage share in selected manufacturing industries and *per capita* GDP see Lydall (1975), Table 14, p. 61.

aggregate view, in which $\bar{v}$ and $\bar{w}$ are calculated across all OMFs in the whole economy. If we break the economy down into separate industries (all working under EPM competition), we must distinguish different values of $\bar{v}$ and $\bar{w}$ for each industry. We may then write $\bar{v}_j$, $\bar{w}_j$ for the corresponding values of (actual or hypothetical) OMFs in industry $j$.

Now, although we may continue to assume that $\bar{v}_j = \bar{w}_j$, there is no reason to expect that $\bar{v}_j = \bar{v}$ and $\bar{w}_j = \bar{w}$. Since value added may be divided into a price and a volume component, we may write

$$\bar{v}_j = p_j \bar{q}_j = p_j / \bar{n}_j \qquad (9.5)$$

where $p_j$ is the competitive price of a unit of real value added in $j$, $\bar{q}_j$ is average output of real value added in OMFs in industry $j$, and $\bar{n}_j = 1/\bar{q}_j$ is the average labour input per unit of real value added in the same group of OMFs. Similarly, the average imputed wage per OMF in $j$ may be expressed as

$$\bar{w}_j = h_j w_o \qquad (9.6)$$

where $w_o$ is the economy-wide imputed wage of an OMF of minimum skill and $h_j$ is the ratio of the imputed wage of an OMF in $j$ to the minimum OMF wage, which may be equated with the unskilled worker's wage.

When there is equilibrium in industry $j$, $\bar{v}_j = \bar{w}_j$, which implies, by substitution from (9.5) and (9.6), that

$$p_j = \bar{n}_j h_j w_o \qquad (9.7)$$

But we may write $\bar{u}_j = \bar{n}_j h_j$ and describe $\bar{u}_j$ as the unskilled-labour-equivalent of the labour cost of producing one unit of real value added in an average OMF in industry $j$. Then

$$p_j = \bar{u}_j w_o \qquad (9.8)$$

and, for any two industries $j$ and $k$, the equilibrium price ratio is given by

$$p_j / p_k = \bar{u}_j / \bar{u}_k \qquad (9.9)$$

This result is analogous to Ricardo's assumption that prices are proportional to unit labour costs at the no-rent margin of production. But Ricardo's assumption implies, as we saw earlier, that the profit–wage ratio is constant across all firms. In our model, the Ricardian assumptions are reversed. The price of real value added (excluding rent) is proportional to labour cost at the zero-profit margin, i.e. in the OMF, while rent per unit of output, which is assumed to be independent of the size of firm, must be added to the cost of value added, just as material costs are added, to arrive at the price of the finished product. In this model, therefore, final prices depend on (1) the OMF labour cost of real value added, and (2) the rent component of cost, both cumulated over all stages of production. The theory is designed to account for relative prices of real value added (excluding rent), and hence for the division of aggregate income between wages and profits. It offers no new contribution to the theory of rent.[20]

A further implication of the theory is that, if we start from a position of general equilibrium, an equiproportionate rise in money wages in all industries will lead to an equiproportionate rise in the money prices of all products, with no change in output, employment, the structure of real wages, or the aggregate wage share. This conclusion, of course, abstracts from the possible effects of a rise in money wages on the demand for money, interest rates, public finance, international trade, or international movements of capital.

*Conclusions*

It should be emphasized that the whole of the discussion of this chapter is set within the framework of EPM competition. The effects of imperfect competition in product markets will be considered in Chapter 10. Under conditions of EPM competition there are imperfect markets for both private technique (know-how) and capital. As a consequence, despite freedom of entry and the existence of uniform product prices, firms are unable instantaneously to take full advantage of potential economies of scale. They need time to accumulate know-how and internal capital, which are the essential prerequisites for

---

[20] In Marx's theory of relative prices in Volume I of *Capital*, prices are assumed to be proportional to labour costs, without any reference to marginal considerations. This requires that the ratio of the combined sum of profits and rents to wages should be constant across all industries, which is not the same as assuming a constant profit–wage ratio unless, for some unusual reason, the rent–profit ratio were also constant.

obtaining outside finance. Hence when there are potential internal economies of scale, firms in an industry will vary in size, depending on their age and past profitability, as well as on the efficiency of their owners and managers.

In order to demonstrate some of the implications of this approach I have made a number of simplifying assumptions about the nature of the functions relating value added per worker and the average wage to the size of the firm, and also about the function describing the size distribution of firms. While these assumptions are unlikely to be precisely accurate as a description of reality in all its complexity, it seems reasonable to believe that they capture some important characteristics of that reality. The major implications of the model—in particular the relative stability of income shares and of the size distribution of firms—do not depend on the functions taking exactly the forms used for purposes of illustration. The crucial assumptions are (1) EPM competition, and (2) persistent internal economies of scale across the whole range of industries. In addition, I have assumed that technical progress is neutral, in the sense that it increases output per unit of labour in the same proportion in each size of firm. The further assumption that in equilibrium value added in the OMF is equal to its imputed wage is also important, since it implies that equilibrium prices of real value added are proportional to labour inputs in OMFs in different industries, and that changes in money wages have a direct (and proportional) effect on changes in money prices of the value added content of output.

The feature of this model which will worry some economists is the absence of substitution between labour and capital within a given size of firm, when there are changes in the wage rate or the rate of interest. (The model allows, however, for differences in capital–labour ratios across firms of different sizes, as well as across industries.) The answer to such criticism is that (1) substitution possibilities within firms of a given size seem to have been greatly overstated in neoclassical theory, and (2) in any case, it is not possible to combine neoclassical substitution theorems, which depend on the existence of perfect competition in factor markets and perfect (costless) knowledge, with a model in which all firms are assumed to be in a state which neoclassical theory would regard as one of disequilibrium. I have chosen to look at the economy from a different standpoint, and I have offered a different vision of the process of growth, the nature of equilibrium, and the effects of these on income distribution. Any theoretical model emphasizes some aspects of reality and underemphasizes others. The important question is whether the theory suggested here goes closer to the heart of the problem of distribution than alternative theories.

Apart from the differences in the foundations of the model, it has some other important economic characteristics. In the first place, the model is not a static model excluding time. The size and performance of every firm are continuously changing for endogenous reasons: as time passes, firms accumulate both know-how and an internal supply of funds, which are the basis for further expansion. But this continuous process of growth and change is compatible with a kind of equilibrium. For each competitive industry consists of a population of firms of different sizes. As established firms grow in size they move up the distribution; but when the total demand for the industry's product is increasing at a sufficient rate, new entrants come into the industry as OMFs, thus maintaining the over-all shape of the relative size distribution. So long as the relative size distribution of firms is fairly constant, and the profit margin varies in a definite way with size of firm, the aggregate wage and profit shares of value added produced in the industry will also be fairly constant; and in this sense also there is an equilibrium.

When value added in the OMF is equal to its imputed wage, the model generates an equilibrium set of prices which—as in neoclassical theory—are equal to marginal costs. But the margin in this model is not the point at which the last unit of each factor of production is applied. Instead, it is the point at which the least productive firm is operating—the OMF. In the OMF all the factors of production are marginally productive, while in larger firms there are economies of scale. Substitutions between factors occur, but they are not crucial to the determination of the margin of production. The reason why, despite their relative inefficiency, OMFs continue to exist is that the growth of larger firms is limited by their imperfect (but growing) technical knowledge and by imperfect capital markets. There is no unique production function available to all firms irrespective of size.

Finally, the model provides a number of links between the 'factor' and the personal distributions of income. The parameter $a$, for example, which partly determines the aggregate wage share, is a measure of the importance of wage differentials between firms of different sizes. Hence, a higher value of $a$ implies wider wage differentials; and vice versa. It is also likely that a country which is in the process of rapid technical change will have a higher value of $a$ than a country with a more homogeneous level of technique.

The parameters $\beta$ and $\rho$, in conjunction with $a$, determine both the average wage share and the size distribution of profits of firms. So long as firms are mainly owned by individual entrepreneurs, the size distribution of profits of firms—after deduction of interest payments—is essentially a size distribution of the profits of individuals; and this provides another link between the model and the personal distribution of income. In the later stages of development, of course, this link is weakened by the conversion of most large firms into companies, shares in which are more widely dispersed, either directly, or indirectly through such agencies as life insurance and pension funds. In addition, differences in the degrees of efficiency and luck of firms, which are important factors in determining their current profits, and consequently their rates of growth, will be reflected in income differences of the owners who, at least in the case of smaller firms, are mainly individual entrepreneurs.

In the next chapter we shall consider what modifications may need to be made to the model by the existence of imperfect competition in production markets. And in the chapter after that we shall examine some of the implications of the model for other aspects of economic theory.

# 10

# IMPERFECT COMPETITION

In the previous chapter I described a model which accounts for the size distribution and rate of growth of firms, income shares, and relative prices in equilibrium. That model is based on the assumption of free entry and perfect competition in product markets (EPM competition). But in industrialized countries only a minor part of national income is generated in industries which approximate to EPM competition. It is necessary, therefore, to consider what are likely to be the effects on income distribution of departures from EPM competition.

It should be noted that our point of reference for defining imperfect competition is not perfect competition but EPM competition. Under EPM competition there are (1) free entry and (2) perfect product and labour markets. Any firm can enter any market, without legal restriction; the individual firm is never conscious of any effect on the market price of its product arising from variations in its own sales; and all firms pay the same rate for a given quality of labour. But EPM competition does not include either a perfect capital market or a perfect knowledge market. Hence the firm is obliged to contribute a substantial proportion of both its capital and its technical know-how out of its own resources, and these resources can be increased only by successful activity extending over time.

What are the principal features which distinguish imperfect competition from EPM competition? In the light of the definition of EPM competition it is clear that there are two major sources of difference: first, there may be restricted entry; and secondly, there may be imperfect product markets. Let us consider these separately.

The second characteristic, which presents little difficulty, may be taken first. In an imperfect product market each firm is conscious that its supply decisions—i.e. decisions to produce and to offer the consequential output for sale—are likely to affect the prices at which it can sell. This may be either because its product is unique in some respect—a differentiated product—or because it already holds a large share of a competitive market. The firm with a differentiated product is strictly speaking a monopolist, and its situation is the limiting case of the firm with a large share in a competitive market. I shall refer to these two types of market imperfection as the differentiated product case and the perfect oligopoly case. There is also an intermediate case, where the product is only slightly differentiated and there are several sellers who are especially sensitive to each other's policies.

We turn next to consider what is meant by restricted entry. The clearest case of restricted entry is a legal prohibition on competitive production or sale of a particular product or group of products. Examples of such restrictions are state monopolies, licensing, and laws regulating patents and trade marks. In many cases state (including local government) monopolies arise out of so-called 'natural' monopolies, e. g. in transport or public utilities. But it is often difficult to decide, once the monopoly has statutory sanction, how much of the monopoly is 'natural' and how much is the result of the law. I do not propose to offer any new contribution to the theory of pricing behaviour under state monopoly. The standard theory of monopoly pricing is satisfactory so far as it goes; but, since state monopolies are usually subject to various legal restraints, the theory needs modification in each individual case. Income distribution in an economy of which a large part is controlled be state monopolies is unlikely to conform to any general theory.

The other kinds of legal restriction on entry, namely, licensing, patents, and registration of trade marks, are, in comparison with state monopolies, of minor importance. Whereas under a state monopoly private firms are usually excluded from a whole branch of industry, these other restrictions limit only certain varieties of activity. Licensing, for example, may prevent location of an enterprise in a certain area; patent protection prohibits the use of a particular process or product design for a limited period of time; and trade mark laws prohibit the use of a specified name or package for a product. Trade marks are closely related to, and can be most usefully regarded as one aspect of, product differentiation. The other two instruments undoubtedly create partial or temporary monopoly rights but, apart from a few exceptional cases, their effect on the distribution of income is probably small.[1] Because of uncertainty about their long-term effects, we shall say no more about them.

Bain (1956) has added to the list of legal restrictions on entry a group of 'barriers to entry' which are economic in origin. For example, since a firm with a differentiated product has a strong interest in preventing a competitor from entering its market, in the sense of offering for sale an almost identical product, it may decide to reduce its own price, or take some other action such as increasing its advertising expenditure, in order to deter competitive entry. A perfect oligopolist, also, has an incentive to consider similar schemes to deter entry into its shared market, especially if it holds a large share of that market.[2] Such policies may have effects on relative prices and the distribution of income, and Bain's empirical studies of their incidence have added considerably to our knowledge about them. But I think that he has somewhat confused the matter by describing the advantages which one firm has over another as a barrier to entry. The origin of this idea lies in the assumption that the 'norm' of a competitive market is one of perfect equality. If we follow the textbook definition of perfect competition, all firms in a competitive market must have the same costs and sell at the same price. From this point of reference, any observed differences in costs between firms selling the same product must be due to market imperfections and hence, according to Bain, to barriers to entry. So we are led to the strange conclusion that economies of scale in themselves constitute a barrier to entry.

The problem is clarified as soon as we shift our reference point from perfect competition to EPM competition. Under EPM competition there are persistent economies of scale; and, both for this and for other reasons, firms which sell the same product at the same price may be of different sizes, and have different costs and different profit margins. Thus inter-firm cost advantages are perfectly compatible with free entry, and it would be self-contradictory to describe a cost advantage as a barrier to entry. Nevertheless, it is a fact that monopolists and oligopolists have an incentive to deter entry. We need, therefore, to consider what sort of effects these incentives will have

---

[1] The effects of patents are shown to be small in most industries by Taylor and Silberston (1973).

[2] This is the case considered by Sylos-Labini (1962).

on their behaviour, and hence on the behaviour of others; and so to infer the likely effects of such behaviour on prices and the distribution of income.

In the light of the above considerations I consider that it is preferable to limit the definition of barriers to entry to legal barriers. The kinds of barriers discussed by Bain are the results of inter-firm competitive marketing strategy and can best be discussed under that heading. It follows that, if we set aside the problem of state monopolies, and if we agree that licensing and patents are usually of small importance in the whole picture, the normal case of imperfect competition is the case of an inelastic demand, due to either product differentiation or oligopoly, combined with free entry. If we can offer a theory to account for prices and the distribution of income under these conditions we shall have covered a large part of the field.

*Product differentiation with free entry*

A firm which sells a differentiated product is, strictly speaking, a monopolist, although its monopoly power under conditions of free entry may be very limited. Free entry, as I have defined it, means the legal right to produce and sell an identical product; and the cases which I am considering are those in which there is no such legal restriction, apart from the trade mark restriction which is inseparable from product differentiation. Thus, when I say that there is free entry into a market for a single firm's differentiated product I mean that other firms could, if they wished, make and offer for sale a product identical in all but name. Free entry into the Coca Cola market, for example, means that there are no legal restrictions on making and selling a product which is identical to Coca Cola apart from the name and the shape of the bottle.

Abstracting from the effects of the trade mark restrictions as such, we may now ask: What is likely to be the pricing policy of a firm which sells a differentiated product under conditions of free entry? This was the question which occupied the centre of the debate about the effects of imperfect or monopolistic competition in the 1930s; and it will be useful to start by considering the answer which was given then and which is still offered as the orthodox view in most modern textbooks.

The orthodox view runs roughly as follows. A seller of a differentiated product has his own market and hence his own immediate demand for the product.[3] This demand curve, like all demand curves for a single product of small importance in total expenditure, is downward-sloping. Hence price is above marginal revenue, and the profit-maximizing firm, which makes marginal revenue equal to marginal cost, will set a price for its product which lies above marginal cost. If sales at this price yield the firm above-normal profits and there is free entry, new firms will be attracted into the market, offering a closely similar product. This process will continue until all firms which are subject to free entry are making normal profits. This implies that every such firm ends up with a demand curve tangential to its (long-run) average cost curve and hence that prices and costs are above their minimum level.

This description of a rational firm's behaviour is, on the face of it, a very curious one. It implies that firms are completely myopic, giving no consideration to any consequences of their decisions beyond the most immediate. This is, of course, a carry-over of the standard static method used in the analysis of competitive equilibrium. But while there might be some justification for the use of that method in a model of perfect competition, where the firm is assumed to have no control over its environment, there is no justification for using it in a model of imperfect competition where, by clear assumption, the firm has the power to influence its environment in a variety of ways. For example, a firm which has its own differentiated product, with its own demand curve, possesses an area of the market in which it is, up to a point, the master. Since the firm is a 'price-maker', it may be expected in fixing its price to have regard to all the important consequences which are likely to

---

[3] There has been much argument about the range of other things which are assumed to be constant when constructing such a demand curve. If we are to keep a clear separation between different steps in the analysis, I think that we should employ the strictest definition of *ceteris paribus*, namely, that *everything* else is believed by the firm in question to be constant. I call the demand curve which is constructed on this assumption the firm's 'immediate' demand curve. As will be clear in what follows, I am far from suggesting that a rational firm's decisions will be determined solely by the relation between its costs and its immediate demand curve. But I do not think that any useful purpose is served by trying to 'boil down' the wider considerations which enter into a firm's decisions into its demand curve.

flow from that decision. And it must be only too obvious to any firm in that position that, if it raises its price above a certain level, it will be likely to attract competitors, with all the undesirable consequences which follow. Hence the rational profit-maximizing firm with a differentiated product, but subject to free entry, will surely weigh the benefits from raising its price to the level consistent with equality between marginal revenue and marginal cost against the costs, in terms of long-term loss of profits, of thereby attracting new entrants into its market.

It was a long time before this simple argument was formulated clearly and was used to frame a different hypothesis about the price behaviour of firms under imperfect competition with free entry. Even now, myopic behaviour is usually assumed to be normal, and the alternative behaviour—expectations-influenced behaviour—is regarded as a special case. But before we proceed with our discussion of the effects of expectations-influenced behaviour on prices and income distribution it will be useful to recall the other major development in price theory during the 1930s.

This other development was the doctrine of 'full cost' pricing. Strictly, this was not a theory but a description of what appeared from empirical study to be the standard pattern of behaviour of firms operating under conditions of imperfect competition. The doctrine was first enunciated by Hall and Hitch (1939), reporting on the information supplied by thirty-eight business men, mainly manufacturers, and mainly, in the opinion of Hall and Hitch, oligopolists. Most firms in the sample were found to fix their prices without regard to the relation between marginal revenue and marginal cost but by a 'rule of thumb', usually described as the addition to unit direct costs of an allowance for indirect costs and a further margin for profit. Hall and Hitch attempted to rationalize this behaviour by use of a 'kinked' demand curve, and a similar model was suggested simultaneously by Sweezy (1939). The kink occurs at the intersection of two hypothetical demand curves: one in which close competitors do not adjust their prices in response to a change in price by the given firm (our 'immediate' demand curve), and another in which they do so adjust their prices. If, for some reason, an entrepreneur believes that the responses of close competitors are asymmetrical, with no price response when his price is raised but a parallel reduction in prices when his price is lowered, there will be a discontinuity in his demand curve, which will encourage him to keep his price constant.

As has frequently been pointed out, the kinked demand curve model provides no explanation for the position of the kink. All that the model predicts is that, once a price has been established, the kink will tend to keep it constant. But this is not a theory of price determination; nor is it really consistent with the 'full cost' rule, which requires price to be altered in line with changes in costs.[4]

One consequence of the discovery of the practice of 'full cost' pricing has been to encourage economists to search for other goals of business decision-making besides profit-maximization. We now have 'behavioural' and 'managerial' theories of the firm, in which profit-maximization is only one of a number of objectives, or in which other objectives, such as a maximum rate of growth of sales, are emphasized, subject to the attainment of a 'satisfactory', 'acceptable', or 'minimum' rate of profit.[5] While it is no doubt true that firms, like consumers, have multiple objectives, the difficulty about including a number of different objectives is to attribute appropriate weights and trade-offs to the objectives. Moreover, the constraint of achieving a 'satisfactory' profit rate is too vague to be useful. It still seems, therefore, to be a worthwhile task to try to explain the behaviour of firms under conditions of imperfect competition without introducing multiple objectives. Let us then consider whether by placing the profit-maximizing objective in a more realistic framework a useful theory can be developed which will also account for 'full cost' pricing and for other reported patterns of behaviour.

*Expectations-influenced behaviour*

The first step in the direction of a coherent theory of imperfect competition is to purge ourselves of the static method and to

[4] In the end, Hall and Hitch suggested that changes in costs result in changes in the position of the kink. But if 'full cost' determines the position of the kink, which in turn determines price, the kink becomes redundant, except as a possible explanation for price rigidity.

[5] See, for example, Simon (1955), Baumol (1959), Cyert and March (1963), Marris (1964), and Williamson (1967). A useful summary is given in the survey by Silberston (1979).

give an explicit role to expectations.[6] As already mentioned, the static method may have some justification in the analysis of perfect competition, but it is a misleading framework for the analysis of imperfect competition. Whether a firm sells a differentiated product or is a perfect oligopolist, it is conscious of being in possession of a market, or share of a market, which is at

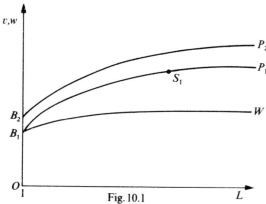

Fig. 10.1

least temporarily its own. It has its own circle of customers; and this is an asset which it will want to safeguard. Hence the firm, by the nature of its environment, must be forward-looking; and its current behaviour must be significantly influenced by its expectations of the future consequences of any decisions taken today.

The areas of possible decision-making under imperfect competition are numerous: they include pricing, advertising, selling, product design, investment in production facilities, plant location, and so forth. But decisions about prices are clearly of very great importance. Let us, therefore, start by assuming—unrealistically—that decisions have already been taken about all other matters and that only the price decision remains to be taken. We continue for the time being with the case of a firm which sells a single differentiated product subject to free entry.

Our firm is, therefore, making a particular product—product $X$—with a particular technique, and it is already of a

---

[6] Many economists have tried to lead economic theory in this direction, notably Keynes (1936), Shackle (1952), and Friedman (1957). In the area of price theory, however, priority should be given to Andrews (1949), Harrod (1952), Bain (1956), and Sylos-Labini (1962).

certain size, measured by employment. Let us also assume that initially, for some reason, the firm is selling $X$ at the price which would exist under EPM competition, i.e. at the price which, with that technique, would yield zero profit to a one-man firm of average efficiency. Without loss of generality we can also assume that the firm itself is of average efficiency. Then the

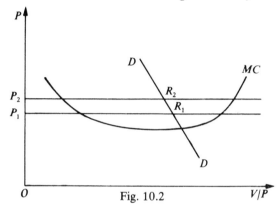

Fig. 10.2

position of the firm, and the effects of alternative price decisions, can be illustrated by Figs. 10.1 and 10.2. In Fig. 10.1 are shown curves, similar to the functions (9.1) and (9.2), which describe how value added per worker and the average wage vary with the employment size of a firm making product $X$. With fixed money wages, there is only one wage function $(B_1W)$, but the value added per worker function, or $v$-function, shifts upwards or downwards as the price of the product (the price of a unit of real value added) is varied. In the diagram are two alternative $v$-functions: the equilibrium EPM function $B_1P_1$, which intersects the vertical axis (through $L = 1$) at the same point as $B_1W$, and a function corresponding to a higher price, $B_2P_2$. The firm is assumed initially to be at point $S_1$.

Figure 10.2 shows the short-term marginal cost function of the firm and its immediate demand curve, i.e. the curve which traces out the quantities which the firm can sell at different prices when there is no change in any other price or in the number of competing firms offering close substitutes. Since Fig. 10.1 measures output per worker in terms of value added per worker, value added is also used as the measure of output in Fig. 10.2, but deflated by the price of a unit of value added to convert to real value added. Consequently, the marginal cost and demand curves also represent prices and costs per unit of real value added. If material inputs (including service inputs from other firms and rent) are constant per unit of output, the marginal cost curve for real value added will simply be the usual marginal cost curve displaced downwards by the unit cost of material inputs (assuming also an infinitely elastic supply of such inputs to the firm). But the demand curve for real value added will have a smaller elasticity than the demand curve for the firm's gross output. The ratio, at any point, of the elasticity of demand for real value added to the elasticity of demand for real gross output will be equal to the ratio, at that point, of the firm's value added to the value of its gross output.

Empirical estimates of the price-elasticity of demand for differentiated products seem to be almost totally lacking. But, in the light of the low price-elasticities which are normally found for those products for which estimates have been made, it seems unlikely that the (negative of the) price-elasticity of demand for most differentiated products is greater than 3. A typical ratio of value added to gross output value in manufacturing is about one-third. Hence it seems probable that for most differentiated products the price-elasticity of demand for real value added is less than unity. But this is not an equilibrium position for a firm which fixes its price in order to equalize marginal revenue and marginal cost.[7] It follows that, if firms selling differentiated products were setting their prices so as to maximize short-term profits, most—or even all—prices would be much higher that they are. Hence there must be some constraint which prevents firms from following the short-term profit-maximizing rule.

And there clearly is such a constraint. It is the probability that, if a firm selling a differentiated product were to fix its price above its existing level, that action would attract other firms to enter its market, i.e. to start producing a product which is closely similar to the firm's own product, and thus to reduce the firm's profit prospects in the future. This constraint, of course,

[7] The profit-maximizing rule for a monopolist is to make $p = m \left(\frac{e}{e-1}\right)$, where $p$ is the price, $m$ is marginal cost, $e$ is the price-elasticity of demand, and $e > 1$. If $e < 1$, the profit-maximizing price will be infinitely large, no matter what the level of marginal cost.

operates only for changes in price in an upward direction; but, so long as the price-elasticity is such as to push a firm to raise its price above the constrained level, the two forces will combine to hold the price always at that level. I shall call this constrained, or 'ceiling', price the no-entry price (NEP).[8]

How can a firm estimate its NEP? This question brings us back to Figs. 10.1 and 10.2. It was assumed that the firm whose characteristics are depicted in those diagrams is initially at point $S_1$, which is on the $v$-function which would exist in equilibrium if the product in question were being sold under conditions of EPM competition. The price corresponding to that function is $P_1$, represented by the distance $OP_1$ in Fig. 10.2. On the assumptions specified earlier, the immediate demand curve for real value added, $DD$, has an elasticity over the range $R_1R_2$ such as to make it profitable for the firm to raise its price above the price $P_1$, e.g. to $P_2$. The effect of such a change in price on Fig. 10.1 would be to shift the $v$-function upwards in the ratio $P_2/P_1 - 1$. The $v$-function corresponding to price $P_2$ is $B_2P_2$.

It is important to understand that the $v$-functions represented by $B_1P_1$ and $B_2P_2$ are entirely hypothetical. There is initially only one firm actually making product $X$: only one point on Fig. 10.1 can actually be observed, namely point $S_1$. The curve $B_1P_1$ shows, in conjuction with $B_1W$, the profit margins which would be received by firms of average efficiency but of different sizes which produced product $X$ with the given technique and sold the product at price $P_1$. Those are also the profit margins which would exist for a group of firms which were all producing $X$ under conditions of EPM competition.

I wish to argue that, in general, it will be very risky for a firm operating under conditions of free entry to fix its price above $P_1$. Potential new entrants into the $X$ market will consist predo-

---

[8] It is sometimes called a 'limit' price, or an 'entry-preventing' price. The first term was suggested originally by Bain (1949) but referred to a price set by a group of sellers acting in collusion. The second term was used by Sylos-Labini (1962). By the use of the term 'no-entry' price I do not mean to imply that at this price there is a guarantee that no new entry will occur under any circumstance. The NEP is the firm's best estimate of the maximum price which it can safely charge without attracting new entry into its market. In making such an estimate, under conditions of uncertainty, an expert firm would balance its estimates of the probabilities of new entry at different levels and at different dates against the cost of forgoing immediate profits by lowering its price.

minantly of firms which are already making products similar to $X$. They will vary in size and in efficiency, but each of them has the same problem of fixing an NEP for its own product. Since their products are similar, it may be assumed that their techniques are similar, so that their $v$-functions have a similar size-elasticity. If they also fix their prices in order to offer to competitors a $v$-function which yields profit margins no more than those obtainable under EPM competition, there will be no incentive for any firm which makes a product similar to $X$ to enter the $X$ market, or to cross over into making any other product in the group which is already being sold on these terms. Thus the set of NEPs for the group of firms making similar products will be such as to produce approximately the same $v$-function for each firm.

It remains, however, to demonstrate that the whole set of $v$-functions is likely to correspond approximately to the EPM equilibrium $v$-function. We may approach the question by imagining that a number of firms of different sizes are selling similar (but differentiated) products at prices which would yield for firms of average efficiency profit margins consistent with a single $v$-function and a single $w$-function. Let that $v$-function be $B_2P_2$ and that $w$-function be $B_1W$ in Fig. 10.1. The whole group of firms is operating under conditions of free entry, both free entry into each other's territory and free entry into the group by firms not at present making a similar product. Under such conditions a group of firms which fixed their prices above the EPM equilibrium level, i.e. so as to offer to the outside world the $v$-function $B_2P_2$ instead of $B_1P_1$, would be likely sooner or later to attract into the group some new entrants. These new entrants could be of any size, not necessarily OMFs. Larger firms with established markets outside the group might well discover that they could make larger profit margins by entering the group than they were currently earning in their own territory: they could 'diversify'. Large new entrants of this sort would present a particularly serious danger to the members of the group. But the ultimate threat to the position of the group is the attraction of new small firms into the market. Since the profit margins of small firms will never deviate far from EPM equilibrium profit margins, small firms will always have an incentive to move into an industry which has raised its

$v$-function above the EPM equilibrium $v$-function. In Fig. 10.1, for example, the OMF which is faced by $B_2P_2$ has an opportunity of making higher profits than on the EPM equilibrium function $B_1P_1$, and the same applies to other small firms of slightly larger size. The ultimate determinant of relative prices, under imperfect competition as well as under EPM competition, is the right of free entry of OMFs and other small firms.

*The role of selling costs*

Up to this point, in order to focus on the process of price determination, I have assumed that the firm has already taken decisions about all other variables. But this is clearly unrealistic, since decisions about prices are interrelated with decisions about many other matters, including especially product design and selling costs. Let us now keep product design and other decisions constant and consider how decisions about price and selling costs are interrelated.

When a firm sells a differentiated product it is almost certain to incur some selling costs on such items as packaging, advertising, and the employment of a sales force. The immediate purposes of these activities are to draw the attention of potential customers to the existence of the product and to improve their opinion of the quality of the product. The major ultimate purpose is to expand sales. But part of the expenditure may also be defensive. ʻOffensive and defensive elements in selling activities cannot really be separated, since the two effects are complementary. Nevertheless, a by-product of selling activities is to strengthen the defensive position of the firm concerned, and one of their main effects may be to raise the cost of entry.

If a firm selling a differentiated product finds it necessary to incur significant selling expenses, the $v$-function for that type of product should be adjusted accordingly. Our original definition of a $v$-function was that it specifies the relation—for a given product, a given technique, a given level of efficiency of the firm, and a given price of the product—between value added per worker and the number of workers employed. Since this definition was designed for a model of EPM competition, it was implicitly assumed that the firm concerned incurred no selling costs, so that outside purchases of material and service inputs included no advertising expenses and inside employment included no salesmen. If we imagine that a firm which sells a differentiated product starts from a position where it has no selling expenses, we can draw a hypothetical $v$-function for that type of product at a given price without subtracting anything for selling expenses. Let us now consider how such a firm can best deter entry. It has two main instruments at its disposal: it can reduce its price or it can start a sales campaign. Either decision on its own will shift the $v$-function downwards—although probably in different ways. But the firm may operate on both instruments simultaneously. It may, for example, estimate that a sales campaign of a certain level of intensity will deter entry so successfully that the price can safely be raised above its original level. In some circumstances, the firm may even be able, by using both instruments, to raise its profit margin *and* raise a barrier to entry at the same time. The possibility of achieving such a result arises where—as is often the case—there is a substantial indivisible element in selling costs, so that, while a rise in price for the large firm more than covers its selling costs per unit, the same rise in price for a smaller firm is not sufficient to cover the selling costs per unit required to maintain a smaller share of the market.[9]

In the light of this discussion it is clear that with product differentiation there is no guarantee that prices and income distribution within the firm will be exactly the same as under EPM competition. So far as prices are concerned, it can be expected that the prices of differentiated products will usually be higher than they would be if the *same* products were sold under conditions of EPM competition. If we take the hypothetical EPM price as our standard, we may say that part of the selling costs associated with product differentiation will usually be passed on to the consumer. But this does not mean that the consumer's welfare is necessarily reduced, since product differentiation, by widening choice, usually raises the consumer's

[9] A firm entering a new market with a differentiated product usually has initial marketing expenses, which are a kind of capital outlay. But these cannot be regarded as a special type of barrier to entry—different, for example, from other initial capital costs—unless such initial marketing costs are in some sense larger than they were for the firms which are already established.

utility level.[10] The effects on income distribution, however, are less certain. If selling expenses are completely passed on, the profit margin remains the same as under EPM competition for the same size of firm of the same efficiency. It is possible that the passing on of selling expenses may have some distributional effects; but they are unlikely to be significant. On the other hand, differentiation of products may accelerate the growth of larger firms and increase the degree of concentration; and, if this happens, it will tend to raise the aggregate profit share.

These conclusions, like empirical predictions from any theoretical model which attempts to capture even a few of the complexities of real life, are not very precise. But they are better than the conclusions which usually emerge from theoretical discussions of imperfect competition, which amount to little more than the statement that 'anything can happen'. The present model is based on the assumption of EPM competition, which already includes inter-firm cost differences arising from differences in firm efficiency and economies of scale, and which allows for imperfect capital and knowledge markets. Thus EPM competition is already several steps on the road to imperfect competition. Yet it can generate a definite equilibrium distribution of income. When the next step is taken, which is to allow product differentiation while retaining free entry in the legal sense, a number of new possible modes of behaviour are naturally opened up. But so long as there is genuine free entry, especially at the level of the small firm, it seems unlikely that product differentiation, even with its accompanying selling costs, makes a major difference to aggregate income shares in comparison with what they would have been under EPM competition.

### Oligopoly

Oligopoly can be clearly defined only in the case of perfect oligopoly, where all firms are selling an identical product. But

---

[10] Some economists believe that product differentiation is 'unnecessary' and adds nothing to social welfare. The test of the market, however, justifies a different conclusion. The only known alternative to the market as a method of determining product variety is the arbitrary rule of an oligarchy. Those who have lived under such conditions are not usually in any doubt about their own preferences.

the market pressures on perfect oligopolists are to a considerable extent matched by similar pressures on those sellers of differentiated products whose degree of product differentiation is, in some sense, small. A precise dividing line between product differentiation without oligopoly and product differentiation with oligopoly can be drawn if we allocate to the former group any firm whose immediate demand curve has an elasticity which is so small that it has no incentive to reduce its price below the no-entry price. This is the type of firm whose behaviour has been discussed under the previous heading. The alternative situation is one in which a firm which sells a differentiated product has an immediate demand curve with an elasticity such as to give it a profit-maximizing incentive to cut its price, provided of course that the assumption underlying the construction of the immediate demand curve is satisfied, namely, that all other things are constant. Since the perfect oligopolist is, by definition, always in this position, it is natural to say that this latter group of sellers of differentiated products are also oligopolists. They may therefore be called imperfect oligopolists.

If we are to account for the price behaviour of oligopolists—whether perfect or imperfect—the first step is to establish that a rational oligopolist firm will follow the same policy of keeping its price at or below the NEP as the non-oligopolist seller of a differentiated product. Although an oligopolist firm does not command the whole market for a given product or group of closely related products it has, by definition, a substantial share in that market. Hence it will have a good enough reason for wishing to deter new entry, and it can safely be assumed that the NEP represents an upper limit on an oligopolist's price. For a group of perfect oligopolists, there is, in principle, only one NEP, although there may be slight differences of view among the member firms as to what that price is.[11] For the imperfect oligopoly group, there is a separate NEP for each different product; but the group of NEPs will bear a close relation to one another and can be expected to move in step.

Let us now consider the choices open to oligopolists in fixing a price below the NEP. Each oligopolist, by definition, has a

---

[11] These differences of opinion about the NEP are partly responsible for the phenomenon of price leadership.

profit-maximizing incentive to cut its price if the price cut evokes no competitive response from other members of the group. If, however, the oligopolist firm expects that any cut in price will be followed by similar cuts by its competitors, the effects on its profits will depend on the elasticity of total demand for the product or, in the case of imperfect oligopoly, of the total demand for a weighted index of the products in the group. It seems reasonable to assume that this elasticity will be such as to provide no incentive for cutting price below the NEP, and hence that an oligopolist firm which expects matching price cuts by its competitors will keep its price at the NEP level. The problem of price policy for oligopolists, therefore, turns on their expectations about the responses of competitors in their group.

It is not difficult to see that a rational oligopolist would expect that its competitors would normally match any price cut below the NEP. The competitors have two main alternatives: to cut or not to cut. If they do not cut, the original price-cutting firm will, by assumption, increase its sales to such an extent as to more than compensate for the price cut. Both its sales revenue and its profits will rise. Hence it will immediately command a larger share of the market and, with its increased profit flow, it will be able to expand its productive capacity more rapidly in the future. Meantime, the experience of the rest of the firms in the group will be exactly the opposite: falling sales revenue, even more rapidly falling profits, and a reduction in the flow of finance for future growth.[12] If competing firms follow the alternative policy of cutting their prices in line with the original price-cutter and if, as we have assumed, the total demand curve for the product or group of products is relatively inelastic, the total real sales of the group will increase, but the profits of all firms will fall. Whether the decline in profits of the responding firms will be greater or less than in the first case depends on a number of considerations. But one rule is general, namely, that the more perfect the oligopoly the more clearly the advantage lies on the side of the second policy; and the more

---

[12] Under imperfect competition, firms usually have excess capacity, i.e. they produce below the point at which their short-run marginal cost curve intersects their horizontal price line. Hence, both increases and reductions in sales, even at fixed prices, will have magnified effects on their short-term profits.

likely that the first firm will come to expect that this will be the response of its competitors to a price cut, and hence that a price cut will only inflict damage on its own interests.

The following conclusions can be drawn from this discussion. Under oligopoly as well as under product differentiation without oligopoly (and with free entry) the rational firm will normally set its price at or below the NEP, except to the extent that selling costs can safely be passed on. If the immediate demand curve is sufficiently inelastic, there is no incentive to cut the price below the NEP. This is the case of product differentiation without oligopoly. If, on the other hand, the immediate demand curve is more elastic than this—which means that we have an oligopoly condition—a potential price-cutter has to expect that competing firms will have an incentive to match any price cut which it makes, and hence to deprive it of any opportunity of benefiting from the price cut. So, on whatever assumption we make about the elasticity of the immediate demand curves, there appears to be no rational basis for reducing the price significantly below the NEP; and hence there is always an advantage in keeping it at or close to the NEP.

*The logic of 'full cost' pricing*

The general conclusion from the previous discussion is that in all cases of imperfect competition with free entry, whether in large or small groups with differentiated products, or under conditions of perfect oligopoly, prices will approximate to the levels which would obtain under EPM competition. There will be some deviations from this rule when selling costs are substantial; but even in this case the starting-point is the EPM price and, provided that there is genuine free entry, especially at the level of the small firm, the price is unlikely to deviate too far from the EPM price in the long run.

The EPM price, adjusted where appropriate for selling costs, is, therefore, the 'standard' or 'normal' price of a product; and the profit margin which a firm can make at that price is its own normal profit margin. This normal profit margin reflects (1) the shape of the $v$-function, which is determined by the technique used in making the product; (2) the $w$-function for that product, which also depends in part on the production technique; (3) the size of the firm which, in conjunction with these two functions, determines the profit margin of a firm of average efficiency; and (4) the actual degree of efficiency of the firm which, when compared with the average degree of efficiency, indicates the profit margin appropriate for that particular firm. In terms of the model, the firm's profit *mark-up* on wages cost when there is EPM equilibrium is (see (A.17) in Appendix A)

$$M_i/W = \theta_i L^{\beta-a} - 1 \qquad (10.1)$$

where $\theta_i$ is the efficiency of firm $i$, $L$ is its employment size, and $\beta$ and $a$ are the elasticities of its value added function and its $w$-function respectively.

It follows that, if a firm can estimate its appropriate profit mark-up, it will be able to deduce the EPM equilibrium price by applying that mark-up to its own unit labour costs. It is not suggested that firms actually attempt to estimate the parameters of (10.1). All that we need to assume is that, from general knowledge of business conditions, to some extent by trial and error, and by observing the practice of close competitors, a firm arrives at an estimate of the mark-up on labour cost which is appropriate for its own product, its own size, and its own level of efficiency.

By applying its normal profit mark-up to its own unit labour costs a firm arrives at an estimate of the EPM equilibrium price of a unit of real value added in that activity. To proceed from there to a corresponding estimate of the EPM price of the product, measured in physical units, it is necessary to add the unit costs of purchased materials and outside services, land rent, and depreciation. If it is assumed that these unit costs are the same for all sizes of firm, the firm can use its own unit costs as the basis for this estimate, which in principle should apply to the unit costs of the OMF.

The above-described method of estimating the EPM equilibrium price of a product, and hence its no-entry price, clearly bears a close resemblance to the kinds of rules of thumb which are used by firms in arriving at 'full cost'. Different variants of these rules seem to be used by different firms, but all start from *the firm's own unit costs* of labour and materials and add one or more mark-ups to them. The resulting estimates may not always be very accurate estimates of the no-entry price, but the method is entirely consistent with a theory of rational pricing under conditions of imperfect competition.[13]

The great practical advantage of the rule-of-thumb method of pricing is that the firm can use a fixed estimate of its normal mark-up for an extended period of time—on the assumption that its production technique and its own relative efficiency are both fairly stable—and apply that mark-up to any variations in labour costs, with an appropriate addition for variations in other costs. This is simply a separation of a parameter from a variable; and economists should be the first to recognize its practical convenience.

### The explanation of multiple objectives

Behavioural and managerial theories of the firm usually suggest that, subject to a profit constraint, firms pursue objectives such as (1) survival, or (2) stability of profits, or (3) a maximum rate of growth. The objectives of survival and stability of profits are not, of course, 'multiple' objectives, unless profit-maximization is originally presented as an entirely static goal. These expectational objectives are central to my model, which emphasizes the importance to the firm of avoiding price increases which may induce new entry. The objective of maximum growth is also consistent with the model. Once a firm has fixed its price, it has fixed its minimum rate of profit (when operating at normal capacity), and it can turn its main attention to the task of expanding its market *at that price*. On the assumption of persistent economies of scale, an expansion of sales at a fixed price will also increase profits and the average profit rate. From the point of view of the managers of a 'managerial' firm expansion of sales, and hence of employment, increases their power and responsibilities, and hence their salaries, their status, and usually their interest in the job. Even if they have no share in profits or a bonus related to either sales or profits, they will have an incentive to encourage growth.

---

[13] The estimate of 'full cost', which is a rough estimate of the EPM equilibrium price, may of course be adjusted for selling costs—and their effects on the probability of entry—and in the light of other *ad hoc* considerations.

While there may well remain other objectives—such as a quiet life, the avoidance of take-over, or the maintenance of a favourable public image—it seems that the major objectives of firms fall naturally into place within the framework of the present model.

## Conclusion

It has been argued in this chapter that, under all conditions of imperfect competition except a statutory monopoly, prices will approximate to those which exist under EPM competition. The crucial condition is freedom of entry—in the legal sense—especially at the level of the small firm. When freedom of entry is assumed, and there is a steady stream of new small firms somewhere in the economy, there is a powerful constraint on static profit-maximization along an inelastic immediate demand curve. Firms which operate under conditions of imperfect competition are inevitably influenced by expectations, and hence they are aware of the dangers of new entry of competitors. In general, this consideration will push them in the direction of limiting the price which they charge to a 'no-entry price', which is approximately the EPM equilibrium price for their product. Some firms, which are particularly sensitive to the risks of new entry, may set a lower price than this; while others, which sell a differentiated product with substantial selling costs, may consider it safe to raise their price above that level, thus passing on part or all of their selling costs to the consumer. But the EPM equilibrium price remains the standard of reference, and the ultimate price, under free entry, is unlikely to deviate very far from it.

We have shown that this system of price-setting is consistent with the practice of 'full cost' pricing. 'Full cost' pricing is a good pragmatic method of estimating the EPM equilibrium price, once the firm has estimated its normal profit mark-up, since it permits the firm easily to adjust its selling price when unit labour and material costs vary.

This model also shows how the objectives which are emphasized by behavioural and managerial theories can be integrated with the central expectations-influenced profit-maximization objective.

# II

# SOME FURTHER IMPLICATIONS OF THE THEORY

The primary purpose of the theory outlined in the previous two chapters was to account for the distribution of income between wages and profits. It has also been shown that the same theory may be used to predict a set of equilibrium prices of real value added (excluding rent) in different industries. When value added is cumulated to the end of each stage of production, and allowance is made for imports, rent, depreciation, and taxes, we may obtain the costs of producing the goods emerging at that stage of production, and hence their market prices. But our theory has a number of other implications for the behaviour of a market economy; and in this chapter I shall consider some of these implications for four particular aspects. These are: growth and fluctuations, inflation, international trade, and public finance.

*Growth and fluctuations*

The dynamic response of an economy to changing conditions depends in part on whether it is operating predominantly under EPM competition or predominantly under imperfect competition. Although various combinations of these conditions are possible, we may, for simplicity, consider separately the two polar cases of universal EPM competition and universal imperfect competition

## EPM competition

*Growth.* It is instructive to start by noting the difference between the pattern of growth of an economy operating under EPM competition and the pattern of growth of an economy operating under perfect competition. In the latter case every firm in equilibrium is, in accordance with static assumptions, already of optimum size; and there is no tendency for any firm to increase or decrease in size, except as a consequence of a change in technique or in relative input prices. Hence under perfect competition the normal expectation is that an increase in demand will be met be an increase in the number of firms supplying the market, not by a change in the size of existing firms.

Under EPM competition, however, the nature of the response will be different. Because of technical and financial constraints on the growth of firms under EPM competition, nearly all firms are always of less than optimal size, if such a size exists at all. Moreover, even in the industries in which there is an optimal size, firms which have reached that size may have a continuing incentive to reinvest their profits, in preference to starting a new firm or distributing all their profits. Under EPM competition, therefore, there is a steady tendency for all profitable firms to grow.

This does not mean, of course, that every firm will increase in size in every time period. For the profits of individual firms vary over time, depending on their efficiency and their luck, as well as on the price of their product, which may be temporarily below its equilibrium level. When individual firms make losses for any of these reasons, their growth will normally be halted for the time being. In addition, there are always some entre-preneurs who, for reasons of temperament or age, have no further interest in the growth of their firms and prefer to use their profits in other ways. But the general expectation is that under EPM competition most firms will be reinvesting part of their profits, together with an appropriate amount of outside finance, and expanding in size over time, independently of any change in technique. And, indeed, this tendency will exist even when the size of the market for each product is constant, although this condition will produce other effects, which we shall consider in a moment.[1]

When technique is constant, when equilibrium prices are ruling, and when there is a stable average reinvestment ratio

[1] Whether the expansion in size of the firm will raise its productivity to a significant extent depends, in part, on the average level of efficiency of entrepreneurs and managers in the country or industry concerned, which will be reflected in the parameter $\beta$ of the value added function. There is reason to believe that social and cultural factors play an important role in determining the average efficiency of firms of a given size in different countries.

(ratio of net investment to profits), the output of each industry will have a spontaneous tendency to grow, even without any net inflow of OMFs. This may be called the 'natural' rate of growth of output; and there is a corresponding natural rate of growth of employment. If the economy-wide natural rate of growth of employment is less than the rate of growth of the aggregate supply of labour, there will be an excess supply of labour which will tend to flow into new OMFs. Under special conditions, this inflow of OMFs will be exactly sufficient to maintain constant the over-all relative size distribution of firms. If, on the other hand, the growth of the aggregate supply of labour is less than the economy-wide natural growth of employment, the labour needs of expanding firms can be met only by a reduction in the number of OMFs. When there is a large initial stock of OMFs, as in the poorer countries, it will usually be sufficient for larger firms to offer new jobs at existing rates of pay in order to attract the required extra work-force. But when the stock of OMFs is smaller, the expansion of employment in larger firms may require a certain upward movement in the real wage, which will induce the proprietors of OMFs to shift from self-employment. Under these labour market conditions the proportion of OMFs, and later of other small firms, will be falling, and the relative inequality of firm sizes will be growing. But in a country which starts with a very large number of OMFs this effect will be barely perceptible for a considerable period of time.

It is conceivable that in some highly industrialized country a continued excess of the natural rate of growth of employment over the rate of growth of the labour supply would eventually eliminate all OMFs. Then the smallest size of firm in the economy would be the two-worker firm. But this position has never yet been reached in practice. Although in some industrialized countries the rate of growth of the labour supply has fallen to a low level, the natural rate of growth of employment has simultaneously been checked by technical progress, which tends to produce a net displacement of labour.

Technical progress has two—partially conflicting—effects on the real wage. On the one hand, an improvement in technique raises the real value of $\bar{v}$, i.e. real value added in an average OMF; and sooner or later $\bar{w}$ will rise to the same degree. On the other hand, rapid changes in technique in particular industries may produce a substantial net displacement of labour in those industries, leading to a temporary rise in general unemployment, and hence a tendency for the growth in $\bar{w}$ to lag behind the growth in $\bar{v}$. This lag in adjustment, which is associated with a high level of 'technological unemployment', is not the result of technical progress as such, the long-term benefits of which are unquestionable, but of disproportionately rapid technical progress in certain industries.[2]

*Inter-industry adjustments.* We have so far been considering changes in the whole population of firms and in their aggregate demand for labour. But under EPM competition each industry has its own natural rate of growth of output, which depends on the parameters of its $v$-function and of its $w$-function, the size distribution of its firms, its reinvestment ratio, and its capital–value added ratio.[3] Only in exceptional circumstances will this rate of growth be equal to the rate of demand for the industry's product. Hence there will constantly arise new temporary conditions of disequilibrium in individual markets.

When the natural rate of growth of an industry exceeds the rate of growth of demand for its product, the product price will fall and the industry's $v$-function will shift downwards in relation to its $w$-function. This is shown in Fig. 11.1 by the fall of the $v$-function to $v_1$, where $\bar{v}_1 < \bar{w}$. Then the profits of all firms in the industry will decline, and may OMFs and other small firms will be making losses. As a consequence, firms of all sizes, but

---

[2] The current tendency to blame technical progress for various social problems—or even for all social problems—is misconceived. Undoubtedly, technical progress creates problems of adjustment. But without further technical progress it will be impossible to give everyone in the world a reasonable standard of living, including sufficient leisure to develop non-economic interests.

[3] The rate of growth of value added in an industry with a fixed technique, a constant capital–value added ratio, and a Pareto distribution of sizes of firms is

$$\eta = a\mu \frac{\beta - a}{\rho - a}$$

where $\eta$ is the rate of growth of output, $a$ is the reinvestment ratio, $\mu$ is the capital-value added ratio, $\beta$ and $a$ are exponents of the value added and wage functions, and $\rho$ is the exponent of the Pareto function. This follows from equation (A.9) in Appendix A.

especially the smaller firms, will tend to leave the industry; the rate of growth of those firms which remain in the industry will be reduced; and the rate of growth of the aggregate supply of the product will decline. Eventually, these adjustments will cause the price of the product to recover, shift the $v$-function upwards, and restore equality between $\bar{v}$ and $\bar{w}$. Similarly, in an industry in which the natural rate of growth is less than the rate of growth of demand, the $v$-function will temporarily shift up,

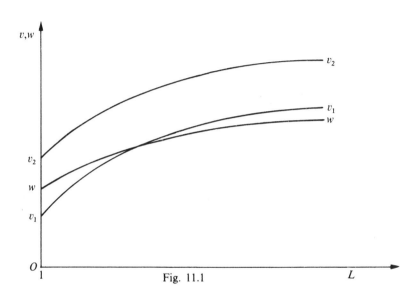

Fig. 11.1

e.g. to $v_2$ in Fig. 11.1 This will increase profits, and hence the rate of growth, of existing firms and encourage a larger influx of new firms, especially of OMFs. Eventually, in these ways, supply will catch up with demand, and price will fall back until equilibrium is re-established, with $\bar{v} = \bar{w}$ once more. While these processes of adjustment may alter the relative size distributions of firms in particular industries, they are unlikely to have a large effect on the relative size distribution of firms in the whole economy.

When techniques change, the processes of adjustment will be of a similar nature, although different in detail. A feature of technical progress is that it is sometimes heavily concentrated in particular industries. When this is so, an improvement in public technique in one industry shifts its potential $v$-function upwards for a given product price. The firms which first adopt the technique will then enjoy exceptional profits so long as the price is held up by the sluggish rate of growth of the other firms in the industry. The consequence is that for a certain period there will be a 'dual economy' in the industry, during which time the pioneering firms will rapidly expand in size along the new and higher $v$-function while the other firms continue to operate on the old $v$-function. But soon the rate of growth of aggregate output will begin to exceed the rate of growth of demand for the product, and, as the price falls, both the old and the new $v$-functions will shift downwards. The firms still using the old technique will then suffer reductions in profits in comparison with their original position, and many will be driven into bankruptcy. The firms using the new technique will eventually squeeze out all those firms which cling to the old technique, their workers will become unemployed, and the original $v$-function will cease to exist. By this time, the new $v$-function will have shifted downwards, the $w$-function may also have shifted upwards to some extent, and equality will have been re-established between $\bar{v}$ and $\bar{w}$.

The classic example of this process is, perhaps, the destruction of the handloom industry in Britain during the first half of the nineteenth century. But technical changes are always occurring and tending to produce technological unemployment. All such technical improvements, as we have shown, eventually lead to a reduction in the product price relative to other prices. Hence the real price of value added rises in other industries. If real wages in those industries were to remain constant, their growth rate would accelerate and they would gradually absorb the unemployed displaced from the technically progressive industries. But if money wages are sticky downwards, the fall in the money prices of products of the technically progressive industries will raise real wages in other industries, and their rate of growth will consequently be retarded. In these circumstances, technological unemployment arising in particular industries may create a temporary condition of general unemployment, which will continue until either the pressure in the labour market causes the real wage to fall back to its equilibrium level, or improvements in technique in all industries lead to a general rise in $v$-functions relative to $w$-functions.

*Fluctuations in demand.* If we abstract from the influence of government and of the rest of the world the principal origin of fluctuations in aggregate demand is changes in the level of private investment. Under EPM competition most firms are likely to be small or medium sized, and the dominant form of ownership will be the unincorporated enterprise. Hence the bulk of investment is likely to be financed out of retained profits, i.e. out of 'inside finance'. In the limiting case, where there is no outside finance, investment depends entirely on current (or immediately preceding) profits and on the proportion of profits which are retained. When the latter ratio is stable, as seems to be empirically plausible, investment depends simply on the level of profits. Our model suggests that, under conditions of general equilibrium, the share of profit in aggregate value added is fairly constant over medium periods of time. Hence both the level of investment and the rate of growth of output will also be fairly constant; and there is no reason why there should be significant fluctuations in aggregate demand.

There are two factors which are likely to upset this pattern of steady growth. The first is the impact of technical progress which, as has been shown above, may in some circumstances generate fairly prolonged technological unemployment. The existence of such unemployment creates an opportunity for an expansion of real demand which would not otherwise exist. The second factor is the growth of the role of outside finance, especially in the first instance through the development of banks. This creates the possibility of expanding the money supply and hence, with a given money wage, of increasing the level of real investment.

*The loan market.* As a first approximation, we may assume that the demand for outside finance comes entirely from firms. Loans are needed by firms to supplement their retained profits in order to finance investment. The amount of loans demanded will depend on (1) the level of retained profits, (2) the maximum gearing ratio, and (3) the loan rate of interest.[4] Let us define the maximum gearing ratio (MGR) as the ratio of outside to inside finance when the rate of interest is at its absolute minimum level. In Fig. 11.2 the demand for loans at a minimum rate of interest (*OC*) is *OB*, equal to aggregate profits multiplied by the MGR. If profits and the MGR are constant,

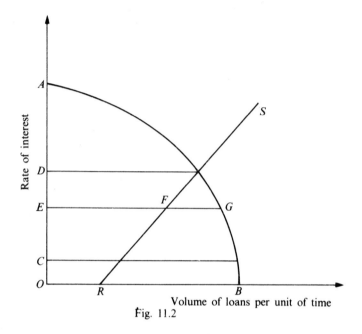

Fig. 11.2

the demand for loans will decline as the rate of interest rises, slowly at first but later more rapidly, until it reaches zero at some finite rate of interest (*OA* in Fig. 11.2). This maximum rate of interest will be somewhat below the marginal rate of profit on investment in the most profitable firm.

In the absence of a government sector and a foreign sector, the major normal source of supply of loans is net saving by households, i.e. the excess of household saving over household investment. But an additional source of loans may be created by an increase in the money supply in excess of the amount

---

[4] All three variables are likely to vary for different sizes of firm. For simplicity, however, this aspect may be ignored.

required to satisfy the transactions demand for money.[5] In Fig. 11.2, *RS* is the household supply of loans and, when the money supply is growing at a rate which exactly satisfies the transactions demand for money (which may be called a 'neutral' rate of growth), the equilibrium rate of interest will be *OD*. But, if the money supply increases at a rate above the neutral rate, equal to *FG* per unit of time, the rate of interest will fall below the equilibrium rate to *OE*. As a consequence, investment will be in excess of voluntary saving, prices will rise, the *v*-function will shift upwards in relation to the *w*-function, and firms will make windfall profits. These profits will be just sufficient to fill the gap between investment and voluntary saving.[6]

But, when profits rise, the volume of inside finance also increases, and consequently the demand for outside finance. Hence, in the next period, the line *AB* will shift to the right. Whether the line *RS* will also shift is uncertain. While the real wage per worker will have fallen, the number of workers employed will have increased, so that real income per worker-family may have moved in either direction. But, since distributed profits will have increased, there is likely to be some increase in the supply of loans. Nevertheless, the outward shift of *AB* is likely to be greater than the outward shift of *RS* and, as a consequence, there will be a tendency for the loan rate of interest to rise, unless there is a sufficient further increase in the rate of growth of the money supply.

It is easy to see that this situation is unstable. Prices are rising, unemployment is falling, real wages per worker are falling, the money supply has increased but, unless it continues to increase, perhaps at an accelerated rate, there will be a tendency for the rate of interest to rise. If outside or inside pressures compel the banking system to restrict the rate of growth of the money supply, the interest rate may suddenly rise above its natural rate, and investment will fall below the level of

---

[5] If all household savings are deposited in savings banks there will be no 'asset' demand for money. I shall consider the role of the asset demand for money at a later stage.

[6] Since part of the increase in the money supply will be absorbed by the increased transactions demand caused by the rise in product prices, the increase in profits will be somewhat less than *FG*. An exact model would require precise specifications of the time-lags between initial changes in the money supply, the rise in profits, and the growth in the transactions demand for money.

voluntary saving. Then there will be a deflationary movement, which will reduce prices, shift the $v$-function downwards until it intersects the $w$-function, cause widespread bankruptcies and closures of small firms, and increase the level of unemployment.

It seems clear that a sufficient remedy for cyclical fluctuations under conditions of EPM competition—in a closed economy with a small government sector—would be to establish stable control over the money supply. Monetarist policy is, therefore, appropriate under these conditions.

### Imperfect competition

There are two peculiar features of imperfect competition which are likely to affect the response of the firm to changes in the level of aggregate demand. The first is that, since each firm is aware that the markets for its existing products are limited, it will not automatically reinvest its profits in expanding its productive capacity; instead, it will need first to estimate the probable increase in demand for each of its products. Secondly, prices under imperfect competition are not determined by immediate supply and demand conditions in product markets, as under conditions of EPM competition, but by reference to no-entry prices (NEP). According to the theory, the NEP depends on the labour and material costs (including rent and depreciation) of a hypothetical OMF of average efficiency. Hence, in a closed economy with constant technique, NEPs depend ultimately on the levels of money wage rates and land rents. So long as money wage rates are constant, the only effect of changes in aggregate demand on prices under imperfect competition will be through changes in rents, which are likely to be insignificantly small in the short run. As an approximation, therefore, we may assume that prices under imperfect competition in a closed economy with constant technique (and no changes in taxes) will move in line with money wage rates.

We must also consider the influence of a third factor which, although not intrinsic to imperfect competition, has been historically associated with the rise in importance of this type of product market. Imperfect competition has tended to spread as the average size of firms has grown, and this trend has been associated with a trend towards incorporation. Consequently, the spread of imperfect competition has been associated with the growing importance of non-bank external finance, raised by means of the issue of shares and bonds. Simultaneously, for other reasons, there has been an enormous growth in the size of the government bond market. Thus, imperfect competition has in practice become the dominant market relationship at a time when the capital market was both large and increasing in size.

The combined effect of these three differences between EPM competition and imperfect competition is to modify significantly the pattern of dynamic response of firms to changes in aggregate demand and the money supply.

When under imperfect competition aggregate demand is expanding at a steady rate, the growth in demand for each product will vary around the average. Those firms which experience a rapidly growing demand will usually try to supplement their internal funds by a larger call on external finance. If they are restricted by gearing limits, they may increase their retained profit ratio, raise equity shares, or merge with a firm which has surplus funds. Although these decisions may sometimes cause anxiety to existing shareholders, the incentive to take advantage of rising demand will usually be sufficient to overcome shareholder resistance. On the other hand, firms which experience a rate of growth of demand for their products which falls below their financial and technical capacities for expansion will be obliged to search for ways to make profitable use of those capacities. They may, for example, redesign their products, attempt to open new markets, introduce new products, diversify into new activities, or take over firms which are short of growth capacity. All of these decisions are difficult and risky, and the continued growth of these firms is by no means so readily assured as it would be under EPM competition.

It might be supposed that these difficulties of matching supply and demand at a detailed level would tend to make an imperfect competition economy more unstable than an EPM competition economy. But, as an offset to this, firms under imperfect competition tend to be larger, to have more managerial experience, to have more capacity to plan their activities efficiently and, above all, they control a more clearly defined market of their own. As a consequence there is less danger under imperfect competition than under EPM competition that an expansion of demand for a particular type of product will produce a large overshoot of supply.

On the other hand, when there are money-financed changes in the level of aggregate demand, the responses of firms operating under imperfect competition are likely to be different from the responses of firms operating under EPM competition; and in these circumstances the imperfectly competitive economy may be more unstable. To illustrate these differences, let us start, as before, from a position in which there is general unemployment. Under EPM conditions this is likely to be associated with $v$-functions which intersect $w$-functions in certain industries, so that $\bar{v} < \bar{w}$ in those industries. In pre-Keynesian theory this situation would be described as a state of disequilibrium in the labour market. But under imperfect competition, on the present theory, prices are fixed at the NEP, which ensures that $\bar{v} = \bar{w}$ at all times; and there is never a disequilibrium, in this sense, in the labour market. But unemployment may nevertheless exist, and it will usually be associated with firms working below their 'capacity'.

The concept of 'capacity' has no clear meaning under EPM competition. In the short run, firms operating under EPM competition will adjust their outputs in order to try to make short-run marginal cost equal to price; and, if the price falls below its previous level, output will fall. When this adjustment has been made, each firm will be at its short-run optimum position and, in short-run terms, there will be no 'excess capacity'. Nor can we say that there is excess capacity in long-run terms, because under EPM competition there is in most industries no optimum size of firm to serve as a benchmark of ideal capacity. Under EPM competition, therefore, most firms are *always* operating at a size below the size at which they would prefer to operate in an ideal world of perfect markets for capital and technical knowledge. Hence we cannot say that, when there is a fall in demand, firms operating under EPM competition have less incentive to expand than previously. The constraint which limits their investment decisions is the decline in their profits as a source of funds, not a reduced incentive to expand.

Under imperfect competition, on the other hand, where price is fixed at the NEP (*OP* in Fig. 11.3), there is a clear point of short-run 'full capacity' operation, namely the output at which short-run marginal cost equals price (point $Q_1$ in Fig. 11.3). While firms will not normally raise output above that level, unless they believe that their long-term market position depends on maintaining customer goodwill by so doing, there is no guarantee that demand will always be sufficient to bring

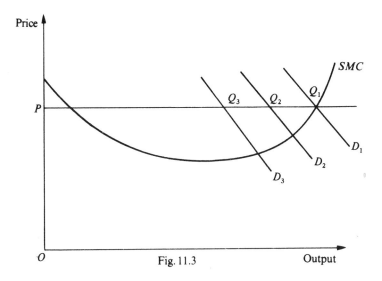

Fig. 11.3

them up to that level of output. Indeed, because of fluctuations in demand, most imperfectly competitive firms are usually producing below capacity, e.g. at points $Q_2$ or $Q_3$. When this is the case, an increase in aggregate demand will shift the output of these firms closer to capacity, and the effect of this will be not only to increase their profits—as under EPM competition—but also to remove their previous inhibitions against using their profits for the expansion of capacity, i.e. for investment. This 'accelerator' mechanism, which exists only under imperfect competition, will magnify the initial increase in demand and lead to a cumulative expansion of output.

The accelerator mechanism also operates in a downward direction, when aggregate demand has started to fall, e.g. from $D_2$ to $D_3$ in Fig. 11.3. The strength of the cumulative decline in demand will depend, however, on the degree to which investing firms are willing to take long views. There will inevitably be some tendency for firms which are confronted by increasing excess capacity to reduce their investment decisions. But, if firms have confidence that demand will revive within a fairly short period of time, e.g. because of a government commitment to a policy of high employment, the fall in investment demand will be less extensive. It was, perhaps, the absence of such a reassurance in the early 1930s, when imperfect competition had already become the dominant feature of the market in the industrialized countries, that was responsible for the deep and prolonged decline in demand which produced the Great Depression.[7]

The intractability of the Great Depression to purely monetary measures was in part the consequence of the growing importance of the capital market, which was associated with the rise of imperfect competition. When the stock of marketable securities in a country is large in relation to its national income, the basis is laid for the influence on the rate of interest of an 'asset' demand for money. This may be explained in terms of Keynes's 'speculative' demand or, more simply, as a form of transactions demand related to the stock of marketable assets. Since marketable securities are occasionally marketed, these asset transactions inevitably generate a transactions demand for money.[8] In any case, for whatever reason, the existence of a large stock of marketable securities imposes a brake on the effect on the rate of interest of an increase in the supply of money. It was, of course, this consideration which led to Keynes's shift of emphasis, between the *Treatise on Money* and the *General Theory,* from monetary to fiscal policy as the principal method of lifting an economy out of depression.

[7] Similar problems have arisen also from the 1974 oil price rise which, in conjunction with a weak import propensity in some major oil-producing countries, has undermined the capacity of governments in other countries to ensure full employment.

[8] If the asset demand for money is treated as a transactions demand, the total demand for money may be expressed as $M_d = aY + bA$, where $Y$ is the money value of national income and $A$ is the money value of marketable assets. At any moment of time, $A = R/r$, where $R$ is the income from marketable assets and $r$ is their average income yield. Hence $M_d = aY + bR/r$, which is effectively the same as Keynes's liquidity preference function, without requiring his 'boot straps' theory of the speculative demand.

There are, therefore, certain special characteristics of imperfect competition which make an economy of this type peculiarly vulnerable to instability and, in conjunction with a large stock of marketable assets, unresponsive to monetary stimulation. But, to offset this, an economy operating under imperfect competition can more easily be stabilized by government policy, because firms are larger, can plan their investment programmes in relation to their own markets, and are, for both these reasons, more capable of taking long-term views. Hence, a government programme of demand stabilization and indicative planning may be expected to be more successful under imperfect competition than under EPM competition.

*Inflation*

Under EPM competition an increase in aggregate monetary demand, no matter how caused, will raise product prices faster than money wages. Hence, $v$-functions will rise in relation to $w$-functions, and in most industries $\bar{v}$ will be above $\bar{w}$. The rise in profits will stimulate investment, expand demand for labour in existing firms, and encourage an inflow of OMFs. As a consequence, unemployment will fall and there will be pressure to raise money wages. But so long as investment is in excess of the amount of saving which would be forthcoming at equilibrium prices, the ratio $\bar{v}/\bar{w}$ will be greater than unity and the profit share will be abnormally large. Under these circumstances, a rise in wage rates will be largely passed on in prices, with the ratio $\bar{v}/\bar{w}$ remaining constant. This corresponds to the model outlined in Keynes's *Treatise on Money*, as well as in 'Keynesian' distribution theories, where a rise in investment raises profits through an increase in product prices relative to wages. But this is only a short-run disequilibrium situation, which cannot continue indefinitely.

Under imperfect competition, on the other hand, our theory predicts that prices are always held in the region of the NEP, which implies that $\bar{v} \approx \bar{w}$. This corresponds to Hicks's 'fixprice' economy. When demand increases in such an economy, output expands but prices are constant. The growth of output reduces excess capacity and increases profits; and investment is stimulated for both these reasons. So demand continues to increase cumulatively, and unemployment falls. But at some point wages begin to rise, and the wage increases are passed on in price increases so as to maintain the equality of $\bar{v}$ and $\bar{w}$. The inflation is then described as 'cost-induced', although it started originally from a rise in aggregate demand.

All actual economies are a mixture of industries operating under EPM competition and imperfect competition. Hence, it is unlikely that any inflation will be either purely demand-induced or purely cost-induced. In a typical industrialized country, in which the bulk of manufacturing and service industries operate under conditions of imperfect competition, an expansion of demand has no immediate effect on the price of real value added in these industries. But it soon raises the price of value added in primary industries, including the prices of imports of such products; and since these price increases raise the NEPs of firms in manufacturing and services, they are then passed on in the prices of their products, Hence, even without any change in wages, there will be some inflationary effects of an increase in aggregate demand. Very soon, however, this rise in prices will combine with the fall in unemployment and the growth in the profit share to provoke trade union demands for increases in wages which, being largely successful, will give a further twist to the inflationary spiral.

The special contribution of this theory to the understanding of inflation is that, by drawing a clear distinction between EPM competition and imperfect competition, it shows why under imperfect competition the price of real value added is adjusted in line with increases in the wage rate. It seems likely that in the *General Theory* Keynes had implicitly moved away from perfect competition to a 'fixprice' model such as I have outlined. Although he did not recognize it, this was the second major shift in his thinking between the *Treatise* and the *General Theory*.

### International trade

Consistent with the standard assumption of perfect knowledge, the usual assumption of neoclassical theory is that technical knowledge is the same in all countries. At any one time, all countries face the same production functions, and their firms choose which combinations of the factors of production to employ in each industry, taking into account the relative prices of the factors. The ultimate outcome, therefore, depends on the available supplies of the different factors in each country and on the structure of demand for the different products. When there is free trade, the structure of demand adjusts to relative product prices, and, if all products and capital were exportable at zero cost, real *per capita* incomes would differ only to the extent that *per capita* supplies of natural resources varied across countries.

The predictions of this theory are not very plausible, even when we allow for the non-exportability of services, for costs of transport, and for imperfect mobility of capital. In particular, it is impossible to reconcile the theory with the great and persistent disparities of *per capita* income between different countries, or with the pressing demand of the poorer countries for improved arrangements for the transfer of technology.

When we drop the assumption of perfect knowledge of technology, we open up a new dimension to the discussion. Then the comparative advantage of country $A$ in producing product $X$ may depend not only on its factor resources but also on its level of technique. Moreover, technical knowledge can change, independently of relative factor supplies. In this theory much emphasis has been placed on the role of practical experience in the improvement of 'private' technique, the kind of technique which is internal to the firm. Hitherto, changes in 'public' technique have been taken for granted, as being given exogenously and freely available to all. This may be a satisfactory approach for an isolated country. But once it is admitted that public techniques vary across countries, it becomes necessary to qualify the concept of a public technique. We must then redefine public techniques by saying that they are fully public only within a single nation; but they are costly to transfer across national boundaries.

The crucial factor responsible for between-nation differences in public techniques, as for within-nation differences in private techniques, is the pooling of common experiences within a socio-economic group. Private technique grows within the firm, as a consequence of shared experience by the members of the firm. National technique grows within a nation, the members of which share common territory, language, culture, system of education, and media of communication.

Although national barriers to the spread of techniques are breaking down, there are still very great national differences in the level of technique. Moreover, for historical reasons, the degree of difference varies across products. British woollens, whisky, and biscuits are still technically superior to competitive products; Germans excel in precision engineering; Japanese in electronics; and so forth. But there is no reason of relative factor supplies why these countries should be permanently specialized in these directions. Indeed, the Japanese, who are experts in the rapid import of technology, have demonstrated that they have the capacity to excel in almost every industry.

With the growth of imperfect competition, differences in private techniques internal to the firm come to play a greater role in determining international trade flows. Each make of motor car, for example, embodies a collection of private techniques. It is, therefore, not in the least surprising that countries which have similar factor proportions should exchange products of the 'same' industry. This is one of the phenomena which it is difficult for neoclassical theory to explain, but which is easily explained by the present approach.

Another implication of the theory is that the pattern of comparative advantage can change more rapidly than would be expected if it were due entirely to differences in relative factor supplies. If technique advances more quickly in industry $X$ (relative to other industries) in country $A$ than in the same industry in country $B$, country $A$ gains a greater comparative advantage in industry $X$. These changes may occur frequently under modern conditions, so that international trade is in a constant state of flux. The result is that industrial structures of individual countries are under much greater pressure to adjust than they were in earlier times.

Finally, the proposed theory of product pricing under imperfect competition may throw some light on the apparent decline in recent years in the profit margins on exports of manufactures. The explanation for the pricing of differentiated products (as well as for oligopoly pricing) is that prices are governed by the NEP, which depends on the production cost of an actual or hypothetical OMF. But an essential link in the argument leading to this conclusion is the assumption that the price-elasticity of demand for the product is low enough to provide no incentive for the firm to reduce its price below the NEP. While this seems a reasonable assumption for domestic sales, it is probable that the price-elasticity of demand for differentiated products in export markets is often greater than this, because imports usually occupy only a small part of a national market, at least in the industrialized countries.

Another consideration is that import suppliers from different countries are subject to differential movements in their levels of wage rates, exchange rates, and labour productivity, so that their NEPs, in terms of the importing country's currency, are constantly changing in relation to one another. Such conditions must lead to instability of relative prices of imports, even when each supplier is adhering to its normal practice of charging the NEP appropriate to its national conditions; and the consequence may well be that prices in import markets are, on the average, depressed below the NEP appropriate to each country.

If it is the case that, for these reasons, profit margins on exports of manufactures tend to be lower than domestic profit margins, the rapid growth of international trade in manufactures during recent decades will have been partly responsible for the trend towards a reduction in aggregate profit shares and average profit rates in industrialized countries. Moreover, since larger firms play a preponderant role in exports of manufactures, the same factor will have depressed the relative profit margins of larger firms and reduced the slope of the manufacturing $v$-functions in these countries.

*Public finance*

The theory predicts that, in equilibrium, $\bar{v} = \bar{w}$ in each industry. Under EPM competition, this equality will constantly be disturbed by changes in conditions of supply and demand, so that perfect price equilibrium is unlikely to be attained except for short intervals of time. Under imperfect competition, on the other hand, when firms determine their selling prices by reference to the NEP, the approximate equality of $\bar{v}$ and $\bar{w}$ will be maintained at all times. Hence, while all changes in taxation which upset the preceding relation between $\bar{v}$ and $\bar{w}$ will tend eventually to be passed on, under EPM competition the period of adjustment to such changes may be prolonged, while under imperfect competition the adjustment will be instantaneous.

If we confine our attention to conditions of imperfect competition, which are dominant in industrialized countries, the theory predicts that the following fiscal changes will be rapidly passed on to the final buyer: changes in taxes or tariffs on materials used by industry[9]; taxes on the employment of labour which are also levied on OMFs; and value added taxes, if imposed on all firms irrespective of size.

On the other hand, taxes which discriminate in favour of OMFs may not be fully passed on. For example, company profits taxes are not in general payable by OMFs. Hence the theory suggests that such taxes will not be passed on, except in so far as the reduction in expected future profits reduces the incentive for the establishment of new OMFs and raises the NEP. For similar reasons, if social security contributions are levied on the employment of workers in large firms but not on OMFs, these extra costs may be only partly passed on.

We must remember, however, that, according to the theory, the rate of growth of output and employment ultimately depends on the flow of internal finance. Any taxes on large firms which are not passed on in prices, such as company profits taxes, will reduce the flow of internal finance, and hence of 'high-powered' savings. Hence, governments which rely on private enterprise to undertake the major part of industrial investment, but at the same time impose high corporate profits taxes, are pursuing contradictory policies. If regard for equity is the main reason for levying corporate profits taxes—in addition to income taxes on dividends—this objective may more consistently be combined with the objective of faster economic growth by levying taxes on each shareholder in respect of his share of retained profits.

In general, the theory is consistent with the assumptions usually made in empirical studies of tax incidence that taxes on goods and 'finished' services are passed on to the ultimate consumer, while taxes on income are paid by the recipients of income.

[9] With traditional first in-first out methods of cost accounting there will be some time-lag between changes in material prices and product prices.

# PART III

## THE SIZE DISTRIBUTION OF INCOMES

# 12

# LONG-TERM TRENDS IN SIZE DISTRIBUTION

In Part II there was presented a model of the structural charac-teristics and growth of firms, which is designed to account for the shares of wages and profits in a given economy at a given moment of time. At the root of the model lies the assumption that value added per worker and the average wage normally increase monotonically with the size of firm. These relations are sum-marized in the $v$-function and the $w$-function respectively. As in any theory which claims to account for observed phenomena by postulating the existence of underlying structural relations, the implication of the theory is that, since the $v$-function and the $w$-function are likely to be fairly stable in the short term, the shares of wages and profits are also likely to be fairly stable over those periods of time. There is no suggestion, however, that these shares must be permanently constant, since there is no reason why the parameters of these underlying functions should not change gradually over time. Indeed, I have expressly argued that, since an improvement in technique shifts the real $v$-function upwards, there is likely to be some period of time during which firms will be distributed across two (or more) $v$-functions, and that in this situation the slope of the observed cross-section $v$-function will be greater than the slopes of either the old $v$-function or the new one. The purpose of this chapter is to consider how far this model helps to explain long-term changes in the distribution of income during the process of economic development.

As soon as we open the topic of income distribution in the early stages of economic development, we are confronted by the problem that the dominant kinds of factor income in poor countries are not the categories of wages and profits which are used in the above model, but two different categories of income, namely, land rent and self-employment income. To a large extent, also, these two categories overlap one another, since most of the self-employed are peasants and many of them own a part or the whole of the land which they cultivate. There is, therefore, little to be gained by trying to apply the model directly in order to explain factor shares in poor countries.

It is possible, however, to follow a different approach to the problem. Although aggregate income in poor countries cannot be divided meaningfully into wages and profits, the distribution of income by size of income can be measured, and inequality coefficients derived from such statistics can be compared with the corresponding coefficients for richer countries. In Chapter 8 I summarized the results of some recent analyses of cross-section measures of inequality, and found that these suggest that relative inequality rises during the early stage of economic development and declines persistently in the later stages. Although this inference about historical changes cannot be fully justified by a cross-section analysis, such evidence as we have about changes in the degree of inequality in the more industrialized countries during the past half-century are consistent with the latter part of the conclusion. If we assume that the cross-section pattern of income inequality, which is in practice a dispersion of income size across households or other income units, reflects changes in the degree of inequality during the process of economic development, we may proceed to consider whether the theory presented in Part II can be used to account for that pattern of changes. This is the task to which the present chapter will be addressed.

Thus the question to which we wish to find an answer is this: How can we account for the apparent tendency for the degree of income inequality to widen during the early stages of economic development and then gradually but persistently to decline in the later stages of economic development? More precisely, how can we account for the kind of pattern of *differences* in inequality—which we also assume to be a pattern of *changes* in inequality—exhibited in Table 8.1 above? According to those estimates, the Gini coefficient of household pre-tax incomes reaches a maximum at a level of *per capita* GNP of approximately $250 at 1971 prices. It may also be noted that the shares of both the top 5 per cent and the top 20 per cent of households reach a maximum at a *per capita* income level of about $200, while the share of the bottom 20 per cent of households reaches a minimum at a *per capita* income level of about $500. These are the major observations which need to be explained.

*Kuznets's hypothesis*

The first attempt to explain observed trends in income distribution during the process of development was made by Kuznets (1955). He suggested that the economy be divided into two separate sectors with different characteristics, sectors which he identified with agriculture (sector A) and nonagriculture (sector B). He further assumed that the *per capita* income of sector B is always higher than that of sector A, and that the inequality of income of sector B is either equal to or greater than the inequality of income of sector A. With the help of a few arithmetical examples Kuznets then showed that if population steadily shifts from A to B, the direction and the extent of change of the degree of inequality of income in the whole population will depend on (1) the levels and changes in the inter-sectoral income differential, (2) the levels and changes in the inter-sectoral inequality differential, and (3) the proportion of the population which has moved from A to B. One of his most interesting discoveries was that, even if the *per capita* income differential between sectors A and B remained constant and the degree of inequality within each sector was always the same, the transfer of population from A to B would produce an initial widening of inequality in the whole population, followed at a later stage by a reduction in inequality. Let us consider the reasons for this phenomenon a little more closely.[1]

The major implications of the Kuznets model may be most clearly appreciated if we start by assuming that, while there is significant inter-sectoral inequality, there is no intra-sectoral inequality in either of the two sectors, i.e. that everyone in sector A receives one level of income and everyone in sector B receives another higher level of income.[2] For example, let sector A income be $100 and sector B income be $200, and let the total population of income recipients consist of 100 persons. Initially, the whole of this population is assumed to be in sector A and their total income is therefore $10,000. Now assume that people begin to shift from A to B and that their incomes are adjusted accordingly. After one person has shifted, total

---

[1] In the following discussion I have drawn on ideas and examples contained in an earlier paper (Lydall, 1977).

[2] I shall consider later the reasons for the existence of such an inter-sectoral income differential.

income will have risen by $100 to $10,100, the share of the top 20 per cent of persons will have risen from 20 per cent to 20·8 per cent, and the share of the bottom 20 per cent of persons will have fallen from 20 per cent to 19·8 per cent. Inequality, on any measure, will have increased. As the process of population transfer continues, the total income—and hence the average income—of the population will continue to increase; and the share of the top 20 per cent of persons will go on rising until exactly 20 per cent of the population has shifted from A to B. At that point aggregate income will be $12,000, the share of the top 20 per cent will be 33·3 per cent, and the share of the bottom 20 per cent will be 16·7 per cent.

After 20 per cent of persons have shifted to B, the income share of the top 20 per cent of persons will begin to decline; and this share will go on declining until everyone has shifted to B, when it will reach the same level of 20 per cent at which it started. But the share of the bottom 20 per cent will not stop falling at the same point at which the share of the top 20 per cent stops rising. In this example, the share of the bottom 20 per cent of persons will go on falling until 80 per cent of persons have shifted to B. At that point aggregate income will be $18,000, the share of the top 20 per cent will be 22·2 per cent, and the share of the bottom 20 per cent will be 11·1 per cent. Thereafter, the share of the bottom 20 per cent will begin to recover, finally reaching 20 per cent again when everyone has shifted to sector B.

Although this is a very simplified model, it nevertheless has some interesting features. First, it shows that, even with no intra-sectoral inequality, a continuing transfer of population from a low-paid sector to a high-paid sector will result in an initial increase in the share of income received by the top 20 per cent of the population, and that this will be followed after some point by a decline in that share. Similarly an initial fall in the income share of the bottom 20 per cent of the population will be followed after some point by a recovery in their share. Second, it shows that the turning-point in the share of the top 20 per cent comes earlier than the turning-point in the share of the bottom 20 per cent. If an actual economy exhibited these same patterns of changes, a superficial study of these facts might lead to the following conclusions: (1) the initial effect of economic development is to make the rich richer and the poor poorer; (2) even when the income share of the rich is no longer increasing (but is still at a high level) the income share of the poor continues to fall, so that further economic development continues to make the poor poorer; (3) there is, therefore, no 'trickle down' of the benefits of economic growth. The model suggests, however, that such conclusions may be misleading.

Even if we allow for the existence of some intra-sectoral inequality of incomes and for changes in absolute income levels in each sector, the pattern of changes in upper and lower income shares will not be fundamentally affected, provided that the degree of intra-sectoral inequality is similar in both sectors and the ratio of mean income in sector B to mean income in sector A is constant. In an example given in my previous paper (1977) it was assumed that mean income in sector B is always twice mean income in sector A, and that individual incomes in each sector are distributed lognormally with a standard deviation of the logarithm of income of 0·65. When all persons are in sector A, the share of the top 20 per cent is 42.4 per cent, the share of the bottom 20 per cent is 6·8 per cent, and the Gini coefficient is 0·35. Exactly the same figures reappear at the end of the transfer process, when all persons are in sector B. But the share of the top 20 per cent rises initially, reaching 45·9 per cent when 40 per cent of persons have transferred, and then declines; while the share of the bottom 20 per cent falls initially, reaching 5·7 per cent when 50–60 per cent of persons have transferred, and then recovers. The Gini coefficient reaches a maximum of 0·40 when between 30 and 50 per cent of persons have transferred.

Kuznets was puzzled by the tendency shown in some of his examples for the income share of the bottom 20 per cent of persons to go on falling, apparently indefinitely. Since this was contrary to the available evidence that the degree of inequality in some industrialized countries had been either fairly stable or declining for several decades, Kuznets was led to infer that the degree of intra-sectoral inequality within sector B must decline during the process of economic development. But, as the above examples have shown, it is not necessary to make this assumption in order to produce a decline in the general degree of inequality and a rise in the share of the bottom 20 per cent of persons after some point in the transfer process. Kuznets lacked empirical information about changes in the share of the bottom income groups, and he was not aware of the facts now revealed by cross-section analysis, such as those shown in Table 8.1 above, that the share of the bottom 20 per cent of persons begins to turn up later in the development process than the point at which the share of top 20 per cent begins to decline. If he had had such information he would have realized that his model was in fact a remarkably good representation of actual trends.

*A revision of the hypothesis*

Although Kuznets's two-sector, or dual economy, hypothesis is a useful one, I believe that it would be improved if the definitions of the sectors were changed. In line with the emphasis in Part II on the effects of technical changes on income shares it would be more appropriate if, instead of using an agriculture–nonagriculture dichotomy, the economy were divided according to the nature of the techniques used in the two sectors. It is true that economic development has always involved a transfer of population from agriculture to nonagricultural activities. But the essence of the development process is the introduction of new techniques; and this may occur in principle in any industry. There is no rule which ensures that agriculture is always backward, nor that all nonagricultural industries are progressive. Hence a more appropriate two-sector division of the economy might be into a 'traditional', or technically backward, sector and a 'modern', or technically progressive, sector. The traditional sector would consist of enterprises (not necessarily complete industries) which initially use mainly traditional pre-industrial techniques, and the modern sector would consist of enterprises which use modern technology and methods of organization. Clearly, the peasant farmer with his wooden plough, animal power, and lack of scientific knowledge is in the traditional sector while the factory is in the modern sector. But the traditional sector also includes the artisans, as well as a large number of people engaged in commerce and other services, including primitive transport and construction; while the modern sector includes the mechanized farmer, modern rail and road transport, and mechanized or capital-and-skill-intensive services in commerce, finance, and government administration.

The reason for drawing a fairly sharp line of division between these two sectors is that differences of technique and organization are the cause of large differences in labour productivity; and these differences in labour productivity are reflected in differences in the incomes of the persons drawing incomes from each sector. At any given set of price ratios it is differences of technique and organization, rather than the nature of the industry, which mainly determine the relative incomes generated in different sectors. In practice, most early advances in modern technique were made in manufacturing, where the scope for changing methods, combining factors in different proportions, and organizing on a large scale were much greater than in agriculture or services. Even today this is still the case in most developing countries, so that the modernization of such countries requires the development of a manufacturing industry. But as modern techniques spread through a country they begin to affect all industries and all types of enterprise to some degree. Traditional farmers begin to use improved seeds, fertilizers, and weed-killers; artisans begin to use electric power and new materials and components purchased from the factory sector, such as machine-spun yarn, metal screws, and modern paints and glazes; rickshaws become pedicabs and eventually motor scooters. In agriculture, productivity begins to rise as soon as the excess population on the land starts to move away. This is partly the natural result of the removal of labour which has a very low marginal product, but perhaps mainly the result of the greater surplus, flexibility, and scope for reorganization which is created by the reduction of population pressure and the associated fragmentation of landholdings. In addition, in so far as the division between sectors is also a division between industries, i.e. of products, the effect of a more rapid growth in *physical* productivity in sector B is likely to change relative product prices and hence to raise the *value* productivity of sector A.

Although the modernization process eventually spreads in all directions, its initial effects are concentrated in a limited number of enterprises, which constitute what I have called the modern sector. These enterprises are at first like islands in a sea of technical backwardness, and there is a sharp contrast between their productivity and the productivity of the mass of traditional enterprises. In Adam Smith's well-known example, (1, 7) a pin factory using no power but only division of labour was said to be able to raise output per man by a factor of 200 or more. More realistically under modern conditions, value added per man in a textile factory in a poor country is often four or five times as great as in the rest of the economy. But these modernized enterprises themselves are in a constant state of development and change. The model of the growth of firms which was outlined in Chapter 9 is a model of firms in the modern sector, which are not fixed in a predetermined mould but are continually growing and changing as a result of improving know-how, the reinvestment of profits, and the adoption of new techniques.

The distinction which I wish to draw, therefore, between a modern and a traditional sector is between (1) a group of enterprises which uses and continually improves modern techniques of division of labour, power, and machinery, and (2) a group of enterprises in which the use of these techniques is slowed down or prevented by ignorance, natural and legal obstacles to the use of better methods, and the vicious circle of low productivity and low investment. But in both sectors there is continual development and change from the moment that a modern sector comes into existence.

A country which passes through the whole range of industrial development may start with a *per capita* GNP (in 1971 prices) of as little as $50 and reach eventually a *per capita* income of $2,000 or more. Even with due allowance for the difficulties of comparing GNP estimates across countries at different levels of development, it is by no means unrealistic to say that the people in rich countries have 10 or 20 times as much income per head as those in poor countries. But the whole of this enormous change cannot be satisfactorily explained by means of the earlier two-sector model. If, for example, we were to give people in sector B an income ten times as great as the income of people in sector A, the income share of the top 20 per cent of persons would reach a maximum of 71 per cent after the first 20 per cent of persons had shifted to sector B, and the share of the bottom 20 per cent would reach a minimum of 2·4 per cent when all but they had shifted to sector B. These figures are unrealistic; and in any case—Adam Smith's pin factory notwithstanding—the gap between average productivity in the modern and the traditional sectors in poor countries is not usually as great as 10 or 20 to 1.

It seems, therefore, that it would be more realistic to make the following assumptions: (1) in a poor country there is initially a substantial difference between productivity in sector B and productivity in sector A, but this difference is not so large as the difference between average productivity in the very rich countries and in the very poor countries; (2) as economic development proceeds, productivity in both sectors increases, although not necessarily at the same rate. These assumptions are illustrated, and compared with the previous model, in Fig. 12.1.

In this diagram mean income per income recipent in sectors

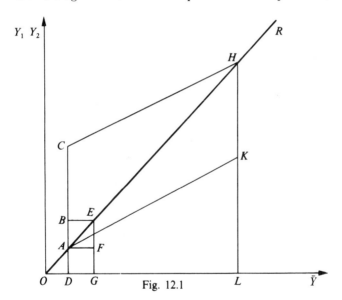

Fig. 12.1

A and B are measured on the vertical axis (by $Y_1$ and $Y_2$ respectively), while the horizontal axis measures mean income per income recipient in the whole economy ($\bar{Y}$).[3] The line $OR$,

---

[3] These incomes are measured for convenience in constant base-year prices. In so far as sectors A and B represent different industries rather than

which is drawn at 45° to the axes, shows points at which either $Y_1$ or $Y_2$ is equal to $\bar{Y}$, i.e. points corresponding to situations in which the whole population is in either sector A or sector B. For our first model, where it was assumed that $Y_1$ and $Y_2$ are constant at all levels of $\bar{Y}$, $Y_1$ and $Y_2$ may be measured by $AD$ and $BD$ respectively. It follows that, at the beginning of economic development, when the whole population is in sector A, the economy is at point $A$. As development proceeds, people shift from sector A to sector B and an increasing proportion of incomes are at the level of $BD$. Mean income in the whole economy moves from point $D$ in the direction of $G$. Eventually, when the whole economy is modernized and everyone is in sector B, mean income in the whole economy is $OG$, equal to mean income in sector B, and the position of the economy is represented by the point $E$.

The unsatisfactory features of this model are (1) the assumption that productivity levels in sectors A and B do not change during the process of development, and in particular are unaffected by the proportion of the population in the advanced sector; (2) as a consequence of the first assumption, mean income in the whole economy cannot rise beyond the initial level of income in sector B; (3) the mean income of the population remaining in sector A falls further and further behind the average income in the whole economy.

An alternative model is represented in the diagram by the lines $AK$ and $CH$. Mean income in sector A at the start of development is still $AD$ but mean income in sector B is $CD$, substantially higher than $BD$.[4] As the population shifts from sector A to sector B, and time passes, productivity in sector B rises with improvements of technique, including learning-by-

different enterprises within given industries, changes in the proportions of persons engaged in each sector are likely to lead to changes in relative product prices, so that income measured at constant prices will not correctly indicate the degree of current income inequality. If income were measured in current prices, the shapes of the lines $AK$ and $CH$ would be affected both by changes in real productivity in each sector and by changes in the relative prices of the outputs of the two sectors as the average income level of the whole economy increased.

---

[4] If $CD$ were the assumed income of sector B in the first model, the swings in income shares during the process of development would be unrealistically wide.

doing, and with economies of scale, both internal and external to the firm. But the rise in productivity in sector B, combined with the withdrawal of part of the population from sector A, tends to raise productivity in sector A. Hence the change in $\bar{Y}$ is influenced by three factors: (1) the rise in $Y_2$, (2) the rise in $Y_1$, and (3) the increase in the proportion of the population drawing incomes from sector B. As development proceeds, the ratio of $Y_2$ to $Y_1$ may increase, decrease, or remain constant; but it is assumed that $Y_2$ is always greater than $Y_1$. When the modernization of the economy is complete, the whole population will be in sector B and its position on the diagram will be represented by the point $H$. As in the first model, inequality of income in the whole economy will at first increase as the proportion of persons in sector B increases, but later it will decline as the proportion of persons in sector A moves towards zero. The exact point at which the Gini coefficient, for example, will reach a maximum will depend on (1) the positions and shapes of the lines $AK$ and $CH$ and (2) changes in the degrees of intrasectoral inequality within each sector.

The lines $AK$ and $CH$, which are not necessarily straight lines, represent 'reduced form' relations between $Y_1$ and $\bar{Y}$, and between $Y_2$ and $\bar{Y}$. In other words, they summarize in a form which is, in principle, empirically observable, the effects of a number of underlying, or structural, relations. The assumed structural relations, which have already been described in words, are as follows: (1) $Y_2 = f_2(t)$, where $t$ measures the time which has elapsed since the beginning of the modernization process and $f'_2 > 0$; (2) $Y_1 = f_1(Y_2, p)$, where $p$ is the proportion of the total work-force engaged in sector B, $\delta Y_1 / \delta Y_2 > 0$, and $\delta Y_1 / \delta p > 0$; (3) $dp/dt = f_3(Y_2 - Y_1) > 0$, given that $Y_2 > Y_1$; (4) $\bar{Y} \equiv (1 - p) Y_1 + p Y_2$. This set of relations between five variables ($Y_1$, $Y_2$, $\bar{Y}$, $p$, and $t$) can be reduced to a single reduced form relation between any two variables by eliminating the other three variables. If we eliminate $Y_2$, $t$, and $p$ we obtain $Y_1 = F_1(\bar{Y})$, and if we eliminate $Y_1$, $t$ and $p$ we obtain $Y_2 = F_2(\bar{Y})$. It is easy to see that, since $dY_2/dt > 0$, $dY_1/dt > 0$ and $\delta p / \delta t > 0$, $F'_1 > 0$ and $F'_2 > 0$.

*A simulated example*

The reduced form model may also be expressed in the following three relations:

$$Y_1 = F_1(\bar{Y})$$
$$Y_2 = F_2(\bar{Y})$$
$$\bar{Y} \equiv (1 - p)Y_1 + p(Y_2)$$

The model could be solved if we knew $F_1$ and $F_2$, and if we were given a predetermined value for any of the four variables $Y_1$, $Y_2$, $\bar{Y}$, or $p$. If we also knew the distribution of income within each sector (which may in principle vary with one or more of the previous variables), we should be able to estimate the over-all degree of inequality of income for any given value of $\bar{Y}$.

The first step towards this objective would be to estimate the functions $F_1$ and $F_2$. To my knowledge, no such estimates have ever been made, although it would not be impossible to produce some useful figures if the necessary research resources were available. In the following illustrative simulation, therefore, I shall rely partly on 'plausible' figures, partly on some indirect estimates (for $F_2$), and partly on the requirement that the behaviour of the pattern of inequality should approximate to that which is shown in Table 8.1.

Some indirect estimates of $F_2$ may be made in the following manner. Let us assume that (1) manufacturing industry is an important component of sector B (or at least that part of manufacturing industry which excludes artisans and traditional workshops) and (2) value added per person engaged in manufacturing is an indicator of mean income per income recipient in sector B. This latter assumption implies that value added per person engaged is similar in other parts of sector B, e.g. in modern agriculture, transport, and other services, and that the number of persons drawing incomes from the sector is approximately the same as the number of persons engaged in the sector, i.e. that there is no substantial number of pure *rentiers*. On this basis, we may use data available in censuses of manufactures to estimate $Y_2$.

The data used for the present simulation were taken from the results of a previous study (Lydall, 1975), in which estimates were made of the relation between value added per person engaged $(V/L)$ and GDP *per capita* $(Y/N)$ in twelve manufacturing industries, based on cross-section regressions over samples of countries ranging in size (depending on the industry) from sixteen to thirty-three. Both variables were measured approximately in 1963 US dollars at current exchange rates. For the poor countries in the sample, the estimates of $V/L$ were based on data for larger establishments only, so excluding artisans and small workshops, but for the richer countries the data usually covered all establishments. All the regression equations were in the form $\log V/L = a + b \log (Y/N)$ and this form seemed to give a satisfactory fit to the data. Although the twelve industries covered by this study clearly do not accurately represent the whole of manufacturing industry, they are not a seriously biased sample, especially for industries in the poorer and medium-level countries.[5] Since the estimated parameters for the textile industry fell approximately in the middle of the two sets of parameters for the whole group of industries, and since the textile industry is a significantly large industry in countries at all levels of *per capita* GDP, it may not be seriously misleading to take the results for this industry as representative of the whole of manufacturing and hence, as a further step, of the whole of sector B.

For the purpose of this model it was necessary to re-estimate the regression for the textile industry, replacing the variable $Y/N$ by $Y/L^*$, where $L^*$ is the total work-force. Estimates of $L^*$ can be made only approximately, since the number in the work-force is defined in different ways in different countries (it is especially difficult to define in poor countries, where almost everyone except very young children is economically active). In general, each country's own definition of the work-force was followed, and the population in the relevant year was multiplied by the work-force participation ratio shown in a nearby census year or years. The resulting regression estimate for the textile industry, across a sample of 31 countries with *per capita* levels of GDP ranging from less than $100 to over $2,500, was as follows (with standard errors in parentheses):

[5] The industries covered (with International Standard Industrial Classification numbers in parentheses) were: processed meat (201), textiles (231), knitwear (232), footwear (241), clothing (243), made-up textiles (244), wood products (251), oils and fats (312), non-ferrous metals (342), sundry metal products (350), electrical goods (370), and precision instruments (391).

$$\log V/L = 3 \cdot 86 + 0 \cdot 55 \log Y/L^* \qquad R^2 = 0 \cdot 81$$
$$\quad \ (0 \cdot 352) \ \ (0 \cdot 05)$$

On our previous assumptions, this may be regarded as an estimate of $F_2$, where $V/L = Y_2$ and $Y/L^* = \bar{Y}$.[6]

Compared with the function $F_2$, the function $F_1$ is inherently more difficult to estimate. In the poor countries sector A consists of innumerable small enterprises in agriculture, artisan work, construction, and services, about which there is usually very little statistical information.[7] Even in richer countries sector A is the sector of small workshops, farms, retailers, construction, and services enterprises, which are less adequately covered by statistics than the larger and more successful enterprises.[8] It is possible, nevertheless, that some estimates of $F_1$ could be made, directly or indirectly, if sufficient research resources were allocated to this task. For the purpose of the present simulation I have chosen an $F_1$ function which yields a pattern of changes in inequality approximating to that shown in Table 8.1[9] The proposed function is

$$\log Y_1 = 1 \cdot 457 + 0 \cdot 725 \log \bar{Y}$$

This function implies that $Y_1 = \bar{Y}$ (and hence that the whole economy is in sector A) when $\bar{Y} = \$200$ at 1963 prices. This corresponds to a *per capita* GDP of about \$65 (since the workforce participation ratio in very poor countries is about $32 \cdot 5$ per cent). The function also implies that, as $\bar{Y}$ increases, value productivity in sector A grows more rapidly than value produc-

---

[6] It is easy to criticize this estimate; and no great claims are made for it. The major criticisms are: (1) the textile industry may not be representative of sector B; (2) a cross-section regression may not represent the behaviour of productivity in sector B within a single country over time; (3) conversion of individual country currency values to dollar values at current exchange rates may give misleading results; (4) value added measured in censuses of manufactures is biased upwards by the inclusion of services purchased from outside firms. Despite all this, I doubt whether more refined estimates of $F_2$ will turn out to be greatly different.

[7] This is one reason why such enterprises in urban areas are sometimes called the 'informal' sector. See, for example, ILO (1972).

[8] It is not suggested that all small enterprises are technically backward. This is both empirically untrue and contrary to the assumptions of the model in Chapter 9. But, for the most part, technically backward enterprises are small.

[9] As a result of more extensive experiments, the function used here differs slightly from that used in Lydall (1977).

tivity in sector B. This conclusion, although surprising at first sight, may be explained by a tendency for the terms of trade of agriculture and services to rise in comparison with those of manufactures during the process of development.

The final assumption required for our simulation relates to the nature of the intra-sectoral distributions of income. Since from inspection of Table 8.1 it appears that the Gini coefficient is in the region of 0.35 both in very poor countries and in very rich ones, it was assumed that this degree of income inequality represents the degree of intra-sectoral inequality in each sector. If we add a further assumption that incomes in both sectors are lognormally distributed, the corresponding value of the standard deviation of the logarithm of income is approximately 0.65.[10]

The final simulation is, therefore, based on the following assumptions:

(1) $\log Y_1 = 1.457 + 0.725 \log \bar{Y}$
(2) $\log Y_2 = 3.86 + 0.55 \log \bar{Y}$
(3) $\bar{Y} \equiv (1 - p)Y_1 + pY_2$
(4) incomes in both sectors are distributed lognormally with $\sigma(\log) = 0.65$.

The results of this simulation are summarized in Table 12.1.

The table shows that, as average income in the whole economy rises from $200 to $5,000, mean income in sector A rises from $200 to $2,063, mean income of sector B rises from $875 to $5,138, and the share of the work-force in sector B rises from zero to 95.5 per cent. The Gini coefficient starts at 0.35 when mean income in the whole economy is $200, rises to a maximum of 0.46 when mean income is in the region of $1,000, and thereafter declines continuously. The share of the top 20 per cent of incomes also reaches a maximum when mean income is in the region of $1,000; but the share of the top 5 per cent reaches a maximum at a mean income of about $600, while the share of the bottom 20 per cent does not reach its minimum until mean income is about $1,750. Despite the fact that the lowest income groups lag behind in relative terms until this late stage, the mean income of those in the bottom 20 per

---

[10] In practice, the equation for $F_1$ was chosen after making this intra-sectoral distribution assumption, not before.

TABLE 12.1

*Simulation of changes in inequality during
the process of development*

| Mean income ($US 1963) | | | Per cent of work-force in Sector B | Gini coeffi-cient | Percentage income share of: | | |
|---|---|---|---|---|---|---|---|
| Whole economy Y | Sector A (Y₁) | Sector B (Y₂) | | | Bottom 20 per cent | Top 20 per cent | Top 5 per cent |
| 200 | 200 | 875 | 0 | 0·35 | 6·8 | 42·4 | 16·0 |
| 400 | 331 | 1,281 | 7·3 | 0·42 | 5·8 | 49·0 | 22·2 |
| 600 | 444 | 1,601 | 13·5 | 0·45 | 5·3 | 51·2 | 23·1 |
| 800 | 546 | 1,875 | 19·1 | 0·46 | 5·0 | 52·0 | 22·9 |
| 1,000 | 642 | 2,120 | 24·2 | 0·46 | 4·9 | 52·1 | 22·4 |
| 1,500 | 862 | 2,650 | 35·7 | 0·46 | 4·6 | 51·1 | 21·1 |
| 2,000 | 1,062 | 3,104 | 45·9 | 0·45 | 4·6 | 49·7 | 20·0 |
| 2,500 | 1,248 | 3,510 | 55·4 | 0·43 | 4·7 | 48·3 | 19·1 |
| 3,000 | 1,425 | 3,880 | 64·2 | 0·42 | 4·9 | 47·1 | 18·4 |
| 4,000 | 1,755 | 4,545 | 80·5 | 0·39 | 5·5 | 44·8 | 17·2 |
| 5,000 | 2,063 | 5,138 | 95·5 | 0·36 | 6·4 | 42·9 | 16·2 |

cent rises nearly sixfold between the beginning of the development process and the point at which their income share is at a
minimum, namely from $60 to $403. Thereafter, their incomes
increase both absolutely and relatively.

A comparison of Table 12.1 with Table 8.1 shows that the
general pattern of changes in inequality is similar. For the
purpose of this comparison the mean income levels in Table
12.1 should be converted to the *per capita* GNP levels shown in
Table 8.1 by multiplying the former figures by the estimated
share of the work-force in the total population.[11] This share
ranges on average from less than 0.35 at the lowest income
levels to over 0·40 at the highest income levels. In terms of *per
capita* GNP the maximum point of the Gini coefficient is at

[11] It is necessary in principle to make two further adjustments, namely, to
convert the 1963 dollars of Table 12.1 into the 1971 dollars in Table 8.1, and
to adjust the value added data of Table 12.1, derived from censuses of
manufactures, to a GNP definition of value added. It happens that these two
adjustments are of approximately the same order of magnitude, so that we
can treat the Table 12.1 figures as if they measured value added at 1971
prices on the GNP definition.

about $250 in Table 8.1 and at about $350 in Table 12.1, while the corresponding turning-points for the share of the top 5 per cent are $200 and $200, for the share of the top 20 per cent $250 and $350, and for the share of the bottom 20 per cent $500 and $750.[12] These figures show that, although the pattern of ˙rning-points in the two tables is not identical, it is close enough to justify the view that the model represents an important part of the mechanism of economic development.

*Conclusions*

It has been shown that it is possible on a number of plausible assumptions, some of which are supported by statistical evidence, to construct a model of a two-sector economy which exhibits a pattern of changes in income inequality similar to that which is found from a cross-section analysis of country data. In particular, a continuing transfer of workers from a low-paid (traditional) sector to a higher-paid (modern) sector will tend to increase the measured inequality of income in the early phases of this transfer (or modernization) process and to reduce the measured inequality of income in the later phases. Hence, it is possible that empirical data showing such changes in income inequality may be accounted for by the existence of two sectors with the suggested characteristics. This interpretation of the observed facts is strengthened by the discovery that the pattern of changes in income shares revealed by the two-sector model is remarkably like the pattern of observed changes in income shares, especially the tendency for the shares of the upper income groups to reach a maximum at an earlier point in the development process than the point at which the share of the lowest income group reaches a minimum. While the simulation results are consistent with the view that the model captures certain crucial features of the development process, they do not prove that the model is correct or adequate. One may only claim to have taken the first few steps towards the construction of such a model.

Even if the model is accepted as providing at least a partial explanation of observed trends in inequality during the process

---

[12] The estimated turning-points in the model in terms of *per capita* GNP are very approximate, since the share of the work-force in total population varies considerably across countries at the same level of *per capita* GNP.

of development, it does not follow that all future trends must exhibit the same pattern. There are three principal points in the construction of the model at which questions may be raised about the validity of the assumptions. The first question arises over the assumption that there are necessarily two distinct sectors. Is it inevitable that the process of modernization should involve the creation of more advanced enterprises separate from traditional enterprises? Why should not the process of modernization raise the productivity of all enterprises approximately at the same rate? The answer seems to be that there are at least some technical factors which make it very difficult to spread technical improvements evenly over all enterprises. The introduction of modern technique usually requires a considerable reorganization of production arrangements, including both the factor composition and the methods of organization of the enterprise. It is difficult to make such changes successfully in a piecemeal or step-by-step fashion, and attempts to do so may result in an inefficient use of scarce capital and skills. Nevertheless, it may be possible to overcome some of these problems. The invention of small power units, small machines, and methods of co-operation between enterprises has already helped to ensure the survival of many small enterprises; and this movement could go further. But poor countries which suffer from severe shortages of capital and skills will continue to face the dilemma that an even spread of their resources over all enterprises will usually prove to be less efficient than a greater degree of concentration, while pursuance of the latter policy creates uneven development and a tendency towards greater inequality of income.[13]

Secondly, one may question the inevitability of the assumption that inter-sectoral differences in productivity entail inter-sectoral differences in income. Clearly, if incomes could be held constant across sectors even when inter-sectoral levels of productivity varied widely, inter-sectoral differences in productivity would have no effect on the over-all degree of inequality. The separation of incomes from productivity might be achieved if all enterprises were nationalized and all employees were

[13] The Chinese communists have been torn by this dilemma, sometimes concentrating resources in large modern plants and sometimes spreading them out over the countryside.

prepared to accept equal rates of pay irrespective of the productivity of their enterprises. There is no evidence, however, that this result has actually been achieved in socialist countries. Just as the capitalist employer finds that, sooner or later, he is obliged to share the fruits of productivity gains with his workers, so the communist state finds that it also must give incentives to workers to be more productive.

Of course, the system of progressive income taxes, which is prevalent in most developed capitalist countries (but not to the same degree in communist countries), is one method of breaking the link between productivity and incomes. But there are signs that the countries which have raised the degree of progressivity of income taxes the most are also those in which productivity is tending to grow most slowly; and it may be that those countries have understimated the importance of incentives. There seems to be a limit to the extent to which incomes can be separated from productivity without adverse effects on the size of the national income and the resources available for raising standards of living in the future.

The final assumption which needs to be examined is the assumption that intra-sectoral inequality is constant during the process of development. It must be admitted that the assumption made for the purpose of the simulation model was arbitrary. There is no 'law of nature' which decrees that the personal distribution of income within each sector should remain constant (in relative terms) over long periods of time. Nevertheless, there are clearly some real factors which influence the degree of intra-sectoral inequality in any economy.

The size distribution of household income within a sector of a market economy depends on (1) the proportionate shares of aggregate wages and profits, (2) the personal distribution of wage and salary incomes, (3) the personal distribution of profit incomes, and (4) the composition of households and hence the composition of household income. In the early stages of economic development it seems probable that the $v$-function of the modern sector shifts upwards more rapidly than the $w$-function of that sector, so that the share of profits in that sector rises. There may also be a tendency for the inequality of personal income from each source to widen. There is no reason, however, to assume that household composition changes in a manner which is likely to affect significantly the size distribution of household incomes. In the later stages of development, the three factors which tend to widen intra-sectoral inequality in the modern sector in the early stages will all move in the opposite direction. The share of profits will fall as the $w$-function catches up with the $v$-function; the dispersion of wage and salary incomes will become smaller as the supply of skilled workers increases; and the dispersion of personal incomes from profits will decline as individual proprietors give way to corporate businesses with more widely distributed share ownership.

For these reasons, it seems likely that the pattern of changes in over-all income inequality is affected by an intra-sectoral component as well as an inter-sectoral component. Broadly, we may expect that intra-sectoral inequality in the modern sector follows a similar path to that which is followed by inter-sectoral inequality.

The question may be raised, however, whether there is any necessity that economic development should proceed within a capitalist market framework. Since the introduction of complete state socialism would eliminate the profit component of private income, the effect would be to reduce the degree of inequality, unless this effect were offset by a widening inequality of the labour component of income. It is true that labour income inequality increased dramatically in the Soviet Union during the Stalinist period, but this pattern has not been followed in other state socialist countries. Nevertheless, the most remarkable feature of socialist countries is that, except for some of the countries in Eastern Europe, no information at all is published about the degree of inequality of income. If socialism is so successful in reducing inequality, it is surprising that more information is not given about its results in this direction.

The problem of economic development is essentially a problem of applying new techniques; and this depends ultimately on releasing the energies of people with initiative and organizational capacity. The free market can achieve this result when it is supported by a sympathetic and uncorrupt government. The communist state has also shown that it can achieve important results, at least in the early stages of industrialization. Whether a non-market form of socialism can produce a high standard of life for its people is an unresolved problem for the future. The market economy is the only known method of combining division of labour and decentralization of decision-making; and decentralization of decision-making is the only long-term guarantee of technical progress and a reasonable level of personal freedom. These wider issues cannot, therefore, be avoided when it is proposed to reduce economic inequality by abolishing the market.

# 13

## INCOMES FROM EMPLOYMENT

The first two parts of this book were concerned with the distribution of income between 'factors', or at any rate between wages and profits. In this respect we followed traditional economic theory, which has been directed principally at the problem of factor rewards and factor shares. From the point of view of my own theory there is also some logic in this approach. Since all incomes are initially generated within enterprises, it is a natural first step to ask whether there are economic laws which determine the division of value added between broad categories of income such as wages and profits. But in the last chapter the analysis began to shift away from an exclusive concern with the 'factor share' aspect and to take some account of the dispersion of income between persons; and in this chapter and in the succeeding one we shall concentrate on the problem of explaining the distribution of personal incomes by size. My method will be to consider employment, self-employment, and property incomes separately, on the grounds that the determinants of the dispersion of these types of income are largely, though not entirely, different. Finally, I shall have some remarks to make about the factors which influence the distribution of family incomes from all sources. But in this chapter we shall be concerned entirely with incomes from employment.

### The importance of employment incomes

In principle, one might include under the heading of employment incomes both the payments made for hired labour (including supplementary costs such as employers' pension contributions, holiday pay, and so forth) and the imputed incomes from the labour of the self-employed. In practice, however, since the imputation of the labour element in self-employment income can be based only on the corresponding incomes of hired labour, the data used for constructing and testing theories of the dispersion of labour incomes are usually data about wages and salaries. In poor countries aggregate wage and salary income is usually only a small part of total personal income, since the bulk of labour income accrues to the self-employed. As economic development proceeds, traditional peasant and artisan enterprises give way to larger firms, in which a clearer separation is made between wages and profits. In the most highly industrialized market-economy countries the proportion of employment income to total personal income amounts to as much as 70 per cent, while self-employment income shrinks to only 10–15 per cent. The remainder is income from rent, interest, dividends, and government transfers, of which the property component is often as little as 10 per cent of the total. If the labour element in self-employment income is imputed by making some rough estimate of the opportunity cost of labour, the share of labour income in total personal income in these countries rises to as much as 80 per cent and the share of property income falls to as little as 15–20 per cent.[1]

It is a natural next step to ask whether some estimate can be made of the proportion of total personal income dispersion which is attributable to the dispersion of employment incomes. But it is impossible to give a definite answer to that question. The difficulty arises not only from a lack of sufficient data but also, more fundamentally, from the fact that the question is not as precise as it sounds. If people were divided into one group who received only employment incomes and another group who received only non-employment incomes, one could proceed by calculating the proportion of the total variance of income which is due to the inclusion of the first group. But we cannot separate the population into income groups of such homogeneity. Alternatively, we might ask: Supposing that there were no incomes from sources other than employment, what would be the dispersion of income in the economy, and how would it compare with the existing degree of dispersion? But if we were to assume out of existence all non-employment incomes, we should end up with a large number of zero or very low incomes, in addition to the incomes of the normally employed population; and the distribution of income might shift

---

[1] Inclusion of net retained profits of companies in personal income would raise the property component to some extent.

from being hump-shaped to being reverse-J shaped, which would be considerably more unequal on any measure of inequality. Although this would be an answer to the question, it is not an answer which makes very much sense.

Despite the impossibility of giving a unique answer to the original question, there can be no doubt that the dispersion of employment incomes is an important contributory factor to the over-all dispersion of incomes in the more industrialized countries. In such countries, as already mentioned, the proportion of employees in the work-force is large. In addition, the dispersion of earnings of employees is usually substantial. Here again, if we wish to give greater precision to that statement, we are faced by awkward problems of definition. If we include in the population of employees all those who receive any wage or salary, no matter how small, in a period of a year (for example), we shall find many small incomes of those who normally work part-time and of those who, for some reason, only worked for part of the year; and this will widen the degree of measured dispersion of income. If, on the other hand, we decide to exclude part-time workers, or those who worked for only part of the year, or juveniles, or females, or any other low-income group, we shall reduce the degree of measured dispersion. A pragmatic, but not perfect, solution to the problem is to use tax data, which have the advantage of being officially assessed and which exclude very low incomes below the tax exemption limit. Such data for the United Kingdom, for example, show that in 1972/73 the ratio of the ninth decile of pre-tax employment income to the median was 1·67 for males, 2·04 for females, and 1·92 for both combined. The corresponding ratio for the total income of tax units—consisting of single persons and married couples—was 1·83.[2] From this comparison it seems that the dispersion of employment incomes in the United Kingdom is not very different from the dispersion of total incomes, at least for the bottom 90 per cent of incomes; and that, even in the absence of non-employment incomes, the degree of inequality of pre-tax income would remain substantial. We also know that the degree of inequality of pre-tax employment income in the

[2] The estimates for employment income are derived from Royal Commission on the Distribution of Income and Wealth, Report No. 3, p. 156. The estimate for the total income of tax units is taken from Report No. 1, p. 36.

United Kingdom is similar to the degree of inequality of such income in many other industrialized countries, including some communist countries.[3]

### Characteristics of employment income distributions

Before we consider alternative theories of the dispersion of employment incomes it is desirable to study the characteristics of the distribution which is to be explained. Since I have examined this question at some length elsewhere (Lydall, 1968b), the present discussion can be brief. There is a great variety of possible definitions of employment income distributions. On one side they vary in their population coverage, according to whether they include or exclude such categories as males, females, adults, young people, full-time workers, part-time workers, employees in particular industries or regions, and people of different races. On the other side, they vary in their definition of income. Some include wages of manual workers only; others include both wages and salaries; and others give the total income of employees from all sources. Some distributions measure income for the previous year, some for a month, some for a week, and some report the average daily rate over the previous month. The number of variants and combinations of variants is almost endless. And these differences of definition usually make a considerable difference to the measured distribution of income.

Consider, for example, two alternative definitions used in the 1950 United States Census of Population. One income distribution shows the number of persons with *any* wage or salary income received during 1949; the other is confined to those who were at work during 1949 for at least 50 weeks. Naturally, the first distribution contains a great many more persons—more than 10 million extra males and nearly 6 million extra females—than the second; but the most important difference is in the shape and degree of dispersion of the two distributions. The first distribution includes far more persons with small, or even very small, wage or salary earnings than the second; and hence the first distribution has a much thicker

[3] See Lydall (1968b, Table 5.6). If it were possible to estimate employment income on a post-tax basis, its degree of inequality in the United Kingdom might well be less than in many communist countries.

lower tail than the second. Indeed, in the case of females the first distribution has such a thick lower tail that it is almost a plateau from zero to beyond the—scarcely noticeable—mode.[4]

In general, measured relative dispersion of employment income is increased by including both males and females, adults and young persons, full-period and part-period workers, full-time and part-time workers, or any other mixture of groups which differ significantly in their income characteristics.[5] In the normal case where income taxes are progressive, pre-tax income is clearly more dispersed than post-tax income, although for people with mixed incomes the attribution of income tax to different sources of income would inevitably be somewhat arbitrary. Relative dispersion is also affected by the period of measurement of income, since many workers experience temporary fluctuations in their incomes over short periods, which average out over longer periods.

In the light of the great diversity of definitions of employment income distribution I suggested in my earlier study (Lydall, 1968b, 60) that it is necessary to make one particular type of distribution the principal target of analysis. The selected distribution, which I called the Standard Distribution, covers male adults working full-time and for the full period in all industries except farming; and the income measured is pre-tax money wages and salaries. It was found that the Standard Distribution tends to have a characteristic shape: it is humped, positively skew, and approximately lognormal, but usually with somewhat thicker upper and lower tails than the lognormal.[6] The upper tail is often quite well fitted by the

---

[4] See *1950 United States Census of Population*, Report P-E No, 1B, Tables 22 and 23.

[5] A part-period worker is one who works for less than some minimum number of days or weeks in the measured period; a part-time worker is one who normally works for less than some minimum number of hours in the week or day. Thus full and part-time workers can be either full or part-period workers—making four different combinations, or even more if finer classifications are used.

[6] The number in the lower tail is sometimes exaggerated by peculiarities of the method of measurement. In the United States example quoted above, many of the persons who worked for 50 weeks but reported very low employment incomes were clearly people with additional income from self-employment. In other words, their wage or salary income was not the income which they would have received for 50 weeks of employment. Some of them, also, may have been part-time workers.

Pareto formula from about the eightieth percentile upwards.

The analysis of employment income dispersion can be conducted at two principal levels. On one level, we may ask: Why do individual earnings differ? Here the theoretician may propose the investigation of such factors as ability, education, and experience. He may also construct models, such as those created by human capital theorists, which bridge the gap between fairly simple assumptions about human behaviour and more complex outcomes like those which are observed. On a second level, however, we may be primarily concerned with the following question: Why does the Standard Distribution have the shape which has just been described? In particular, why is it approximately lognormal with a Pareto-type upper tail? To answer this question, we must search for the same fundamental determining factors as in the first case; but we need to go further. We need to be able to show how the factors combine not only to produce the individual results but also the group results. Moreover, the existence of a particular shape of distribution has led to the suggestion of certain types of theory—stochastic process theories—which have no role to play in the first type of analysis.

These questions have been discussed with increasing intensity during the past two or three decades and a number of different theories have been proposed. Broadly, they fall into four categories: (1) theories which ascribe most or all of the differences between incomes to chance (Stochastic theories); (2) theories which ascribe most or all of the differences between incomes to voluntary choice (Choice theories); (3) theories which focus on the role of personal characteristics, family environment, schooling, experience, and other events which affect an individual's development (Personal Characteristics and Development theories); (4) theories which ascribe most or all of the differences between incomes to the structure of job opportunities in firms and institutions (Job Structure theories). These four types of theory are not mutually exclusive. Choice theories may admit that initial personal characteristics are of some importance; personal characteristics and development theories may allow for the effects of chance and choice; and job structure theories do not exclude the influence of abilities or educational qualifications on the final decision about who gets a particular job. Despite these overlaps, however, I think that it will be useful to discuss each of these types of theory separately.

## Stochastic theories

Stochastic theories are of two kinds. In both kinds of theory it is assumed that the variable under consideration is subject to a series of random shocks in successive time periods; but in one theory these shocks affect the future expected value of the variable, while in the other they do not. In the former case the series of shocks generates a Markov chain or random walk; in the latter case there is only transitory variation around a constant trend, such as has been emphasized by Friedman (1957). An indefinite repetition of a first-order Markov stochastic process, with a constant distribution of the probability of change, may generate an asymptotically stable relative size distribution of the variable; and when particular assumptions are made about the character of the probability distribution of change, that distribution may be normal, lognormal, or Pareto.

For example, if we assume that

$$y_t = y_{t-1} + u_t \qquad (13.1)$$

where $y_t$ is a person's earnings in year $t$ and $u_t$ is an independent normally distributed random variate with $\bar{u}_t = 0$ and a constant variance, an indefinite repetition of this process will generate a distribution of earnings which converges towards the normal distribution over time. The closeness of approximation to a normal distribution in year $T$ will depend on the relative importance of $u_t$ and $y_0$ (the distribution of $y$ at the beginning of the stochastic process) and on the value of $T$ (the number of years which have elapsed since the process began). If, instead of actual earnings, $y_t$ measures the logarithm of earnings, the process defined by (13.1) will generate a distribution which converges towards the lognormal. If, in addition, $\bar{u}_t < 0$ and there is a lower bound to the level of income, the stochastic process can generate a distribution which converges towards a Pareto function.[7]

At first sight, the Markov chain theory seems to offer a simple approach to explaining the observed characteristics of

---

[7] For a model of this sort see Champernowne (1953).

the Standard Distribution of earnings. But there are a number of difficulties. In the model defined by (13.1), the variance of the observed distribution increases steadily over time, because of the cumulative effect of the additional variance contributed by $u_t$. But this is inconsistent with empirical evidence on the stability over time of relative size distributions of earnings. The problem can be overcome by suitable adjustments to the mathematical assumptions of the model, e.g. Kalecki's (1945) assumption that there is a negative regression of $y_t$ on $y_{t-1}$, which is just sufficient to offset the variance-increasing influence of $u_t$. But Kalecki's assumption has no theoretical justification; and the empirical evidence in its favour—the so-called 'regression to the mean'—can be explained more simply by the existence of transitory fluctuations, combined in many cases with errors of measurement which have effects equivalent to transitory disturbances. A second objection to the Markov chain model, when applied to earnings from employment, is that there is no reason to assume that an increase or decrease in a person's earnings in one period is completely carried forward into the level of his expected earnings in future periods. One can think of many events which affect earnings in a single period but which have no—or very little—effect on future expected earnings. Indeed, there are some kinds of events, e.g. working very long hours of overtime in a particular week, or completing a particular piece-work job, which are likely to have a negative effect on expected earnings in the following period.

There is a third objection to this type of theory which is perhaps more fundamental. Since the desired shape of the distribution can be obtained only by an indefinitely prolonged repetition of the stochastic process, the initial distribution of income, which is presumably the result of initial personal abilities or other resources, fades into insignificance in the Markov theory. But each new cohort of earners enters the labour market after many years of upbringing and education, and it is unrealistic to assume that these early years outside the stochastic earnings process have no influence on subsequent earnings.[8] In addition, there are reasons to believe that the

[8] A stochastic model which allows for cohort effects was outlined in an important paper by Rutherford (1955).

underlying abilities, health, energy, and other qualities of individuals change in a systematic way as they grow older.

Rejection of the Markov chain theory of the distribution of earnings does not necessarily entail exclusion of any stochastic effects of the Markov type. There can be no doubt that many of the chance events of life have permanent effects on the future of the individual experiencing such events. Individual careers, and hence earnings, are often profoundly affected by a particular conjuncture, such as the influence of a teacher, the opportunity to take a particular job at a particular time, or the introduction of a new technique at the moment when the person concerned is most able to profit by the expansion of the opportunities which it creates. Most of the great men and women of history would have been of no special consequence if they had been born in a different epoch. Hence stochastic processes must remain a component of any comprehensive theory of individual earnings.

The second type of stochastic theory—the Friedman type—is less ambitious. It does not pretend, on its own, to account for the whole of the observed differences in earnings. But it does draw our attention to the fact that measured earnings in any single period of time may differ from the average earnings of the same individual over a longer period of time. Since the reasons for these temporary variations are not fully identified, they are aggregated under the heading of 'chance'. Transitory components of income, including measurement errors, may be regarded as a kind of statistical 'noise', which is an illusory addition to the degree of income dispersion. From this point of view it would be preferable to exclude transitory deviations of earnings and to focus on the dispersion of 'permanent', or long-term normal, earnings. It is only these earnings which can be explained by a deterministic theory, and it is these earnings which are relevant for normative judgements about the degree of inequality. The relative importance of transitory earnings varies across occupations and it increases as the length of the period for which earnings are measured diminishes. Unless allowance is made for this factor, comparisons of the degree of dispersion between occupations and between sets of data which refer to different time periods may be vitiated.

This argument is of considerable importance, and it has been too much neglected. It is not, of course, a theory of income dispersion but a partial theory of *observed* income dispersion. There still remains the problem of explaining the dispersion of permanent income. Moreover, if there is a Markov element in earnings as well as a transitory element, the problem of separating out the two elements empirically is extremely difficult, and perhaps impossible without rarely available longitudinal data. This is a problem which still awaits a satisfactory solution.[9]

It scarcely needs saying that stochastic theories, which are designed to account for the general shape of the size distribution of incomes, contain no explanation for the earnings of particular individuals. This is the primary focus of attention of the next group of theories.

*Choice theories*

Whereas stochastic process theories imply that the individual is helplessly adrift on a sea of random events, theories of choice insist that the individual can control his own destiny. In order to sharpen the point of the argument, choice theories sometimes assume that everyone is really equal in his abilities and opportunities, and that the dispersion of actual outcomes is entirely a reflection of individual decisions made freely and rationally. When the model takes this extreme form, it follows that all observed inequalities of income are illusory: they may be what we measure, but such measurements do not directly reveal the underlying reality. Since some economists believe that economics is the Science of Choice, it has been claimed that choice theories of income distribution are the only true economic theories. But this is no more than a debating point. The real issue is whether distributions of income can be entirely explained by a model of rational choice or whether other factors play a significant part.

Two variants of choice theory have been suggested. In the first (Friedman, 1953) individuals are confronted by a choice of methods of organizing society. Under some arrangements incomes will be more risky and under others more certain. In

---

[9] A useful first step in this direction was taken by Thatcher (1976). See also Lillard (1977).

the former case the variance of observed annual incomes will be greater than in the latter case. If people are risk-averters they will try to make arrangements to stabilize their incomes, e.g. by hiring themselves to an employer at a steady wage, while if they are risk-lovers they will be happy to accept wide annual fluctuations in their incomes. If the majority are risk-averters the organization of economic life may be arranged to give them what they want; and the observed distribution of income will be relatively equal. If the majority are risk-lovers, the opposite situation may obtain, and the observed distribution of income will be relatively unequal.

There is clearly a grain of truth in this theory, although it has not been developed further since it was first proposed. The main gaps in the theory are (1) the absence of any explanation of the reasons why in some historical periods or societies the proportions of risk-lovers and risk-averters should be different, (2) the methods by which the preferences of these two (or more) groups are reconciled, and (3) reasons for assuming that the degree of observed income variability is mainly the consequence of rational utility-maximizing choice rather than of technology or the inherited structure of property relations.

The second variant of choice theory—human capital theory—has generated a large literature and has become a major contender for recognition as the only truly economic theory of earnings distribution.[10] The theory has been admirably expounded on a number of occasions and its predictions have been carefully tested in a variety of ways.[11] The basic assumption of the theory is that the discounted present value of the lifetime income of an individual may in some circumstances be increased by expenditures (investments) on his education or training.[12] The circumstances in which such investments are profitable will depend on their productivity and on the rate of discount, but it is assumed that for most people the marginal

---

[10] Becker (1964, 66) went so far as to claim that human capital theory is 'the means of bringing the theory of personal income distribution back into economics'. See also Mincer (1976, 136).

[11] Excellent surveys have been made by Mincer (1970, 1974, 1976). See also Becker (1964) and Chiswick (1974),

[12] The theory has also been extended to cover expenditures on such things as health and migration. But these are not given major emphasis in the earnings models of human capital theory.

rate of return on $1 invested in education or training is always greater than the rate of discount for some positive amount of investment. If all individuals of a given age could borrow at an equal rate of interest and all were equally aware of the possibilities of profiting by investment in themselves, one would expect that all young people would borrow in order to invest in themselves up to the point at which the marginal rate of return on investment in themselves was equal to the rate of interest. If, in addition, the productivity of such investment were the same for everyone, everyone would invest an equal amount in themselves and everyone would have an identical profile of lifetime earnings.

Investments in human capital may have two kinds of effect on income during the period of investment. Investments which take the form of expenditures on tuition fees or other outlay costs will not reduce current income, although they may be associated with a reduction in current consumption expenditures; but investments which take the form of reducing the amount of time or effort devoted to current paid work will be reflected in a reduction in current earnings. Both types of investment, however, will increase potential future earnings (so long as their marginal rate of return is greater than zero). If the members of a society are distributed over different age groups, the effect of decisions to invest in human capital will be to reduce the measured earnings of young people—in so far as their investments require a reduction of time spent on current paid work—and to increase the measured earnings of older people. A cross-section survey of incomes in such a society would then show a dispersion of current incomes, even though every member of that society was in fact equal in his or her lifetime income expectations. The measured earnings inequality of such a society would, therefore, be illusory. It would merely reflect decisions by young people to invest in themselves.

Thus far, the logic of the theory is impeccable and the argument is interesting. Its great virtue is that it draws our attention to the naivety of aggregating income distributions across age groups. But the argument tends to be spoiled by the over-enthusiasm of its supporters. Because they want to make as much room as possible in their model for the influence of free choice, they tend to disregard evidence that people differ in their productive abilities, in their real opportunities, in their knowledge of those opportunities, or in their abilities to make rational choices affecting their future incomes. Hence the basic models of human capital theory are built on assumptions of equal abilities, equal opportunities (including equal rates of interest on personal loans to finance investment in human capital), and above all *long-term equilibrium*, which implies equal and accurate knowledge of the future effects of current investment decisions. It is true that Becker (1967) and others allow in principle for differences in the productivity of investment in different people (for which they have appropriated the word 'abilities') and differences in the rate of interest on loans (for which they have appropriated the word 'opportunities'). But there is reluctance to admit the existence of difference in other abilities or opportunities, such as abilities which increase earnings without necessarily increasing the productivity of years of education, or opportunities arising from the home environment or the cultural group to which the individual belongs, which have nothing directly to do with the availability of personal loans.

Human capital theory has successfully demonstrated that the average earnings of people with different numbers of years of schooling *could* be explained by the hypothesis of free investment choice in a perfect market, with equal abilities or abilities independent of the investment decision.[13] But the implied rate of discount revealed by empirical tests of this model is lower than would be expected from other evidence. Moreover, this variant of the model does not explain why different people choose to invest different amounts in their (or their children's) education. In order to account for these variations—and hence for the shape of the distribution of observed earnings—it is necessary to bring back differences in abilities and opportunities, even if only in the restricted senses mentioned above.

When the schooling model is applied to individual earnings data—at least in the United States—it appears to explain less than 10 per cent of the total variance of earnings.[14] So the

[13] See, for example, the discussion of the 'schooling' model in Mincer (1970).

[14] See Mincer (1970, 1974). This figure is biased downwards by the inclusion in earnings of small amounts received by persons employed for only part of the year.

emphasis of human capital theory has tended to shift to considering the influence of on-the-job training, or work experience. It is a well-established empirical fact that relative earnings tend to rise fairly rapidly during early years of work, and that the rate of change of earnings diminishes as the number of years of work experience increases, eventually becoming negative in most occupations.[15] Human capital theorists have offered a choice-theory explanation of these phenomena also. The necessary assumptions of the theory are: (1) work experience raises productivity, at least in early years, but by different amounts in different occupations; and (2) people have a free choice between occupations in which work experience is more or less productive. It follows that, if there are equal initial abilities and a perfect capital market, each person will choose an occupation which gives him the same discounted present value of the expected profile of earnings. Observed differences in earnings in different occupations and age groups will, therefore, be illusory, since everyone—by assumption—is entirely equal in his discounted lifetime earnings.

As before, one must admit that there is an element of truth in this theory. Young people—or their parents—do have a certain amount of choice between occupations; and one of the factors which influences that choice is the 'prospects'. For example, there are some 'dead-end' jobs, or jobs which require very little training, in which the initial rate of pay is higher than in jobs which have better long-term prospects. In such cases a choice has to be made between the importance of immediate and ultimate advantages. If there were perfect knowledge and a perfect capital market, no one would ever be made worse off by such a decision and everyone would make the optimal choice.[16]

But the difficulty with this Panglossian view of the world is

---

[15] It is an important achievement of Mincer that he has succeeded in redirecting attention from the role of age to the role of years of work experience in determining earnings. He would probably wish to give some credit for this discovery to the fact that he was using a human capital approach to the problem.

[16] On these assumptions the market would presumably allocate people to different occupations in the required proportions by adjusting the lifetime expected earnings profiles of different occupations. But it would be impossible to guarantee that the market would reach equilibrium unless there were some imperfections such as differences in personal abilities or estimates of the future.

that it overlooks too many defects in its own assumptions. Apart from the fact that people differ in their effective abilities, especially by the time that they reach the age at which they make a choice between occupations, many of them are prevented from making optimal choices by imperfections in the capital market or by imperfections in the scope of their knowledge of available alternative occupations, of their likely investment requirements, and of their likely earnings profiles. It is, indeed, absurd to assume that young people from different social classes in any country are confronted by the same menu of choices of occupations at the same prices. Moreover, tastes for different items on the menu have usually been greatly influenced by the prejudices of parents and by childhood experiences.[17]

Mincer and others have found that, when years of work experience are included as an explanatory variable, the proportion of the variance of individual earnings which is explained statistically is substantially increased. Using a large sample drawn from the 1960 United States Census of Population, consisting of white urban non-farm and non-student males aged up to 65 years, Mincer (1974, 92) found that years of schooling alone accounted for only 7 per cent of the variance of the logarithm of 1959 annual earnings; but, when years of work experience were also included, the proportion increased to about 30 per cent.[18] This is an important finding, which is in line with the emphasis placed in earlier studies (e.g. Lydall, 1968b) on the role of age as a factor influencing earnings. But the fact that earnings vary with years of experience is not necessarily evidence in favour of human capital theory as against alternative explanations of this phenomenon.

In order to use these results to support human capital theory it would be necessary to establish that the only or major reason

[17] In the United States, for example, many studies have shown that the educational and job choices of young people are correlated with social class. See Phelps Brown (1977, Ch. 7), who also refers to evidence of a similar situation in the Soviet Union (pp. 232–3 and 246–7).

[18] The additional inclusion of the logarithm of the number of weeks worked raised the proportion to over 50 per cent. But this is a rather misleading figure. It might have been better to have confined the analysis to persons working for 50–52 weeks, so as to exclude the influence of the number of weeks worked, which is largely irrelevant to the problem of what factors determine earning capacity.

why earnings increase with experience is that in early years of experience either the worker or his employer incurs a cost by allowing work experience to occur. Human capital theorists normally assume that the worker bears most or all of the cost; if this were not so, the human capital model would cease to apply, at least in any straightforward manner. But in what sense does a worker incur a cost in order to benefit from work experience? The cost is not an outlay but an opportunity cost. The argument is that the worker gaining work experience is forgoing an opportunity to enjoy higher earnings by doing work which does not carry with it the benefit of work experience. Thus, in order to isolate the cost of work experience, it would be necessary to have a reasonably wide range of opportunities of combining work with different amounts of work experience. It is easy to think of examples of jobs which seem to offer very advantageous opportunities for work experience, e.g. being personal assistant to a highly skilled executive, and, at the other extreme, of jobs which are 'dead-end'. But most jobs seem to be in an intermediate position. Indeed, if this were not so, there would be no general tendency—as in the statistics used by Mincer—for earnings to increase with years of experience. But in so far as all jobs offer similar opportunities for gaining valuable work experience, there is no opportunity cost in taking one job rather than another.

Human capital theorists have not given much attention to this problem, nor offered direct evidence to support their assumptions. They simply assume that work experience has to be paid for by lower earnings in early years. But it may be argued that work experience is a kind of external effect, a benefit not paid for through the market. The accumulation of personal know-how is a process similar to the accumulation of know-how by the firm, which was discussed in Chapter 9. In both cases, know-how can be increased mainly by practical experience, which requires time. But to receive practical experience one must be engaged in practical economic activity: to gain work experience, one must work. And, if the work is to generate useful experience, it must be 'serious' work, i.e. work which is productive. Beginners are nearly always less productive than experienced workers, but they usually produce something of value. In any case, there is no choice between being a beginner and not being a beginner, just as there is no real choice between starting an enterprise as a one-man firm and on a large scale. Beginners may have a limited range of choice between occupations with slightly more and slightly less scope for advancement; but it seems quite unrealistic to assume, as Mincer does (1974, 49), that the whole difference between a beginner's earnings and the earnings level achieved after about eight years of work measures the opportunity cost of work experience in the first year.[19]

This suggested method of estimating the opportunity cost of work experience is indicative of the peculiar assumptions which human capital theorists tend to make about human behaviour. Suppose that two individuals have different histories of years of education and earnings, and that we have a complete record of their education costs and earnings over their whole lives. By comparing these two records we may be able to find a unique rate of discount which equalizes the present value of each record at a given age for each individual. If such a unique rate exists, we may call it the internal rate of return on investment in human capital. But now we want to partition the earnings records into two parts—the part relating to the schooling period and the part relating to the employment period—and to estimate how much investment occurred during individual years in the second period. Since we have no direct estimate of the earnings forgone by an individual in the first year of his working life, we simply assume that his maximum earnings capacity in that year was equal to (1) what his earnings capacity would have been if he had had no education plus (2) the return (at the already calculated internal rate) on his accumulated investment in education. The implication is that investments in education raise the productivity of the individual concerned without any time-lag and without any work

[19] A comparison of Table 3.1 in Mincer (1974) with his Chart 4.2 shows that the ratio between a beginner's earnings and his assumed opportunity earnings is about one-half for each group of years of schooling. But if all beginners are investing half their opportunity earnings, where are the occupations in which they could actually make such earnings? In practice, the figures used by Mincer for beginners' earnings refer to the annual earnings of persons of a specified age, many of whom were employed for only part of the year (mainly for the obvious reason that beginners do not all enter the work-force on January 1).

experience: a Ph.D. is a better bus driver, for example, than a high school graduate from the very first day of his employment.

But this is contrary to all reason. The essence of education—as distinct from technical training—is that it creates in the individual a capacity to learn: to learn faster, and to learn more complicated things than can be learnt by people without such education. The economic effects of education are that, up to a point and on the average, people with more advanced education can absorb technical instruction and general information relevant to their work more quickly than those with less advanced education; indeed, in many cases they can absorb technical instruction which could scarcely be absorbed at all by persons without the necessary prerequisite education. Hence, we cannot partition the effects of education and experience in the simple sequential manner assumed by Mincer. Most of the rapid growth of productivity of more educated workers during their years of work experience is attributable to their prior education rather than to the quantity or quality of training received during their years of work experience.[20]

The conclusion which may be drawn from this review of human capital theory is that the shape of the age, or experience, profiles of earnings of people with different amounts of schooling is influenced by more complex factors than those which are emphasized in the theory. Men and women are not machines; even less can they be regarded as if they were government bonds, whose value accumulates by compound interest. People differ in their inherited abilities, in their family backgrounds, in their schooling, in their job opportunities and job experiences, and in their luck. There is an important element of truth in human capital theory—the truth that at least some people have a certain degree of choice about their careers. Within this group, some may choose careers which yield early income gains

[20] In line with this way of thinking Thurow (1976) argues that the level of prior education is regarded by employers as an indicator of the cost of training an employee. Hence, in his opinion, the 'job queue' is largely an educational ranking of job seekers. But careful employers will not be so simple-minded as to assume that all educational qualifications are worth as much as they pretend to be worth. Some studies (e.g. Taubman and Wales, 1973) suggest that college dropouts do better than those whose graduate. The 'screening' function of education is examined critically in Layard and Psacharopoulos (1974).

and others may choose careers which yield later income gains; and, if we take a cross-section of their earnings in any single year, we shall get a spurious measure of the degree of underlying inequality of lifetime incomes. But the importance of this factor depends on how many people have an effective choice of careers, and within what range. Human capital theory simply assumes that everyone has perfect freedom of choice of all possible careers and, in many models, that there is perfect knowledge and a perfect capital market. As an exercise in showing what might happen in such an imaginary world, the theory is not without interest. The theory also serves to remind us that changes in the degree of freedom of choice will have repercussions on economic behaviour. For example, a squeeze on skill differentials, which is not accompanied by a corresponding reduction in the cost differentials of acquiring skills, will be likely eventually to reduce the supplies of skilled workers. Since freedom of choice is intrinsically valuable, it is important to study its economic effects. But the aim of preserving or widening freedom of choice is not served by pretending that the existing world is already one of perfect freedom of choice.

Because human capital theory is directed exclusively towards deducing the outcome of free choice by individuals under exogenously given constraints, it cannot account for the nature of those constraints. Hence the theory has considerable difficulty in explaining the observed shape of the size distribution of earnings without relying on 'sociological' factors. At one stage there was a tendency to assume that the distribution of years of education is normal, or positively skew. If education is normally distributed, the 'schooling' model implies that earnings will be lognormally distributed; if education is positively skew, the earnings distribution will be more skew than a lognormal distribution. But why should years of education be distributed in either of these ways? That is a 'sociological' question. In any case, as admitted by Mincer (1974, 135), the distribution of years of education in the United States is now negatively skew.

An alternative approach to the problem, suggested by Becker (1967), was to rely on exogenously given distributions of 'abilities' and 'opportunities', and on the correlations between these two distributions. But this is a major retreat towards 'sociology'. If it turns out, as it seems to do, that abilities and opportunities are much more important than rational choice in determining the general distribution of earnings, human capital theory must be prepared to accept a more restricted role than it has claimed hitherto.

### Personal characteristics and development theories

By contrast with human capital theory, this approach to the explanation of the distribution of earnings emphasizes the personal and social limitations on personal choice. In so far as this approach has tended to exclude any role for personal choice it is an incomplete theory—perhaps a biased theory. But the theory has been struggling to establish the importance of factors which are usually excluded from Markov chain and human capital theories and this may have led to an underestimate of the importance of the factors of chance and choice.

The assumptions of this theory are: (1) the productive capacities of individuals depend on their abilities and their opportunities; (2) under equilibrium conditions in the labour market earnings will be correlated with productive capacities. Hence earnings depend ultimately on abilities and opportunities. Abilities may be assessed at different points in an individual's life. In principle, they exist at birth in the form of abilities which are wholly or predominantly genetically determined. From the moment of birth onwards, however, abilities are greatly influenced by the child's experiences, i.e. its environment or the interaction between itself and its environment. The child's environment is part of its 'opportunities'; and, as a consequence, abilities assessed at any time after birth are an amalgam of original abilities and actual opportunities up to the time of assessment. The interaction between accumulated abilities and new opportunities continues throughout life; but there are certain crucial turning-points in the lives of individuals. The first of these is the family into which he or she is born; a second series of turning-points may be entries in different types of schools; and a further turning-point is the kind of occupation chosen for first employment. Other important turning-points may occur later: for example, an opportunity to join a rapidly expanding firm, to migrate, to switch careers, or to take a managerial position.

Freedom of choice at the first turning-point is zero: a child cannot choose its family. Yet family influence on a child's career is usually of enormous importance.[21] Parents pass on to their children, especially to their very young children, their own attitudes, prejudices, limitations, verbal skills, interests, standards of conduct, and much else. As has been abundantly demonstrated, children from manual-worker homes generally lack the abstract verbal skills, and hence practice in the corresponding ways of thinking, which are typical of middle-class homes. They often have less stimulus to read, to experience art or music, or to engage in intellectual conversations. Their lives are usually less carefully structured and their time is less efficiently used to widen their interests and horizons. These are not, of course, the only qualities that matter in human beings. Solidarity and practicality may be more important in some circumstances than middle-class individualism and intellectualism. But it is the latter qualities which usually count more in determining earning capacities in all modern societies.

But the variation of family characteristics is much greater than the variation between manual-worker and middle-class homes, or even between 'socio-economic classes' as they are normally measured. Within each socio-economic class there is a considerable variation in outlook between parents with different home backgrounds, abilities, religion, ethical and political attitudes, racial group, geographical region, size of city, and so forth. And there is an ultimate residue of parental variation which goes beyond all easily measurable factors. So long as the family remains a basic institution of society, its influence on the attitudes and abilities of children will continue to be of overwhelming importance.

By comparison with the family—and all that goes with it—the role of the school is usually of less importance. There is no reason to doubt that the qualities of schools affect children's attitudes, habits, behaviour, and effective abilities.[22] These

[21] See Phelps Brown (1977, Chaps. 7 and 9) and his references to the extensive research findings on this topic such as those reported in Davie, Butler, and Goldstein (1972).

[22] Statistical support for this proposition is summarized in Psacharopoulos (1975). As he points out, the measurement of school quality is a matter of some difficulty. Hence the magnitude of the effects of school quality on children's abilities is debatable. But the direction of influence is undoubted.

qualities are not simply academic qualities but also, and perhaps more important for most children, the inculcation of good habits of work, good manners, a judicious mixture of solidarity and competitiveness, the provision of opportunities for self-expression, and so forth.[23] But most of the statistical analysis of the effects of schooling on abilities and earnings has been concentrated on the effects of the number of years of schooling, and this seems to have encouraged a simplistic belief that the effects of years of schooling are independent of other characteristics of the student. Yet it is obvious to any teacher that the effects of an extra year of schooling on students depends on their abilities and attitudes, and in some cases on their economic circumstances. Since abilities, attitudes, and economic circumstances favourable to the effects of education are usually correlated with the period of education, it is clearly misleading to attribute the whole of any apparent effects of education to the period of education.[24] In the case of earnings, there is the additional difficulty that what may appear to be effects of education may be in part the effects of (1) personal qualities which make for success in both education and employment and (2) the screening role of education, which means that jobs with better earnings prospects are allocated to people with longer periods of education.

Although no statistical study has yet been able to take account of all these factors at the same time, it has been found in the United States that the inclusion of cognitive ability usually reduces the apparent effect of education on earnings by 10–20 per cent; and the introduction of additional variables reduces it still further.[25] Since the crude contribution of years of education to individual earnings in the United States is already rather small, these results suggest that the importance of the period of education as a cause of earnings inequality in that country was previously much exaggerated. But the situation may be differ-

[23] Gintis (1971), in a paper which is in many respects perceptive, is pleased to describe good work habits, manners, discipline, and the like as qualities required only by 'bureaucratic and hierarchical' organizations. In my view, such modes of behaviour are preconditions of any viable human society.

[24] This is one of the unfortunate by-products of human capital theory, so long as human capital theorists try to avoid introducing what they call 'sociological' considerations.

[25] See Psacharopoulos (1975, Chap. 3).

ent in other countries, especially in those with a much greater dispersion of years of education. A number of studies in different countries have suggested that the rate of return to years of education is greater at the lower end of the education range; and from some studies it seems that the relative contribution of ability and other variables to the' crude apparent effect of education is greater at the higher end.[25] If these two relations are combined, they suggest that the net contribution to productive capacity of raising the minimum level of education in poor countries may be large, whereas the effect of raising it to higher levels in rich countries may be small.

The next major turning-point after schooling is the choice of an occupation. Occupations vary considerably in earnings prospects and, at normally assumed market rates of discount, in the net present values of those prospects.[27] But young persons' choices of occupations are heavily influenced by their parents' knowledge of available alternatives and by their parents' attitudes; and there is a general tendency for children to follow fairly closely in their parents' footsteps. Consequently, occupational classes and relative incomes are, to a considerable extent, handed on from generation to generation. Although there are many individual exceptions to this rule, there is an element of inertia about the system which is hard to break, even in communist countries.

For the individual, the choice of an occupation is probably the most important turning-point in his career after his initial 'allocation' to a particular family; and there is a considerable element of luck about the detailed outcome. Knowledge of occupational prospects is uncertain, especially detailed knowledge about the prospects of working for a particular firm or institution. But a firm or institution which expands rapidly after the worker has joined it will offer good prospects for promotion to positions of higher skill and responsibility, while a stagnant or declining enterprise will offer indifferent or poor prospects. Since it is impossible for the new entrant to make accurate forecasts about the future expansion of each enterprise, there is a large element of luck in the ultimate outcome of his choice. Moreover, since a large part of the know-how which the worker accumulates by work experience is specific to his

[26] See, for example, Hause (1972).   [27] See Phelps Brown (1977, 240).

own enterprise, so that mobility between enterprises is restricted, the effects of the initial choice of employer on lifetime earnings may well be cumulative, with persistent divergence between the earnings of a worker who happened to join a good firm and the earnings of his colleague who happened to join a bad firm.[28]

Further important turning-points in the individual career include the choice whether to continue in the first or existing employment, the choice whether to move into self-employment and set up on one's own account, and the choice whether to seek or accept promotion to a managerial position. By no means every worker has effective choices of this sort, but there is a sufficient minority to make a significant difference to the identity of the individuals who occupy the available jobs. Thus, if we wish to provide a full explanation of the earnings of individuals, we cannot omit these turning-points and the factors which influence the actual choices made. In the absence of the very detailed information needed to account for individual choices—which may in any case contain a substantial random element—we may well find that some kind of Markov chain of stochastic processes provides the best explanation for the general pattern of outcomes. But it would be inappropriate to assume that these processes operate regularly every year in a worker's lifetime, let alone over an indefinitely prolonged period of time. Finally, we must allow for the fact that measured earnings in a single period, even a period as long as a year, may include a significant transitory component.

The data requirements for testing these hypotheses and for estimating the contributions of different abilities, opportunities, and choices are enormous. Ideally, one would need information from a large and representative sample of individuals, with measurements of their annual earnings, in several different years over lifetime; the days and hours worked in those years; demographic and health data; occupation, industry, and size of firm at different stages of life; parents' background and other characteristics; abilities of various sorts (not just IQ); quantity and quality of education; history of promotion opportunities and choices made; attitudes to work; and willingness to

[28] Cf. the theories of dual labour markets in Reder (1969) and in Doeringer and Piore (1971).

work harder or accept greater responsibility for the sake of higher earnings. A sample which contained a large number of identical and fraternal pairs of twins would also permit an analysis of genetic influences, although the data requirements for ensuring that such an analysis is reliable are very great.[29] No such data are available at present, even in the United States which is remarkably productive of socio-economic sample data. One of the difficulties is that representative samples usually contain only a limited range of data while samples with a wide range of data have, up to now, been restricted to unrepresentative groups of the population.

A sample of United States males which is unusually rich in information has recently been analysed by Hause (1972), Taubman (1976a), Taubman and Wales (1973), and Lillard (1977). The sample is the NBER-TH sample, drawn from white males who volunteered for the U.S. Air Force pilot, navigator, and bombardier programmes in 1943 and whose abilities were tested at that time. In 1955 a questionnaire was sent to 12,000 of these men, and in 1969 a further questionnaire was sent to a subset of that sample. Data on earnings in up to five different years were eventually collected for nearly 5,000 men, together with a wide range of information about their education, family background, the education of their parents, and to some extent about their attitudes to work and risk-taking. The sample is not representative of all males of the given age group (mainly consisting of men born between 1917 and 1925) since the members were all volunteers for the Air Force, they were not accepted unless they had completed high school (or the equivalent), and they were in the top half of the ability range. In addition, they have all had military experience and those with good conduct discharges had the opportunity of subsequent education under the G.I. Bill. The final sample, of course, includes only those who responded to the questionnaires.

Analysis of the NBER-TH sample has produced some important results. In one group of analyses (summarized by Taubman, 1976a) which were designed to account for annual

---

[29] Ideally, they should include detailed information about the parental treatment of twins reared together and about the character of the home environment of twins reared apart.

earnings in 1955 and 1969, it was found that, even with the inclusion of over forty independent variables, the proportion of the variance of annual earnings explained was not more than 19 per cent in 1955 and 32 per cent in 1969 (or 20 per cent and 33 per cent respectively when the dependent variable was the logarithm of annual earnings).[30] Of the part of the variance explained, both education and ability accounted for a significant amount—approximately the same each—but in total they explained less than 'the conglomeration of family background, attitudes, and non-pecuniary preferences' (Taubman, 1976a, 208). Within this latter group important identified influences on earnings were religion (especially the effect of being Jewish, which raised earnings by more than a third), attendance at a private school (associated with very large increases in earnings), and non-pecuniary preferences (which, when positive, reduced earnings by a considerable amount).[31] These results imply that, of the part of individual earnings which has so far been explained statistically in the United States, variables such as cognitive ability and years of education are less important than other abilities, cultural factors, and the quality of schooling. Elsewhere I have suggested (Lydall, 1976) that there may be a bundle of abilities and attitudes which influences people to show more or less drive, determination, and related qualities; and I gave this group of personal characteristics the title of the D-factor. That the D-factor is something distinct from cognitive ability and years of education is well known to parents, teachers, and employers; and it would not be surprising if the D-factor were more important in determining earnings—and indeed some other indexes of success in life—than either cognitive ability or years of education. Taubman's results are fully consistent with that

[30] Most of the independent variables were dummy classificatory variables. Earnings included the earnings of the self-employed, thus giving an upward bias to the variance of earnings.

[31] Taubman argues that, since the effect of private schooling becomes insignificant when the level of the respondent's net worth is included in the regression, attendance at a private school is a proxy for parental wealth. But this does not follow. It could be the case that attendance at a private school helped to promote earnings and hence net worth, especially for the self-employed. Lillard (1977) suggests that part of the reason for the higher earnings of Jews is that they are concentrated in New York City; but the size of city was included as one of Taubman's dummy variables.

view. Little work has been done so far to measure the D-factor (or similar concepts) for individual persons, and virtually nothing is known about the relative importance of genetic and environmental influences in determining its size. But it seems probable that the D-factor, unlike cognitive ability, is preponderantly influenced by the environment, especially by the attitudes of parents and by experiences during early years at school.

A recent study by Lillard (1977), also using the NBER–TH sample, brings out some other aspects of the determinants of earnings. Lillard used data for up to five years of earnings, measured at intervals over the working lives of the sample members and, by pooling these observations, was able to estimate average age profiles of earnings for men of different cognitive abilities and years of education. These profiles, unlike those estimated from most previous studies, are longitudinal profiles for a constant sample of individuals, and consequently more directly relevant for estimating the effects of age or experience on earnings. Lillard's results on this aspect are consistent with those of Mincer (1974), which were based on cross-section analysis, in showing the great importance of age or experience as a factor influencing observed earnings.[32] All groups of ability–schooling combinations show an upward trend in earnings with age, which is concave and possibly asymptotic to a maximum at or after the age of 50. But men with either more cognitive ability or more education have steeper rates of increase, sometimes starting from lower levels; and ability and education are interactive, i.e. those who are both more able and more educated have steeper earnings profiles than would result from adding together the average effects of ability and education.

Lillard has also shown that, at least in the NBER–TH sample, human wealth is substantially more equally distributed than annual earnings, or even than earnings in a given age group; and this conclusion provides some justification for the argument of human capital theorists that observed earnings distributions are, at least in part, misleading. But the variance

---

[32] Lillard did not use years of experience as an explanatory variable, since his major objective was to examine differences in human wealth, which required him to discount earnings back to a common age.

of human wealth according to Lillard's estimates remains considerable and, surprisingly, only 10–12 per cent of it can be accounted for by measured differences in ability, schooling, and a group of background variables consisting of father's and mother's education, number of siblings, number of childhood family moves, and religion.[33] Most of the unexplained residual seems to be peculiar to the individual, in that it reflects a permanent upward or downward displacement of the individual's annual earnings in comparison with those predicted by the measured explanatory variables. Since the NBER–TH sample is truncated for both cognitive ability and schooling, these results probably underestimate the importance of ability and schooling in the determination of the distributions of both earnings and human wealth in the United States; and the importance of differences in schooling must surely be larger in many other countries in which the dispersion of years of schooling is greater. But it is evident that, until other factors are identified and measured satisfactorily, both the variance of individual earnings and the variance of human wealth will remain largely unexplained.

These conclusions are supported by the results of Taubman's further analysis of a large sample of United States white male twins, born between 1917 and 1927, who served in the military and were still alive in 1974.[34] The sample contains about 1,000 pairs of identical twins and about 900 pairs of fraternal twins. From a comparison of regressions of the logarithm of 1973 earnings on years of schooling within each group of twins and between all members of the sample Taubman (1976b) concluded that earnings are influenced to a considerable extent by genetic endowments and family background as well as by years of education. Moreover, the influences of genetic endowments and family background shown in his results go much further than in results from analyses in which IQ is used as an indicator of genetic influence and the socio-

[33] These factors—including apparently age—account for 30 per cent of the variance of annual earnings; but in the variance of human wealth the influence of age is inevitably removed. This is consistent with Mincer's finding that years of experience explain more of the variance of earnings than years of schooling.
[34] The sample is known as the NAS–NRC twin sample and its characteristics are summarized in Taubman (1976b, 1976c).

economic status of the family (usually father's occupation) is used as an indicator of family background. Taubman's efforts to divide the joint influences of genetic endowment and family background into their two component parts are debatable and depend—as he admits—on several at present unverifiable assumptions. But the general tenor of his conclusions about the importance of hitherto unmeasured personal characteristics and the importance of family background (and possibly genetics) in determining these characteristics is fully in accord with my own conclusions from other evidence.

Before concluding this section, it is necessary to show how the personal characteristics and development theory can account for the general shape of the size distribution of earnings. The essence of the theory is that many different factors play a part in determining earnings. In the simplest case, where all factors are in play at the same moment of time, the outcome will depend on (1) the distribution of each factor and (2) how the factors combine to produce their total effect on earnings. For example, if each factor were normally distributed and uncorrelated, and earnings could be predicted by the equation

$$y = a_1 f_1 + a_2 f + \ldots + a_n f_n \qquad (13.2)$$

where $y$ is earnings and $f_i$ is the value of factor $i$, then the distribution of earnings would be normal. If, however, the earnings function were

$$y = f_1^{a_1} f_2^{a_2} \ldots f_n^{a_n} \qquad (13.3)$$

and the factors were normally distributed and uncorrelated, earnings would be lognormally distributed. But if there is also some positive inter-correlation between the factors, (13.3) would generate a distribution which is more positively skew than the lognormal.

There is abundant evidence to support the view that factors such as cognitive ability, family background, and education each play some part in determining earnings. And it is also well-known that these three factors are positively inter-correlated. Although cognitive ability, as measured by IQ and similar tests, is usually adjusted to be normally distributed, it seems likely that family background, if it could be measured quantitatively, would be positively skew; and in most countries the distribution of years of education is positively skew. Hence, there is every reason to expect that the combination of these three factors alone would produce a positively skew distribution of earnings. And, since the effects of these factors are probably at least to some extent multiplicative rather than additive, they would tend to make the earnings distribution more positively skew than the lognormal.

There are several other factors which influence the distribution of earnings and which are likely to contribute to its positive skewness. First, there are other important abilities besides cognitive abilities, such as those which I have described as the D-factor. Second, there are dynamic stochastic changes which affect the career of an individual, especially at crucial turning-points. And third, there is the 'hierarchy' effect which arises from the managerial structure of organizations and which may be the major explanation of the Pareto upper tail of the earnings distribution.[35]

Before we pass on to consider the fourth and final type of theory, let us review the results achieved by the previous three theories. Markov process theories can, with suitable adjustments to their parameters, account approximately for the existing over-all shape and stability of the distribution of earnings of, say, the Standard Distribution of full-time full-period adult non-farm males. But the parameter assumptions required for this result are arbitrary, and in any case the theory is intrinsically unable to make a prediction about the effects of socio-economic endowments or choice decisions on the earnings of an individual worker. It is in this area that we find the potential strength of human capital theory, while the theory of personal characteristics and development can claim to be able to provide useful explanations in both areas. But neither of these latter theories has so far been able to account for more than about a third of the variance of full-time earnings of male adults, at least in the United States, and most of this is due to the inclusion of age or experience as an explanatory variable. While it seems unlikely that further progress can be made by human capital theory, which has already fully exploited the evidence of the influences of schooling and years of work experience in its own

[35] The hierarchy model is discussed further in Lydall (1968b, 125–33). See also Phelps Brown (1977, 309–10).

favour, there is probably some scope for improvement of the predictive power of the personal characteristics and development theory, if other personal abilities besides IQ can be measured and if more detailed information about family upbringing can be obtained.

An extension of research in these directions would make it possible to reach a fuller understanding of the effects of family and other social environments on the development of basic personal abilities and character. But final earnings depend not only on basic personal abilities and character but also on the range of job opportunities. While the distribution of young people entering the labour market according to their qualities is the supply side of the market, the structure of job opportunities is the demand side. The career of an individual worker of given abilities and character depends on the occupation which he chooses (or is pushed into), the types of industry and enterprise for which he works, and ultimately on the degree of managerial responsibility which he achieves within his employing firm or institution. The availability of occupations and the levels of pay and prospects for promotion which they offer may be called the job structure.[36] I shall now consider what factors influence the job structure and how the job structure affects the earnings of the individual worker.

*The job structure*

Let us start by imagining what would happen in an economy in which there was only one occupation, for example, harvesting coconuts. In such an economy there would be little use for the skills of reading, writing, and arithmetic, let alone for the skills obtained by more diverse or advanced studies, such as foreign languages, medicine, or physics. Nevertheless, it might well be found that children who had been to school for a few years became more consistent and productive workers than those who had no schooling. While schools are often assumed to exist mainly for the purpose of imparting specific skills, their most

---

[36] Thurow (1976) uses the term 'job distribution' for a somewhat similar concept. Although I do not exactly follow Thurow's account of the genesis of the job distribution, nor agree that it is given independently of the vector of supplies of effective abilities, I wish to acknowledge the stimulating effect of his book on my own thinking.

important job in practice may be to build character. In any case, the productivity of individual coconut harvesters would clearly depend on a number of their personal characteristics: their health, strength, other physical qualities, mental ability, preferences, and, not least, the D-factor—the factor which makes people work in a methodical and determined way, overcoming distractions, myopia, and temporary boredom or fatigue. If all workers were self-employed (with no shortage of natural resources) or all were employed on piece-work wages, it seems reasonable to assume that the distribution of earnings in terms of coconuts would depend on the distributions of different abilities and qualities of character.

Now let us change the assumptions and imagine an economy in which there is a wide range of occupations, but in which everyone is self-employed. There are coconut harvesters, rice farmers, merchants, lawyers, doctors, and so forth. The existence of all these specialized occupations is the consequence of trade and the division of labour. Because of the technical nature of each occupation there are differences in the productive effects of different basic abilities and qualities of character, and also of specific skills which are most efficiently imparted to children and young people in schools, such as literacy and numeracy. A literate and numerate rice farmer, for example, will be able to plan his work more effectively; a merchant must be able to read, write, and do arithmetic; and lawyers and doctors must be able to read documents and reference books, speak and write with precision, plan their own activities and advise their clients how to plan theirs. For any given level of technique in each occupation there is a certain range of combinations of preliminary education (including training) and effective productivity, which depends in turn on the valuation placed on outputs of different quality; but there is often a threshold of prerequisite education below which it is impracticable to enter a given occupation in a given society. When this is so, it seems reasonable to assume that the lifetime earnings of an occupation will be approximately sufficient to repay the costs of the prerequisite education and training at some normal rate of interest.

But while the costs of prerequisite education and training may provide a floor below which equilibrium earnings cannot fall, they do not impose a ceiling above which equilibrium earnings cannot rise. There are two reasons why earnings may exceed the level required to compensate for prior education and training costs. In the first place, the productivity of some occupations may be especially responsive to abilities or qualities of character which are scarce. These scarcities may be natural—as with musical or sporting abilities—or contrived—as in the case of restrictions on entry into medical schools. In either case, the supply price of workers to the occupation will contain a substantial element of rent. The second reason why earnings may be more than sufficient to cover prior education and training costs is that occupations differ in their degree of earnings variability and that uncertainty increases with such variability. These variations are both age- or experience-related and stochastic. For both reasons a young lawyer or doctor, for example, is likely to face a more uncertain earnings prospect than a young office clerk, although even in the latter case there may be great uncertainty about promotion prospects. Since for most people uncertainty is a real cost, average *ex post* earnings in the more uncertain occupations are likely to be larger in equilibrium than in the more certain occupations.

If every young worker had equal and accurate knowledge about job prospects in all occupations and no risk-aversion, and if there were a perfect capital market, the discounted lifetime earnings of each occupation not requiring scarce basic abilities and qualities of character would be equal. But because of imperfect knowledge and risk-aversion, the discounted value of lifetime earnings in occupations requiring longer periods of prior education and training, and consequently having a greater degree of variation in earnings with experience, will tend to be greater than in occupations requiring shorter periods of prior education and training. In this manner, the technical characteristics of each occupation in part determine both the age-profile of earnings in that occupation and the discounted value of that profile at a standard rate of interest.[37]

[37] Since the more highly educated, especially those from educated families, usually have more accurate information about the long-term prospects of different jobs and tend to have a lower rate of time preference (one of the most important effects of education is to increase the 'telescopic' faculty), they will

If we finally move from an economy of self-employed one-man firms to an economy of firms of varying size, in which the majority of workers are employees, there is a further influence on the job structure. As is well known (see also Appendix B), there is a positive relation between size of firm and the average wage. There are probably two main reasons for this. The first is that larger firms are more complex organizations and generally more capital-intensive. Consequently the workers in a large firm are usually responsible for more valuable machinery and for a greater throughput of materials than in a smaller firm of the same industry Since the results produced by a worker in a large firm depend to a greater extent on his work intensity, accuracy, and care than the results produced by a worker in a small firm, the large firm employer will usually be willing to pay his workers more, in order to give them an incentive to work efficiently.[38] The second reason is that larger firms have a larger proportion of technicians, supervisors, managers, and specialists, and a larger hierarchical structure of management, and this raises average earnings per employee in comparison with average earnings in smaller firms.

Thus the job structure which confronts a young worker choosing his first occupation is a complex pattern of jobs requiring different amounts of prior education and training, and offering a considerable range of different earnings prospects at different ages.[39] Most workers do, in fact, have only a limited

---

more often choose the occupations with better long-term prospects, for which in any case they are usually better qualified. If, in addition, they have easier access to personal loans or gifts, e.g. from parents, they will have several advantages in securing access to the jobs with the highest net present values at some standard rate of interest.

[38] The rational basis for paying more to employees who have more responsibility is that the quality of most employees' work is affected by incentives. It is, therefore, especially important to give incentives to those employees whose decisions or actions are likely to have the largest effects on the value of output. This corresponds to the 'scale of operations' factor mentioned by Mayer (1960) or the 'time span of discretion' mentioned by Jaques (1956). Reder (1969) has suggested that it is relevant also to consider the 'sensitivity' of the employee's decisions or actions, i.e. the extent to which his decisions or actions can alter the outcome of the process which he controls.

[39] Doeringer and Piore (1971) have suggested that the labour market is divided into a 'primary' high wage sector and a 'secondary' low wage sector. A division of this kind certainly exists in poor countries, where there is a strong contrast between wages and conditions in modern—especially large-scale—enterprises and wages and conditions in the traditional or 'informal'

area of choice by the time that they come to exercise that choice. Their options have long ago been restricted by the attitudes of their parents to alternative ways of life, types of education, and types of occupation. Those with less education, or with a poorer quality of education, or with a more limited family background, suffer not only from an actual restriction on their range of choice, but also from more limited knowledge about the choices still available to them, so that they are less well equipped to make an optimal choice. Not surprisingly, it is mainly the children of better educated parents who are encouraged to persist with their education, to keep their options open, to take long-sighted views about alternative careers, and hence to qualify themselves for the jobs which offer the best prospects. But the situation has changed considerably during the past generation in the more highly industrialized countries. With a wider spread of educational opportunities and wider know-ledge of alternative career requirements and prospects, children from all strata of society are beginning to compete for the better-paid jobs. Unless there are fully offsetting changes in the job structure, which seems unlikely, the increased relative sup-ply of qualified people is bound to lead sooner or later to a reduction in earnings differentials.

*Conclusions*

Each of the theories discussed above seems to have some-thing to contribute to an understanding of the dispersion of individual earnings. The distribution of earnings of men aged 50, for example, is surely affected by the following influences: personal characteristics at birth; family and social environment; school quality and length of education; choices of schools and occupations made by parents and by the child; pure luck, both permanent and temporary; the industry and firm of first (or subsequent) employment; opportunities for promotion to positions in the managerial hierarchy; and the existing structure of job opportunities in industries, firms, and other employing organizations. The distribution of earnings

---

sector. But in the richer countries the variation across industries and enter-prises is more continuous. See also Reder's (1969) discussion of the division of the labour markets for 'permanent' and 'temporary' employees.

across all ages and both sexes is much influenced by the dispersion of periods of education, the pattern of education and experience requirements which is consistent with the existing job structure, the effects of education and experience on the rate of improvement of productivity in different occupations, and differential effects of the interaction between the job structure and education-cum-experience requirements of jobs on the earnings of disadvantaged groups, such as women, residents on farms or in backward regions, immigrants, and in some cases people of particular races or religions.

Although it is not possible to incorporate all these factors and their complex mutual interactions into a simple model, there are a few leading ideas which help to give some order to the subject. In the first place, it is possible to show that combinations of a number of explanatory factors can produce a shape of distribution similar to that exhibited by the Standard Distribution. For example, if earnings are the multiplicative product of two or more factors, each of which is normally distributed, the distribution of earnings will be lognormal. Even if the multiplying factors are not normally distributed, but there are many factors, each of relatively small importance and of finite variance, earnings will be asymptotically lognormal. If, in addition, managers' salaries are arranged according to the hierarchical model, the upper tail of the earnings distribution will approximate to the Pareto function. It is, therefore, not necessary to rely on a Markov chain model in order to generate the required shape of distribution.

Secondly, both common sense and accumulating statistical evidence show that the lifetime earnings prospects of the individual depend to a very great extent on the type of family into which he is born. Although genetic factors cannot be ignored, the importance of the family environment is enormous, especially in its influence on the child's attitudes, habits, verbal and other skills, range of interests, aspirations, expectations, and degree of self-confidence. In addition, family economic circumstances affect the ranges of choice of education and occupation. But, as many examples demonstrate, the level of education and the general outlook of the parents are usually more important for a child's future career than their material wealth. A child's most valuable inheritance from its parents is a sense of purpose, together with good habits of living and working in the fulfilment of that purpose.

Thirdly, both schooling and the training obtained through work experience have considerable effects on subsequent earnings, although in both cases quality is probably more important than quantity. Since social policy cannot easily affect conditions within the family, the best prospect for raising the productive capacities of individuals with inadequate family backgrounds must lie in improving the qualities of schooling and training. But, if they are to succeed, the educators and trainers themselves must have a clear view of their purpose. If they do not believe in the importance of good manners, good work habits, self-discipline, and striving for excellence, their pupils can hardly be expected to develop those qualities.

Finally, although the factors affecting the distribution of individual earnings are more diverse than those which were used in the earlier model to account for the distribution of income between wages and profits, there is a considerable overlap between the two sets of factors. In particular, the model of wage and profit shares stressed the importance of (1) the distribution of efficiencies of entrepreneurs, (2) the role of experience in improving the know-how, and hence the productivity, of the firm, and (3) the variation of average wage and salary earnings with size of firm. Moreover, it is the size distribution of firms, generated by the earlier model, which determines the relative importance of large firms, and hence the relative importance of hierarchical management structures in the general job structure.

Much work still needs to be done before the dispersion of individual earnings can be adequately explained empirically. Some of the areas in which further research might prove to be profitable are: (1) measurement of the D-factor and of its influence on earnings; (2) detailed study of the influences of the family and the school on the personal characters—not just the cognitive ability—of children; (3) factors affecting choices at turning-points in an individual's career; (4) the effects of different forms of work experience on productive capacities; (5) methods of selection for employment and promotion; (6) the effect of the type of industry and firm, including size of firm, on the job structure and job opportunities of its employees; and (7) reasons for the existence of dual labour markets or other barriers to labour mobility, which restrict competition and opportunities for improvement and promotion.

# 14

## OTHER SOURCES OF FAMILY INCOME

In this chapter I consider the sources of non-employment income, their aggregation with employment income, and the consequential distribution of family incomes. There are two main reasons for being interested in the distribution of family incomes. The first is that the family is a social unit within which individual incomes are wholly or partially pooled; and the second is that the family is the vehicle for passing on abilities, attitudes, and property rights from one generation to another. The family acts, therefore, both as a means of current redistribution of income and as a means of continuity and redistribution between generations. But the definition of the family which is relevant for the first purpose is narrower, at least in the more industrialized countries, than that which is relevant for the second purpose. Current pooling of income in the richer countries is largely confined to those members of a family who live together, the *residential* family, while inter-generational transfers are made between members of the wider *biological* family. The residential family may be defined as the group of persons who live together, pool their incomes for major household expenses, and are related by blood, marriage, or adoption. In practice, this definition is not very different from the definition of a household, which includes the first two requirements but not the third. On a narrower definition, related persons who contribute less than half of their incomes to the common pool may be treated separately, and this is the definition of a spending unit which used in the American Surveys of Consumer Finances. In practice, this narrower definition is not very different from the nuclear family of husband, wife, and dependent children, with single adult persons being taken separately; which, again, corresponds fairly closely in many countries to the definition of the tax unit. This is sometimes a convenient unit to use, especially when the principal source of data about the composition of income is the tax statistics.

Factor income may be divided into three broad categories: employment income, self-employment income, and income from property ownership. Although employment income as we have seen, is quite widely dispersed, income from the other two sources is usually more unequally distributed, especially income from property. Some illustrative figures for the United Kingdom and the United States are given in Table 14.1. These figures, relating to only two countries, are between twenty and forty years out-of-date; but it is nevertheless probably true in general that self-employment income is more unequally distributed than employment income, and that property income is even more unequally distributed.

TABLE 14.1

*Percentage of total personal income from each factor source received by top 5 per cent of persons, United Kingdom and United States*

|  | Employment income | Self-employment income | Property income | Total factor income |
|---|---|---|---|---|
| *United Kingdom* |  |  |  |  |
| 1937 | 18 | 41 | 60 | 31 |
| 1945 | 16 | 47 | 56 | 25 |
| 1954 | 15 | 45 | 50 | 22 |
| *United States* |  |  |  |  |
| 1937 | 17 | 23 | 54 | 24 |
| 1948 | 11 | 31 | 44 | 18 |

*Sources*: United Kingdom: Lydall (1959), Tables 6, 9, and 11. Share of top 5 per cent of tax units. Employment income includes family allowances and occupational pensions. All government transfers other than family allowances assumed to be received by bottom 95 per cent of persons.
United States: Kuznets (1953), Tables 116 and 123. Share of top 5 per cent of persons derived from data on tax units.

Among the self-employed there are at one end some highly successful professional workers and business owners, and at the other many millions of small traders, builders, and service workers, including people engaged in part-time self-employment. Among property owners also there are at one end those with great fortunes, while at the other end many families receive very small incomes from their savings. Increasingly widespread ownership of houses and durable goods in the richer countries is gradually raising the share of property owned by the lower- and middle-income groups; but the inequality of wealth distribution remains much greater than the inequality of income.[1]

Apart from factor incomes, families also receive government and private transfers. Government transfers are mainly intended to raise the incomes of the poor, and they are consequently more equally distributed than any of the other three types of income. Almost nothing is known about private transfers, but presumably their normal effect is to redistribute income from richer to poorer persons. Since no attempt will be made to provide a theoretical explanation for either of these types of transfer income, the principal aim will be to explain the distributions of self-employment and property income. These two forms of income cannot be treated in complete isolation from one another, since self-employment income usually contains a substantial property component while much property income should strictly include a management component. Moreover, incomes which are initially classified as self-employment incomes are often the historical explanation of property incomes, as for example when an unincorporated business is converted into a company. For these reasons, the discussion which follows will be arranged along historical lines rather than by logical categories. We shall try to show how self-employment, employment, and property incomes evolve from one another during the different phases of development.

## The pre-industrial economy

Most countries have passed through a stage of economic development in which the major industry is agriculture and the major form of property is land. Such societies usually have

[1] See Lydall and Lansing (1959) for a comparative study of income and wealth distributions in the United Kingdom and the United States. These figures, also, are very much out-of-date, and since that time the distribution of wealth in the United Kingdom has become appreciably less unequal. For recent estimates, see Royal Commission on the Distribution of Income and Wealth (1977), and also Atkinson and Harrison (1978).

some trade and division of labour: hence there are merchants, artisans, transport workers, towns, and a government apparatus. The largest occupational group, however, consists of self-employed farmers, although in some societies their independence is limited by serfdom or other legal constraints. It is from the vast reservoir of agricultural self-employed and employed workers that the artisans, merchants, and other self-employed and employees of the towns and villages are recruited.

In such a 'traditional' society, without modern industry, the incomes of the great majority of the self-employed depend to a considerable degree on their land rights. Agricultural landowners and self-employed farmers merge into one another. While a few rich landowners may draw non-participatory (and even absentee) rents from their properties, most landowners are also farm operators. But the over-all inequality of landownership, and hence of incomes, is usually very large. Except in the most tradition-bound societies, this inequality of property tends to increase over time, until such time as the growth of modern industry and modern ideas leads to a solution of the land problem, sometimes by means of a radical land reform. In the long run, however, the continuing growth of modern industry reduces the importance of other forms of property and self-employment income.

Why is the distribution of landownership usually so unequal? In most countries the original distribution of landownership can be traced to a period of conquest and forcible seizure of property rights. The outcome of this phase depends in part on the policy of the ruling monarch, who in some cases yields to a few powerful subjects but in others tilts the balance mildly in favour of smallholders. But once the outline of the initial distribution has been drawn, new processes begin to operate. If we leave aside attempts to redistribute property by force or law, which have sometimes played an important role, the major processes which affect the evolution of landownership are twofold. The first is the fluctuations of fortune; and the second is inheritance.

Even if every family were to start with an equal landholding, equal needs, and equal labour resources, random fluctuations in output would soon produce inequality of landownership.

Suppose, for example, that each family farm had initially a normal probability distribution of annual output, as illustrated in Fig. 14.1 While *OA* is the expected output from each farm, actual output in each year has a probability of deviating from *OA* given by the ordinate of the normal curve at that point.

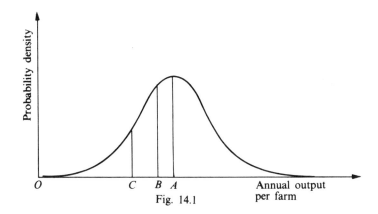

Fig. 14.1

Suppose that the normal consumption of each family is *OB*, so that normal saving is *BA*. If in year 1 a family actually produces *OA*, it will be able to save *BA* and build up a reserve against lean years in the future. But if in year 2 the same family's output falls to *OC*, the savings of year 1 will be insufficient to maintain normal consumption in year 2. The family may borrow from another family which has been more fortunate; but now it will need to have an exceptionally good output in year 3 if it is to repay the debt with interest. If that level of output is not achieved, the family's debt will continue; and the interest charge—which is usually high in these circumstances—will add to its future difficulties. Clearly, a family which is unfortunate enough to experience a succession of bad years will run heavily into debt and its expected net income in future years—after debt repayment—will be correspondingly reduced.

More generally, if $\bar{y}$ is a family's expected income from its farm, $c$ is its normal consumption expenditure, and $d_1$ is the sum required for debt repayment in year 1, the expected net surplus in year 1 is $\bar{s}_1 = \bar{y} - c - d_1$. But if actual income in year 1 is $y_1$, actual net surplus in that year will be $s_1 = y_1 - c - d_1$. Clearly, even if $\bar{s}_1 > 0$, $s_1$ may be $< 0$. If $s_1 < 0$, $d_2 > d_1$, and $\bar{s}_2 < \bar{s}_1$. If $\bar{s}_1$ is small, $\bar{s}_t$ may easily be $< 0$ in some year $t$, and the family farm will be heading for bankruptcy. Because $\bar{s}/\bar{y}$ is normally larger for large farms than for small farms, the probability of bankruptcy is greater for small farms than for large ones. Hence if, as a result of conquest or forcible dispossession, a large number of families have been left with small farms which are only just sufficient to yield a subsistence income under normal conditions, many of these subsistence farmers will be compelled eventually to sell their land and lose their independent status. Landownership will become more concentrated and the number of landless labourers will grow.

In most agricultural economies the general level of expected output varies—for all sizes of farm—from one year to the next, since a good or bad harvest affects all farmers. But the small farmer, close to subsistence, is driven into debt by a bad season while the richer farmer can draw on his reserves or reduce his consumption. In a bad season, food is scarce and the poor farmer has to pay a high price in terms of money for food which he buys or borrows. Even if, in the following season, he has a surplus of physical output, it may not be sufficient at the lower money prices ruling at that time to repay his debt. So fluctuating incomes may have a more serious effect on the fortunes of the poorer farmer.

There are many other reasons why a farm family may fall on hard times. The number of children may multiply; the husband or one of the grown-up children may fall ill or die; animals may be stricken by disease; relatives may arrive and demand support; men may be conscripted by the government; armies may requisition supplies and destroy crops and buildings. In all cases, the small farmer has less chance of surviving and recovering than the larger farmer or landowner. The small farmer is tenacious and hard-working and, by careful control over his consumption expenses, he can often recover from apparently disastrous events; but the long-term effect of all these fluctuations of fortune is to dispossess the small farmer and increase the concentration of landownership.

The tendency towards concentration of landownership is greater where there is initially a considerable inequality of landownership. In general, the more that inequality grows, the more it will continue to grow. For similar reasons, inequality will grow faster in conditions of heavy population pressure than where the majority of farmers have expected outputs well above subsistence.

The second major process of redistribution of landownership in normal times is inheritance. If the inheritance rule is that there should be equal division of land between all surviving children, farms will decline in size and, as more and more farms approach the subsistence level, the increasing risk of running into debt will cause inequality to grow. The rule of primogeniture, on the other hand, will help to preserve the smaller family farms, although at the expense of the younger sons, who will be forced to find other work.

Increasing concentration of landownership may, of course, be counteracted by government policy, including in some cases extensive programmes of land reform. Land nationalization in itself does not eliminate inequality of farm incomes, and even compulsory collectivization does not equalize incomes between collective farms. Complete equality of income for each level of skill would require the nationalization of all farms and the payment of every worker in the country at a standard rate which would be independent of the productivity of his farm. But the most likely effect of such a policy would be a sharp decline in agricultural output, especially the output of animal products. In countries where the expansion of industry and services has been rapid enough to relieve population pressure in agriculture, while at the same time raising agricultural productivity, the problem of the distribution of landownership has become less acute and the share of land rent in total income has declined. This period of transition has sometimes been eased by a programme of land reform, which has also encouraged large landowners to redirect their energies and their assets towards industry.

*The growth of modern industry*

Unlike the distribution of landownership, which is usually made very unequal at an early stage by non-market forces, the distribution of capital—and hence of self-employment income

in modern industry—started historically in the older industrialized countries as an equalizing tendency. The new middle
class was drawn predominantly from the self-employed farmers, artisans, and traders of the traditional economy, as well
as from previously employed workers. The profits of the new
enterprises were small in comparison with the rents of the
larger landowners and, since the new class had a high propensity to save, their consumption level was generally modest.

But now began the great unfolding of the powers of modern
technique, especially of the effects of economies of scale. Freer
trade, cheaper transport, and economies of scale, with ever-
improving technique, raised productivity far beyond all previous experience. Part of the benefits went to labour; but the
profits of the larger firms rose cumulatively, so generating a
new inequality of self-employment income in modern industry.
As shown in the model of competition with economies of scale,
outlined in Chapter 9 and illustrated in Appendix C, the size
distribution of firms may after a period of fifty years or so
become extremely unequal and positively skew. Since in the
model the share of profits in value added is increasing with size
of firm, the inequality of profits is even greater than the inequality of the size distribution of firms. Clearly, if the undivided
profits of each firm continued to be received by a single owner,
the distribution of personal income resulting from an indefinitely prolonged process of expansion of firms would
become increasingly unequal.

But this is not exactly what has happened. While a few
entrepreneurs have kept undivided ownership of their firm's
profits, in the majority of cases they have not done so. Both
outside loans and outside equity tend to grow with the size of
firm, and eventually, in most cases, the interests of the founding
entrepreneur or of his decendants decline to a level of minor
importance. An increasing proportion of business profits
accrues to outside investors, including life insurance companies
and other financial intermediaries which act as channels for the
investment of smaller savings. There have probably been many
reasons for this check to the growth of inequality of *personal*
income, despite a continued tendency for growing concentration of *enterprise* income. A business man's decendants are often
less vigorous and successful than he, i.e. there is a natural

'regression to the mean'; and this effect is supplemented by the style of the children's upbringing and education, which is often debilitating. Business men themselves decide to retire, and to sell off part of their equity in order to reduce their commitment to a single enterprise. And, of course, taxation of estates forces a reduction in the inequality of private wealth. The consequence of all these processes is to convert part of self-employment income into property income, i.e. non-participatory income from bonds or shares.

Part of the observed inequality of property income is the natural result of savings accumulated by employed or self-employed workers for their retirement. But as Atkinson (1971) has shown, on any reasonable set of assumptions this factor alone could account for only a small part of the observed inequality of wealth in the United Kingdom. The same conclusion is suggested by a consideration of the figures in Table 14.1 above. If people aimed by their savings to provide for a constant level of consumption over lifetime, and all of their post-retirement income were property income (i.e. they had no occupational pensions or annuities), one would expect that the share of property income received by the top 5 per cent of tax units would be less than their share in total factor income. But, as the table shows, the share of property income of the top 5 per cent of tax units was in the period covered more than double their share of total factor income. The contrast would be even greater if we allowed for the fact that people do not usually aim to maintain as high a level of consumption after retirement as during working years.[2]

*Family incomes*

The total income of a family—by which we here mean a *residential* family—depends on its size and composition as well as on the sources of income of its individual members. The size and composition of families vary widely: at one extreme there are single persons living alone, at the other there are families

---

[2] As an offset to this, the existence of flat-rate national insurance retirement pensions will increase the proportion of savings for retirement held by the upper income groups. But most of these savings go into pension funds, and the pensions themselves are not counted as property income in the British statistics.

consisting of persons belonging to three or more generations, including brothers or sisters of each generation. In poor countries families are more often of the latter type, especially in rural areas, while in the rich countries families have rapidly shrunk in size and now consist overwhelmingly of nuclear families of single or married adults with their dependent children. One of the functions of the large traditional family is to pool resources and provide welfare services for weaker members. In modern industrialized economies such services are mainly provided by the state; and the growth of these public services has helped to accelerate the decline of the traditional family. Thus the size and composition of the family are in part economically endogenous characteristics of a society.

If it were not for the growth of public welfare services the modern trend towards the smaller family, including an increasing number of single person families, would be reflected in a growing measured inequality of income across families. It is now increasingly recognized that measures of the degree of inequality of personal income which take no account of the size and composition of the income units may be seriously misleading.[3] For welfare purposes, a preferable procedure would be to adjust family incomes for the family size and composition by means of equivalence scales or, as an approximation, by converting family income to income *per capita*.[4]

But in countries in which nuclear families predominate, another problem arises, which is not solved by adjusting family incomes for family size and composition. This is the effects of the family life-cycle. In a fully extended family several generations live together: it contains economically active adults and young persons of different ages as well as dependent children and the old and the sick. If the family is large enough, variations in the age and productivity of the members tend to cancel out and, apart from the influence of macroeconomic events, such as floods, famines, and bumper years, the family's stan-

---

[3] See, for example, among recent discussions of this point, Kuznets (1976); Fiegehen, Lansley, and Smith (1977); and Das (1977). Also Lydall (1978).
[4] The estimate of inequality depends also, in most cases, on whether each family is still treated as a single unit, e.g. for calculating the proportion of the population in a given income group, or whether each person or 'equivalent adult' is so treated. See Das (1977) for detailed discussion of this point, with empirical estimates for the United Kingdom and the United States.

dard of living will be fairly stable. But when the extended family breaks down and different generations, other than dependent children, live separately, the fortunes of the individual depend very much on his position in the life-cycle. Young adults with jobs but no dependent children are moderately well off; married couples with young children have a more difficult time; middle-aged couples, whose children have grown up and whose incomes have risen with age, are on the average the most prosperous group; while many old and retired persons sink back into relative poverty.[5] If everyone passed through exactly the same life-cycle of income, it would be somewhat misleading to measure the inequality of income by aggregating all families, irrespective of their position in the life-cycle. A preferable procedure might be to measure inequality only within life-cycle groups. But even this is not enough if life-cycle patterns vary across different socio-economic groups.

Not only does the level of aggregate income of a family tend to vary with its position in the life-cycle but so also does the composition of its income by source. On the average in the industrialized countries, families consisting of young adults derive most of their income from employment, families consisting of young and middle-aged married couples, with or without dependent children, derive a significant proportion of their income as a group from self-employment, while retired persons derive their incomes predominantly from property and government transfers. There are, of course, many individual exceptions to these average tendencies: most people in fully industrialized countries never derive any income from self-employment, and there may be a few who never derive income from employment. But most younger recipients of substantial property incomes also have earned incomes from employment or self-employment.

There is a general tendency for the relative income inequality of families to increase with the age of the head.[6] Families headed by young adults are usually fairly equally distributed (although there seems to be a trend towards greater inequality in this group in recent years), and the degree of inequality

[5] See Lydall (1955).
[6] See Das (1977), Tables 3.7 and 3.10, for the United States and the United Kingdom respectively.

grows quite rapidly as the age of head rises up to the fifties or early sixties. From sixty-five onwards, relative inequality tends to stabilize, at least in the data available for the United Kingdom. Increasing inequality in the working age groups is probably largely the result of the tendency for employment income to spread out with age up to at least the fifties.[7] But the employment participation of married women is also of great—and increasing—importance for the measured income of the family. Married women contribute significantly to the family income in the early years, before children arrive, and later, when the children are older. Measured inequality of families in the same age group is much affected by the proportion of families which contain working wives, and the recent growth of inequality of income of young families in the United States and the United Kingdom is probably a reflection of decisions by some couples to postpone the birth of children in order that the wife can continue to work.

The high degree of inequality among the retired, on the other hand, is largely the consequence of differences in wealth ownership, which is most obvious at a time in life when current incomes from employment have ceased. It reflects also the more favourable pension arrangements for employees in the upper levels of managerial hierarchies.

The aggregate income of a nuclear family is, therefore, affected by a number of major influences: the family size and its composition; the age of the head; whether the wife works (which is related to the other family characteristics); and the principal sources of income (which are also related to the family life-cycle to some degree). But, if we widen our vision and focus on the biological rather than the residential (or nuclear) family, other factors need to be mentioned. These are the factors of family continuity—genetic, environmental, and property rights—which have been discussed above. There is a complex interplay between these underlying elements of family continuity and the fluctuations of personal experience, which are represented by particular occupations, life-cycle changes, and so forth. In spite of the nuclear fragmentation of families in

---

[7] This is partly the result of promotion in the managerial structure, which is usually in part a function of age or experience.

industrialized countries, there is still a large element of long-term income pooling within the biological family.

## Conclusion

It is unlikely that it will ever be possible to construct a simple theory of the distribution of family incomes. In the previous chapter we discussed the many factors which influence the distribution of employment incomes of individual earners. In the richer countries this distribution accounts for a large part of the inequality of family incomes, while in poorer countries the distributions of landownership and of self-employment incomes are most important. Even in the rich countries self-employment and property incomes represent a substantial proportion of the incomes of families in the top 5 per cent of the array. In addition, government transfers in the richer countries have a considerable effect on the income of those at the bottom of the income scale, while the earnings of wives are especially important in raising the incomes of families in the middle of the distribution.

The current incomes of nuclear families depend to a large extent on the position of the family in the life-cycle. But the lifetime incomes of families are greatly affected by family inheritance of genetic characteristics, environmental influence, and property. In that sense, family continuity across generations is a major influence on the distribution of family income. But there are also many chance factors which may dominate in the individual instance.

# 15

# GENERAL CONCLUSIONS

The search for a theory of income distribution has taken us over a wide field—from aggregate factor shares to the detailed earnings of individual persons—and it has proved necessary in the course of the inquiry to delve deeply into the major theories of economics. In this chapter I shall not attempt to summarize all the conclusions reached in previous chapters but rather to draw out some of the major implications of the analysis. I shall start by considering the crucial points of difference between the assumptions used in alternative theories of factor shares, including my own. Secondly, I shall draw attention to certain phenomena which are inadequately accounted for by previous theories but which can be explained by the present theory. Thirdly, I shall review the suggestions made in this book for improving our understanding of the size distribution of income. I conclude with a discussion of some of the policy issues which arise in relation to the problem of income inequality.

## Theories of factor shares

Every economic theory makes assumptions about three aspects of the real world, namely, about production techniques, the socio-economic or institutional environment, and the motives or tendencies of human behaviour. Hence the major questions which economic theory aims to answer are: how do people behave in relation to the economic side of life in the face of the technical and institutional constraints which confront them; and what is the general social outcome of their mutual interactions? The theories which are considered below may usefully be compared on the basis of the assumptions which they make, and of the answers which they give to these questions.

The technical assumptions of economic theory are concerned with the nature of the production function and they are addressed mainly to two problems: whether the input proportions are fixed or variable, and whether the function permits economies of scale. In most cases, those economists who have emphasized the role of variable input proportions assumed, implicitly or explicitly, the absence of unutilized economies of scale, while those who emphasized the importance of economies of scale were not much interested in the effects of variable proportions. Adam Smith, for example, although not denying variable proportions, placed major emphasis on the scope for increasing productivity through economies of scale, which required freedom of trade and an expanding market. Ricardo's thinking, on the other hand, was dominated by the law of diminishing returns. He was the first to see that variable proportions are needed to determine marginal products; but, since he was preoccupied with the effects of a fixed supply of land, he does not appear to have recognized the importance of economies of scale. Marx accepted both variable proportions and economies of scale; but, while he used economies of scale together with technical progress to predict the growing domination of large firms, his only use of variable proportions was to justify his law of the falling rate of profit. Variable proportions played no role in his method of determining relative values or the distribution of income.

Marshall, like Marx, accepted both these assumptions, and he tried to combine them with competition in the determination of relative prices along neoclassical lines. Despite the self-contradictions which resulted, Marshall was too much of a realist to abandon the assumption of persistent economies of scale. Most neoclassical economists have explicitly denied the existence of unexploited economies of scale, since this would prevent the attainment of equilibrium under conditions of perfect competition. In the model described in this book economies of scale are of pre-eminent importance, while fixed proportions of labour and capital are assumed to hold for a firm of given size in a given industry using a given technique.[1]

The standard institutional assumption of the classical economists—as well as of Marx—was free competition. Adam Smith, of course, was also much concerned with the effects of monopoly. Marshall tried to steer a middle course between

---

[1] Land, on the other hand, may be combined with other factors in variable proportions, and land rent may be explained on Ricardian lines.

perfect and imperfect competition, in contrast to other neoclassical economists who have firmly insisted on perfect competition. The theory presented in this book requires the rejection of perfect competition and its replacement by Entry and Product Market (EPM) competition. EPM competition yields some of the same results as perfect competition without entailing the exclusion of economies of scale. Apart from this, the theory incorporates certain forms of imperfect competition. A crucial conclusion is that prices under imperfect competition approximate in most cases to prices under EPM competition. If this is so, it can be claimed that the theory is a general theory of competition covering a wide range of conditions.

As regards the third set of assumptions, concerned with the motives or natural tendencies of behaviour, Adam Smith is, as usual, more modern than either Ricardo or Marx. Smith gave considerable emphasis to the role of choice in the balancing of costs and advantages, e.g. in his theory of wage differentials; but he shared with Ricardo and Marx the assumption that the total supply of labour is determined by an exogenous law (of population for Smith and Ricardo, of the fixed supply price of labour-power for Marx). Neither Ricardo nor Marx gave much thought to the role of individual choice: they were primarily interested in macroeconomics, and they were content to leave microeconomic problems to be dealt with by non-behavioural axioms about the origins of value. All neoclassical economists, including Marshall, emphasized the role of individual choice and of the personal utility function. Whether utility is of practical importance in determining normal prices depends, of course, on whether long-period supply curves deviate significantly from the horizontal, which is likely to be so, on usual neoclassical assumptions, only where natural resource costs are an important constituent of total supply price. In my theory, people make constrained choices on neoclassical lines, but their scope for choice is limited by imperfect markets for capital and private technique.

Thus the theory presented in this book shares with Adam Smith, Marx, and Marshall a belief in the importance of economies of scale; it shares with all economists except Ricardo and Marx a belief in at least a limited role for individual choice;

but it deviates from all previous theories of general equilibrium by rejecting the assumption of perfect competition.[2]

When we consider more specifically the treatment of income distribution in the different theories, we find that they fall broadly into two groups: residual theories, and general equilibrium theories. Ricardo's was a classic example of a residual theory, and Marx's theory also belongs in that category. Post-Keynesian theories of the Kaldor–Pasinetti variety are residual theories in a different sense. The theories of Adam Smith, Marshall, and other neoclassicals, as well as my own theory, are general equilibrium theories.

The essence of residual theories is that one or more types of factor income are determined separately, without reference to the incomes of other factors, and that a residual factor gets the remainder. Ricardo's theory had two residuals: first, all units of labour-and-capital receive their marginal product on land, with the remainder of the product being paid as land rent; second, labour receives its subsistence wage, and profit is the final residual. In Marx's theory, on the other hand, there is only one major residual: the difference between the socially necessary labour time to produce total output and the socially necessary labour time to produce wage goods. Since the latter is determined independently, surplus value is a residual. Part of surplus value is then paid to landlords, merchants, bankers, and so forth, so that the profits of capitalists are a residual of a residual. No theory was developed to account for this latter division, which Marx regarded as being of little importance.

The key assumption of both these theories is that labour receives a fixed real wage but, since no clear explanation is given as to how this wage is actually fixed at any one time in any one country, the theories stand on shifting sands. In practice, it is true that in the early stages of industrialization there is a large reservoir of potential industrial workers on the farms, and the

[2] This summary of differences in the treatment of three types of assumption may suggest that the present theory owes nothing to Ricardo. But no economist can escape Ricardo's influence, since he was the first to recognize the role of the margin in establishing equilibrium. I have not attempted to classify either Keynes's theory or 'Keynesian' theories in the same manner as the other theories. Keynes himself was a neoclassical in all respects except in his treatment of the capital market, where he uncovered the impossibility of ensuring equilibrium under conditions of uncertainty. Post-Keynesian economists vary in their assumptions.

industrial wage for unskilled workers is therefore related to their alternative income in agriculture. But the Ricardian and Marxian theories of the industrial wage really require a prior analysis of the situation in agriculture, including the influence of such factors as the average man–land ratio, the level of technique, and the distribution of landownership. It is along these lines that an explanation could be found for what Marx acknowledged to be significant differences in customary levels of wages in different countries.[3]

The Kaldor–Pasinetti theory of distribution in a steady state is a theory in which consumption is a residual. If capitalists consume nothing—a strange notion with even stranger implications for policy—wages, which equal consumption, are the residual. Profits are then determined by investment, the level of which is, however, left unexplained.

Walrasian neoclassical theory, with its modern derivatives, is the archetype of general equilibrium theories.[4] The 'factor' distribution of income then depends on the nature of the production function (or functions), the supplies of the factors, the nature of the utility functions, and the distribution of factor ownership between people with different utility functions. While the relevance of all these matters is, in principle, indisputable, the weakness of the theory is that in its exact—and highly detailed—form it yields no predictions of any practical significance, while in its aggregative—and inexact—form it loses its logical coherence. The fundamental difficulty is how to aggregate capital into a 'factor' which is well-behaved in the production function, i.e. which can be held fixed while other factors, and all factor prices, are varying. Moreover, even if the 'quantity' of capital could in some sense be held constant—as a quantity of butter, Meccano, or the like—there is no theoretical expectation that the law of diminishing returns applies when the physical nature of such capital is allowed to vary freely.

[3] In so far as Marx relied on the industrial reserve army of the unemployed to keep wages down to subsistence level and, since the size of this army reflects decisions on investment and technical change, his theory has elements of a theory of general equilibrium. But Marx never reconciled this approach with his axiomatic method of demonstrating that wages are equal to the cost of production of labour-power.

[4] Most of the fundamental ideas of general equilibrium were already present in Adam Smith, although not brought together in a coherent model.

Apart from these unsolved problems, the neoclassical assumption of perfect competition, and the consequent exclusion of increasing returns to scale, is inconsistent with so many of the important facts of economic life that the theory must be rejected for that reason.

The theory proposed in this book retains the possibility of perfect competition in product markets but excludes perfect knowledge of technique and a perfect capital market. This leads to the concept of EPM competition, which permits a combination of competitive equilibrium with unutilized economies of scale. Although a firm's choice of scale of operation at a given moment of time is restricted by limited organizational know-how and a limited supply of internal finance, there is assumed to be a sufficient number of individuals in a position to make a choice between being employed or operating a one-man firm (OMF) to produce equality at the OMF margin between the average earnings of the operator of such a firm and the wage appropriate to the level of skill required to operate an OMF in that industry. The basis of the equilibrium system is, therefore, the productivity of the OMF. If this productivity rises on the average over all industries, because of improvements in public techniques which are independent of the size of firm, the real wage will eventually rise, but the wage share may remain unchanged in the long run. If productivity is changing in different proportions in different industries, or if tastes change, product prices will be adjusted in equilibrium to achieve a distribution of relative earnings in OMFs in different industries which corresponds to the distribution of relative wage rates appropriate to the skill differences between industries. Hence equilibrium prices are proportional to equilibrium implicit wage costs in OMFs. It has also been argued that, even under conditions of imperfect competition, relative product prices will approximate to the same general equilibrium pattern, provided that there is legal freedom of entry at the OMF level.

While this model leads, on the one hand, to a general equilibrium of prices and wages, it also generates an equilibrium distribution at a given moment of time of sizes of firms and hence of wage and profit shares. This is an equilibrium of constrained growth, where the constraints are the amounts of time required to accumulate organizational know-how and profit for reinvestment. Since every firm in such a situation expects a higher rate of profit from expansion, those which are currently profitable will tend to reinvest and grow. Hence growth is endogenous to the model, not an arbitrary imposition from outside.

While the growth of the firm under EPM competition is unconstrained by the market, growth under imperfect competition depends on the ability of the firm to find new markets. When the aggregate national product is increasing, most imperfectly competitive firms will find that their own markets are also increasing; but some will be more fortunate than others. Those firms whose existing markets are not expanding fast enough will need to develop new products or new markets; and this may prove difficult. Since under imperfect competition investment decisions are highly sensitive to the level of capacity use, and since a change in the aggregate level of investment has feedback effects on the level of capacity use throughout the economy, growth under imperfect competition may in some circumstances be subject to wider fluctuations than under EPM competition. It was probably a combination of imperfect competition, a large capital market, and ill-advised government policies which produced the Great Depression. Keynes fastened on the blockage in the capital market as the key problem, but imperfect competition was also an essential ingredient.

The model outlined in this book accounts for a number of important phenomena which are not satisfactorily accounted for by neoclassical theory. These include: persistent growth in the size of firms; the skewness of the size distribution of firms; the stability of that size distribution; the widespread existence of unutilized internal economies of scale; the dominant role of self-finance; the importance of practical know-how and learning-by-doing; and the use of fixed mark-up pricing rules. The model also answers some questions which cannot be answered satisfactorily by neoclassical theory, such as: why wage and profit shares are stable over considerable periods of time; why investment demand is self-renewing, so that the prospect of the stationary state continually recedes; why imperfect competition tends in some circumstances to magnify fluctuations; and why freer trade in manufactures under modern conditions tends to reduce the aggregate profit share.

## The size distribution of incomes

My model of the growth of firms is concerned with the outcome of market relations in an industrial capitalist economy. But in the early stages of economic development this 'modern' sector is small and the bulk of the economy consists of traditional enterprises, mainly in agriculture and services, but also in construction and artisan work. As the share of the modern sector grows, the change in the structure of the economy has significant effects on the size distribution of income. Since the value of output per worker—measured by value added—is at a much higher level in modern enterprises than in traditional enterprises, the transfer of workers from the traditional to the modern sector tends at first to increase the over-all degree of inequality, even if the degree of inequality within each sector is the same and remains constant. But as the transfer process continues, the degree of inequality rises to a maximum and thereafter declines continuously until the whole economy is modernized. We have seen that this mechanism is sufficient to explain the pattern of changes in inequality implied by a cross-section comparison of countries at different levels of economic development, in particular, the tendency for the share of the upper 20 per cent of incomes to reach a maximum at an earlier point than that at which the share of the bottom 20 per cent of incomes reaches a minimum.

It is also possible that there are significant changes in the degree of inequality within each sector during the process of economic development. As the traditional sector loses its surplus of labour, average wages and self-employment incomes within the sector are likely to rise, and land rents to decline. The latter tendency will be encouraged by the growth of modern enterprises in agriculture and the consequential substitution of capital and technique for land. Meanwhile, in the modern sector there will be two different tendencies. On the one hand, the growth of firms and the increasing skewness of their distribution (at least in the early stages of development when conditions approximate to EPM competition) will tend to raise the profit share. On the other hand, the profit share for a given size distribution of firms tends to be higher in the early stages than in the later stages, because there is more diversity of techniques in the early stages. These two tendencies may roughly offset one another, leaving the profit share approximately constant; but there is some evidence to suggest that, at least in manufacturing, the profit share is inversely related to the level of economic development. If this is the position throughout the modern sector, it constitutes an additional reason for the decline in the degree of inequality with economic development.

The major source of income in a modern industrialized economy is wages and salaries, or employment income. The proportion of household income from this source is in many countries as high as 70 per cent. Self-employment income, which is of great or even dominant importance in less developed countries, accounts for only 10 to 15 per cent of personal income in the most highly industrialized countries, while incomes from property and government transfers in such countries are each of the order of 10 per cent of the total.[5] Although self-employment and property incomes are more unequally distributed than employment incomes, the importance of employment income in the total implies that inequality of employment incomes is a major source of total inequality. If all adults were full-time employees with only this source of income, and their earnings were distributed exactly as full-time earnings are actually distributed, the distribution of pre-tax personal incomes would still be very unequal.

Labour markets are far from perfect: there are enormous differences between earnings in different countries, and even within a single country full-time adult earnings for apparently similar work vary considerably between regions, urban and rural areas, industries, and sizes of firm. In addition, women and particular racial groups often receive less than the competitively appropriate wage. But even within a single fairly competitive group, such as white urban males in a single region of the United States, there are very wide differences of earnings.

---

[5] If retained profits of companies were included in personal income, the property component would be higher. Its precise share would depend on whether retained profits were included before or after tax.

Theoretical explanations of competitive differences in earnings have focused on four main influences: pure chance, deliberate choice, the personal characteristics of the earner, and the structure of job opportunities. Although the adherents of each theory have been inclined to emphasize their own favourite explanation at the expense of other alternatives, there can be no doubt that each of these four influences plays some part in determining individual earnings. Chance has both 'permanent' and temporary effects; choice is important when parents or children select schools, occupations, firms to work for, or areas of residence. The personal characteristics of the individual depend on his genetic inheritance and his family environment, as well as on the character of his school and of the firm or organization for which he works. Although these personal characteristics could, in principle, be attributed ultimately to chance and choice within a given socio-economic environment, such an approach would direct attention away from the variables over which policy may have some influence towards variables which are largely outside social control.

While theories of the determination of personal characteristics and of their influence on earnings are concerned with the supply side of the labour market, the job structure introduces the demand side. In its extreme form it says that the structure of job requirements and of rates of pay is determined independently of the supplies of labour of different educational qualifications and skills. But, even if it is admitted, as it surely must be, that supply and demand both play a role in determining relative earnings in different jobs, it is clear that the job structure has a special importance. The exogenous determinants of the job structure include the technical requirements of different jobs, which often prescribe particular educational prerequisites (as a real, not a sham, screening device); the size of firm, which affects the scale of operations of each worker; and the internal organization of firms, which determines the management structure. Some aspects of the job structure may be amenable to modification by institutional reforms, such as changing methods of job training or increasing the degree of participation in decision-making; but experience from widely different social systems suggests that fundamental changes in the job structure cannot be made without sacrificing a great part of the advantages of economies of scale and division of labour.

My theory of employment incomes draws on all these component theories to some degree. But it tends to give prominence to the role of personal characteristics and of their changes over lifetime. Empirical studies of factors influencing the distribution of individual earnings have found—at least in the United States—that cognitive ability and years of education each contribute somewhat less than 10 per cent to the variance of annual earnings, although the actual figure depends on whether the sample is restricted, as it should be, to full-time employees. When years of work experience are added, the proportion of the variance explained is increased by about 20 per cent; but no study of individual earnings of full-time employees in a reasonably competitive group has yet been able to account for more than about a third of total variance. This is a severe blow to human capital theorists, who have been inclined to set aside all other influences besides rational choice. They have tried to save the situation by appropriating the effects of work experience for their model; but in my opinion they have failed to show that most work experience is an opportunity cost, and hence an investment which necessarily yields a subsequent return.

One must not be too optimistic about the prospects of explaining the greater part of the variance of individual earnings. There are a great many influences at work, many of which will remain for a long time, or even indefinitely, in the box labelled 'chance'. Of course, the proportion of the total variance of earnings explained by any factor depends in part on the variance of that factor. The low explanatory power of years of education in the United States is probably partly due to the high minimum level of education achieved by the great majority in that country. In countries which still have mass illiteracy a wider spread of primary education would undoubtedly tend to reduce inequality of earnings below its present high level. I believe that further progress could be made in the explanation of individual earnings if more attention were given to non-cognitive abilities, such as the D-factor (of drive, determination, persistence, reliability, and the like). There may also be other personal characteristics which are important, such as ability to get on well with others, imagination, enterprise, leadership, and ambition. Another area for useful research would be the role of family and cultural influences, the quality of schooling, methods of training young entrants to enterprises, and methods of selection for promotion.

The distributions of property and self-employment incomes are partly by-products of a market economy. In a predominantly agricultural economy the distribution of landownership, and hence of rental income, has a tendency to become more unequal over time as a consequence of fluctuations in the environment . The closer the population is to the subsistence level, the greater the effects of such fluctuations and the stronger the tendency towards increasing inequality. This tendency will, however, be offset to some degree if there is a large emigration of workers from agriculture, and if machinery and improved techniques reduce the importance of land as a specialized factor. In the modern industrial sector there is also a trend towards increasing inequality through the widening size distribution of firms; but this may be partly offset by increasing homogeneity of technique as the modernization process continues. Thus, while the centrifugal forces of chance and growth are important factors in constantly recreating inequality of property and self-employment incomes, there are other influences at work in a modernizing competitive economy which can check these tendencies. The most important source of inequalities of property and self-employment incomes is the inter-generational carry-over of inherited inequality of property ownership.

Inheritance of property is only one aspect of the inter-generational continuity of family income. Other major components are genetic inheritance and the influence of the family on upbringing, education, and occupational choice. In one way or another, despite individual deviations, the biological family tends to perpetuate its own characteristics and hence the level of 'permanent' family income. In detail, however, *per capita* residential family incomes in the richer countries (where the extended family has largely broken down into nuclear families) vary over the family life-cycle. In general, young adults without dependent children are better off than married couples with dependent children, while older married couples whose children have grown up are more prosperous before retirement and less prosperous, or even impoverished, after retirement. In a cross-section study of income inequality of families, even on a *per capita* or equivalent adult basis, life-cycle effects partly obscure the underlying distribution of permanent family income.

*Some policy considerations*

Since the purpose of this book is to provide a theory of income distribution, it aims to be as ethically neutral as is practicable in a scientific study. But all theories have policy implications. For example, a theory which maintained that 90 per cent of the variance of earnings is due to genetic inheritance and 10 per cent to schooling would have different implications for policy from a theory which maintained the opposite of this. Similarly, a theory which maintains that profits arise solely from the ownership of capital has different implications from one which attributes a significant part of profits to enterprise or innovation. Since policy conclusions are to some extent implied by any theory, it seems desirable to consider some of the policy implications of the present theory. In such a discussion, however, it would be idle to pretend that all statements are grounded in ethically neutral scientific reasoning or statements of fact. All hypotheses in the field of social science, and most statements of 'fact', are influenced by ethical considerations. The investigator should, therefore, try to be as explicit as possible about his value premises.[6]

The value premises which underlie the following discussion are mine; but I believe that they are also those of the majority of my fellow-countrymen as well as of the citizens of other countries which have enjoyed a significant period of democratic government. In this value system economic equality is an important objective; but there are also other important objectives, such as respect for the rights of others, freedom for the development of personal talent, freedom of inquiry and thought, tolerance of dissenting opinions, and so forth. Although none of these objectives has complete dominance over all others, there is one objective which is very close to being in that position. This is the principle of equality of *status* of every

---

[6] Myrdal has been pre-eminent in his insistence on this requirement for scientific work in the social field. See Myrdal (1944) and many of his subsequent writings.

individual. Under this principle it is forbidden to discriminate arbitrarily against people of different sex, race, or religion (although some discrimination in the treatment of young people is permitted). It is this principle, also , which requires the maintenance of the rule of law and of strict limitations on the powers of administrators to make decisions about the rights of individual persons or about the scope of their activities. These are some of the 'human rights' aspects of equality of status.

But equality of status also has important implications about equality in the economic and political spheres. So far as the first is concerned, there cannot be said to be equality of status if some people inherit large fortunes while others live in conditions of extreme poverty. On the political side, equality of status implies the right to equal participation in political decisions and, more generally, the right to make decisions about aspects of personal behaviour which do not seriously diminish the equal rights of others.

Even this brief list of some of the implications of equality of status reveals that the concept creates a serious dilemma: the conflict between *ex post* economic equality and the *ex ante* right of choice. This conflict is most acute in three areas. In the first place, freedom of choice implies a substantial degree of freedom in the allocation of personal labour, including, for example, the freedom to decide whether to undergo higher education, freedom of choice of a job, of the degree of work effort, of the level of managerial responsibility, and of the amount of leisure. While these freedoms are constrained in practice, there is a vast difference between the normal constraints on freedom of choice and the administrative allocation of labour. Freedom of choice in this area entails differences in personal productivity (even apart from the effects of predetermined differences in abilities) and, so long as there is scarcity of economic goods, labour incomes will be related in some measure to labour productivity.

Secondly, freedom of choice implies—in the opinion of the overwhelming majority of mankind—freedom for parents to bring up their children, at least in their early years. But, as has been shown above, this entails that non-genetic characteristics of parents will be passed on in considerable measure to their children, thus perpetuating some part of existing inequality.

This is one reason why extreme egalitarians would like to abolish the family. But the family seems likely to survive. Indeed, it is possible that the swing of sentiment against the family in some countries in recent years—which is based on the demand for freedom—may soon move in the opposite direction. In any case, the continuing importance of the family as an institution for child-rearing and for inter-generational continuity is one reason why economic inequality will persist.

The third major area of conflict between equality and freedom of choice takes us to the heart of the debate about the role of the market. The market inevitably entails economic inequality, since the market is a system of economic incentives. Economic incentives are economic rewards and penalties, which are inconsistent with perfect *ex post* equality. But the market is the only known device for creating freedom of choice in a large economy, i.e. beyond the level of a household or a small co-operative. This can be seen most clearly if we consider the alternative to the market, namely, the centrally planned economy. In such an economy all crucial decisions are taken by the central bureaucrats and the political élite: the function of the rest of the population is simply to obey and to fulfil, or over-fulfil, the plan. Of course, in a market economy in which production is largely concentrated in big enterprises most people have little opportunity at present to make decisions about production; and, despite much wishful thinking, this problem cannot easily be overcome. A person does not become a true participant in decision-making by voting for a representative, especially if that representative is nominated by a caucus. But the market does permit the existence of millions of small enterprises, which provide an outlet for those who are most anxious to make their own production decisions. Moreover, in so far as participation in decision-making is possible within large enterprises, it can be effective only if such enterprises operate within a market environment. The most important law of political economy is that decentralization of decision-making is impossible without a market.

Apart from production decisions, people also wish to have freedom of choice in the expenditure of their income. The command economy is intrinsically unresponsive to consumer preferences and functions best under conditions of rationing, shortage, and queues. Quality is at a discount, innovation is slow, and the standard of service is poor. Hence, if one believes that freedom of consumer choice has any importance, there is a further reason why the economy must contain an element of market competition.

In the light of the above discussion we may proceed to consider the implications of my theory of income distribution. According to the theory there is a spontaneous tendency for inequality of income to increase in the early stages of modernization, when the transfer of population from the traditional to the modern sector inevitably widens the inequality of income. In addition, in a market economy the growth of firms in the modern sector, and the resulting increase in the skewness of the distribution of these firms, tend to raise the profit share and to increase the inter-firm inequality of employment incomes. There may also be some tendency for inequality of land-holdings to increase and for the share of land rent to rise. Meantime, the demand for skilled labour increases ahead of its supply, since the supply, consisting of those with practical on-the-job experience, grows more slowly than the number required to man expanding industries.

As modernization proceeds further, the degree of inequality at first stabilizes and then begins to decline. The influence of continued inter-sectoral transfers is of major importance in these changes; but there may also be a tendency for the profit share in the modern sector to fall as the degree of heterogeneity of technique within the sector diminishes. Modernization of agriculture, together with continued emigration of labour from the farms, tends to raise wages and reduce rents, while the supply of skilled workers in the modern sector may also begin to catch up with the growth in demand for such labour. Eventually, as the economy reaches a position of advanced modernization, inequality returns to at least as low a level as that at which it stood at the beginning of the development process.

While this theory is optimistic about the long-term effects of economic development, it also implies that in the early stages of development economic inequality will grow. If this prospect is unacceptable, there seem to be two alternatives. The first is the classic communist policy of nationalization of industry and collectivization of agriculture, which gives absolute priority to economic equality over political equality and human rights. The second is the 'bourgeois democratic' policy of political democracy, land reform, and a major programme of mass education. The choice between these alternatives, however, has not usually depended in practice on abstract considerations of maximum welfare.

When we turn to conditions within the advanced industrialized countries the picture is very different. Average real incomes in these countries have already reached high levels by historical standards, and the conditions of even the poorest groups cannot seriously be compared with those of the majority of people in the undeveloped countries. Nevertheless, there remains considerable economic inequality. The major distributional problems of these countries are the high concentration of inherited wealth at one end and the low earnings of some groups of workers and the low incomes of many retired people at the other. The optimal solution to the wealth problem, consistent with the maintenance of a market economy, is to reduce the rights of private inheritance. The alternative of taxing current wealth, irrespective of whether it has been inherited or accumulated over lifetime, inhibits enterprise and growth and preserves the dominance of old wealth.

The problem of low earnings is partly the result of discriminatory practices in the labour market, but it is mainly a symptom of the failure of educational and job-training programmes. Why is it, one might ask, that in countries where migrant workers (from the farms or from foreign countries) are an important element in the labour force these workers tend to occupy the low-paid jobs while the urban or native-born citizens occupy the better jobs? A serious attempt to answer that question would suggest some practical solutions to the problem of low earnings. Poverty among the retired and inactive, on the other hand, is a problem which can be overcome directly, by government transfers in the short term and by universal contributory pension schemes in the longer term.

If the extreme inequalities generated by inherited wealth and by low earnings capacity and low retirement incomes were eliminated, there would still remain a significant, but tolerable, amount of inequality among the active population. This inequality would reflect mainly differences within the employed and the self-employed groups respectively. My theory suggests that an essential condition for the competitive and efficient functioning of industry is the maintenance of free entry of firms into industry, and especially the maintenance of free entry of one-man firms. This is the point at which competition takes place between the employed and the self-employed, and at which general equilibrium is established between prices and wages. It is therefore important that those who accept the need for a market mechanism, whether they be in communist or in capitalist countries, should direct their attention to this point.

# APPENDIX A

## MATHEMATICAL DERIVATIONS

1. *The aggregate wage share*

If $v$ is average net value added per worker (exclusive of land rent) in firms employing $L$ workers, and $w$ is the average wage in the same group of firms, it is assumed that, over the economy as a whole,

$$v = BL^{\beta-1} \qquad B > 0, \beta > 1 \qquad (A.1)$$

and

$$w = AL^{\alpha-1} \qquad A > 0, 1 < \alpha < \beta \qquad (A.2)$$

In addition, it is assumed that the size distribution of all firms conforms to the Pareto function

$$N = RL^{-\rho} \qquad R > 0, \rho > 1 \qquad (A.3)$$

where $N$ is the number of firms employing $L$ workers of more.

In all the above functions, workers employed include working proprietors, so that the wage in (A.2) is partly an imputed wage. Since the minimum size of firm is the one-man firm (OMF), $L \geqslant 1$. Strictly, the variable $L$ can take only integral unit values; but for simplicity it will be assumed that the functions are continuous.

The density of firms at $L$ is given by

$$-\frac{\mathrm{d}N}{\mathrm{d}L} = \rho RL^{-\rho-1} \qquad (A.4)$$

and from (A.1) the corresponding density of value added per firm is

$$\rho RL^{-\rho-1} BL^{\beta} = \rho RBL^{\beta-\rho-1} \qquad (A.5)$$

Hence, by integration over all firms employing one worker or more, aggregate value added (or national income excluding rent) is

$$Y = \frac{\rho RB}{\rho-\beta} \qquad \text{subject to } \rho > \beta. \qquad (A.6)$$

Similarly, from (A.2) and (A.4), aggregate wages paid in all firms is, by integration,

$$W = \frac{\rho R A}{\rho - \alpha} \tag{A.7}$$

Then the average wage share in national income is

$$S_w = W/Y = \frac{\rho - \beta}{\rho - \alpha} \cdot \frac{A}{B} \tag{A.8}$$

If in addition, as assumed in Chapter 9, $A = B$ in equilibrium, we have

$$S_w = \frac{\rho - \beta}{\rho - \alpha} \tag{A.9}$$

## 2. *The rate of profit of a firm*

The word profit is used here to describe the surplus of net value added over land rent and wage payments, where wages cover all labour costs, including the imputed labour cost of working proprietors.

The 'rate of profit' is derived by the usual (theoretically unsatisfactory) method of dividing current net profit by the value of net capital.

The function (A.1) describes the behaviour of *average* value added per worker in all firms employing $L$ workers. But firms vary in their efficiency, and hence in the amount of value added produced—at fixed prices—by the employment of a given number of workers. It will be assumed that value added per worker in firm $i$, with a specified level of efficiency, is related to the number of workers which it employs by the function

$$v_i = B_i L^{\beta - 1} \tag{A.10}$$

where the parameter $\beta$ takes the same value as in (A.1).

The efficiency of firm $i$ may then be defined as

$$\theta_i = B_i/B \tag{A.11}$$

Since $B$ is the mean of $B_i$, $\bar{\theta}_i = 1$.

From (A.2) and (A.10) the amount of profit of a firm of efficiency $\theta_i$ which employs $L$ workers is

$$M_i = B_i L^{\beta} - A L^{\alpha} \tag{A.12}$$

I shall assume that net capital employed in a firm of average efficiency producing $V$ of value added is given by

$$K = CV^{\gamma} \qquad C > 0,\ \gamma > 0 \qquad (A.13)$$

Since $V = vL$, we may substitute (A.1) in (A.13) to obtain

$$K = CB^{\gamma}L^{\beta\gamma} \qquad (A.14)$$

By combining (A.11), (A.12), and (A.14) with the equilibrium condition that $A = B$, we obtain the rate of profit of a firm of efficiency $\theta_i$, namely,

$$r_i = \frac{A^{1-\gamma}}{C}\ L^{\beta-\beta\gamma}\ (\theta_i - L^{\alpha-\beta}) \qquad (A.15)$$

If the ratio of capital to value added is constant over all sizes of firm of average efficiency, $\gamma = 1$ and (A.15) reduces to

$$r_i = \frac{1}{C}\ (\theta_i - L^{\alpha-\beta}) \qquad (A.16)$$

where $C$ is the capital–value added ratio.

It can be shown that, when $\gamma \leqslant 1$, $dr_i/dL > 0$. Within the structure of this model, therefore, the condition $\gamma \leqslant 1$ is sufficient for ensuring a rate of profit which increases with the size of the firm (its efficiency being held constant).

By combining (A.11) and (A.12) we obtain the profit markup on wage costs of a firm of efficiency $\theta_i$, namely,

$$M_i/W = \theta_i L^{\beta-\alpha} - 1. \qquad (A.17)$$

# APPENDIX B

## PRODUCTIVITY AND SIZE OF FIRM IN MANUFACTURING

A major source of empirical information about value added per worker and the average wage in different kinds of plant or firm is the reports of censuses of manufacturing. Such censuses have now been made in most countries, and one might expect to be able to use them to throw some light on the nature of the relationship between value added per worker (or the wage) and the size of firm. But unfortunately the census data suffer from a number of defects. In the first place, they are confined to manufacturing (including sometimes mining), which is only a part of the whole business field. Secondly, the measure of value added is usually biased upwards on account of the census practice of subtracting from gross value of output only the value of *material* inputs. Service inputs and depreciation are rarely, if ever, subtracted; and it is uncertain how the proportion of these inputs varies with the size of firm.[1] Thirdly, and probably even more serious for our purpose, firms (or more often plants or establishments) are usually classified in size by their number of employees, rather than by a measure of their output.

The classification method is important because it introduces a bias into the estimation of the relation between value added per worker and the size of firm. If firms are classified by their number of workers, there will be a downward bias in the estimate of the regression slope coefficient of value added per worker on size of firm; if firms are classified by total value added (or by total value of output) the bias will be in the other direction. This problem of 'errors in variables' was apparently first noticed in this connection by Steindl (1952).

Of these two biases, the more serious seems to be the bias introduced by using the number of employees as the classifying variable. Most census questions can be answered from accounting data, which are likely to be compiled with a reasonable

[1] For the model used in this book, it would also be preferable if land rent were deducted. But this is unlikely to be an important item in manufacturing.

degree of accuracy by the reporting enterprises or establishments, since these data are needed for normal commercial purposes. But questions about employment cannot generally be answered from standard accounting records. The appropriate information is the aggregate number of worker-hours or worker-weeks used in the firm during the period of account. Since this type of data is not normally kept by firms, the census question on employment is usually limited to asking how many employees were employed on a selected date in the year, or sometimes on the average of several such dates. The consequence is that the census measure of employment is an inaccurate measure of the number of hours worked, being subject to both a possible bias and also substantial random errors.

For this reason, census data selected for consideration in this appendix have been limited to those in which the size classification of firms or establishments is a value-of-output measure, not an employment measure. Although an exhaustive search for suitable data was not undertaken, eligible data were found for three countries of varying degrees of economic development, namely, the United Kingdom, Brazil, and the Republic of Korea. The United Kingdom data are for firms, classified by their 'net output' (i.e. census value added); the Brazilian data are for establishments, classified by their gross output value; and the Korean data are for establishments, classified by their census value added. Summaries of the relevant figures are given in Tables B.1., B.2, and B.3.

The size distributions of firms or establishments are, as expected, highly dispersed and positively skew. None of them conforms exactly to the Pareto function; but the Korean distribution is a good fit to that function for firms with a net output of 2 million won or more (nearly 30 per cent of the total number), and the United Kingdom 1971 distribution fits the Pareto function well for firms with a net output ranging from £20 million to £100 million. At lower levels, in all cases, the Pareto coefficient based on neighbouring points steadily declines, so that the line tracing out points relating the logarithm of firm size to the logarithm of the number of firms exceeding that level is concave.

Figs. B.1a, B.1b, B.2, and B.3 show the relations between the logarithm of net output per worker and the logarithm of size of

## TABLE B.1
### United Kingdom, 1963 and 1971
#### (private manufacturing enterprises employing 100 persons or more)

| Net output of the enterprise (£000) | 1963 | | | 1971 | | | |
|---|---|---|---|---|---|---|---|
| | No. of enterprises | Net output per: Enterprise (£000) | Person engaged (£) | No. of enterprises | Net output per: Enterprise (£000) | Person engaged (£) | Wage and salary bill per employee (£) |
| | $(V)$ | $(V)$ | $(V/L)$ | | $(V)$ | $(V/L)$ | $(W/E)$ |
| Less than 100 | 869 | 74 | 561 ⎫ | 804 | 149 | 1,123 | 899 |
| 100– | 2,229 | 148 | 920 ⎭ | | | | |
| 200– | 2,219 | 314 | 1,125 | 2,562 | 330 | 1,921 | 1,154 |
| 500– | 896 | 699 | 1,234 | 1,379 | 702 | 2,285 | 1,230 |
| 1,000– | 534 | 1,399 | 1,315 | 813 | 1,400 | 2,434 | 1,254 |
| 2,000– | 407 | 3.098 | 1,418 | 578 | 3,106 | 2,597 | 1,308 |
| 5,000– | 121 | 7,083 | 1,457 | 225 | 7,146 | 2,725 | 1,359 |
| 10,000– | 86 | 13,884 | 1,542 | 137 | 14,202 | 2,818 | 1,396 |
| 20,000– | 41 | 29,439 | 1,627 | 92 | 33,201 | 2,944 | 1,476 |
| 50,000– ⎫ | 21 | 69,429 | 1,480 | 18 | 60,622 | 3,192 | 1,457 |
| 75,000– ⎭ | | | | 9 | 88,156 | 2,738 | 1,563 |
| 100,000– ⎫ | 4 | 164,750 | 1,921 | 3 | 117,700 | 2,203 | 1,551 |
| 125,000– ⎭ | | | | 17 | 234,365 | 2,653 | 1,468 |
| All the above | 7,427 | 1,225 | 1,402 | 6,637 | 2,666 | 2,625 | 1,382 |

*Sources*: 1963: United Kingdom Department of Industry, *Report on the Census of Production 1968, Summary Tables: Enterprise Analyses*, H.M.S.O. (London, 1974), Table 45.
    1971: *Business Monitor, Report on the 1971 Census of Production, Summary Tables*, H.M.S.O. (London, 1976) Table 10.

firm and, where available, the corresponding relations for the average wage. In no case are the points exactly on a straight line, as they would be if functions (9.1) and (9.2) were exactly satisfied.[2] But in every case there is a middle range of points falling approximately on a straight line, e.g. those falling between the enlarged points. Firms below this range always show a steeper relation between the logarithm of net output per worker and the logarithm of size of firm. In the case of the United Kingdom this is at least partly the consequence of the truncation of the data at a size of firm employing 100 persons. But in all cases this curvature probably also reflects the bias intro-

---

[2] If $v = BL^{\beta-1}$, it can be shown that $v = B^{\frac{1}{\beta}}V^{\frac{\beta-1}{\beta}}$, where $V = vL$. If, in addition, $w = AL^{a-1}$, it can be shown that $w = AB^{\frac{1-a}{\beta}}V^{\frac{a-1}{\beta}}$.

TABLE B.2

*Brazil 1970*

*(manufacturing establishments)*

| Gross output per establishment (Cr$000) | No. of establish- ments | Net output per establishment (Cr$000) | Net output. per person engaged (Cr$) | Wage and salary bill per person engaged (Cr$) |
|---|---|---|---|---|
| | | (V) | (V/L) | (W/L) |
| Less than 100 | 18,734 | 26 | 3,761 | 1,714 |
| 100– | 8,164 | 61 | 8,180 | 2,758 |
| 150– | 6,749 | 81 | 9,791 | 2,952 |
| 200– | 10,583 | 126 | 11,099 | 3,344 |
| 350– | 5,513 | 202 | 11,998 | 3,642 |
| 500– | 4,655 | 294 | 13,266 | 3,892 |
| 750– | 2,796 | 414 | 14,117 | 4,084 |
| 1,000– | 3,276 | 581 | 15,033 | 4,355 |
| 1,500– | 1,935 | 798 | 16,581 | 4,500 |
| 2,000– | 2,857 | 1,213 | 17,108 | 4,685 |
| 3,500– | 1,271 | 1,911 | 18,570 | 4,988 |
| 5,000– | 1,197 | 2,735 | 18,981 | 4,968 |
| 7,500– | 629 | 4,020 | 21,610 | 5,021 |
| 10,000– | 1,290 | 7,170 | 24,019 | 5,386 |
| 25,000– | 432 | 16,284 | 31,196 | 6,564 |
| 50,000– | 267 | 53,919 | 50,835 | 8,809 |
| All the above | 70,348 | 744 | 21,972 | 5,080 |

*Source: Anuário Estatístico do Brasil, 1975,* Secretaria de Planejamento da Pres-
idéncia da República (Rio de Janeiro, 1975), p. 193.

duced by using output as both a classifying variable and as a
component of the dependent variable. A slight tendency for net
output per worker in the largest firms in Brazil and Korea to
rise above the linear relation of the intermediate range of firms
may also be due to the same cause. Since we do not know how
much allowance to make for these effects, we cannot be certain
whether the empirical relation between net output per worker
and size of firm deviates systematically from a log-linear relation.

The United Kingdom graphs show a tendency for net output
per worker in the largest firms—and more especially those in the
range immediately below the largest—to fall away in comparison with those below them in size. This tendency, which is more
marked in 1971 than in 1963, may be the consequence of one or

TABLE B.3

*Korea 1966*

*(manufacturing establishments)*

| Value added per establishment (won 000) | Number of establishments | Value added per establishment (won 000) | Value added per person engaged (won 000) | Wages and salaries per person engaged (won 000) |
|---|---|---|---|---|
| | | $(V)$ | $(V/L)$ | $(W/L)$ |
| Less than 500 | 5,908 | 306·1 | 47·7 | 35·5 |
| 500– | 5,441 | 724·5 | 88·8 | 43·4 |
| 1,000– | 4,937 | 1,405·5 | 120·7 | 49·1 |
| 2,000– | 1,882 | 2,438·4 | 143·0 | 50·9 |
| 3,000– | 1,672 | 3,849·3 | 156·6 | 52·6 |
| 5,000– | 1,352 | 6,978·2 | 178·7 | 55·4 |
| 10,000– | 945 | 16,565·8 | 216·8 | 64·2 |
| 30,000– | 200 | 38,387·0 | 252·6 | 74·8 |
| 50,000– | 381 | 261,661·4 | 502·7 | 91·3 |
| All the above | 22,718 | 6,874·5 | 275·6 | 66·7 |

*Source:* Economic Planning Board, Korean Reconstruction Bank, *Report on Mining and Manufacturing Census, Series 1—Basic Tables 1966* (Seoul 1967), pp. 164–5.

more of the following: (1) increasing effects of international competition, resulting from tariff reductions, on the earnings of large firms, (2) managerial inability to maintain efficiency in very large British firms, and (3) a misguided attempt to secure the benefits of economies of scale during the 1960s by means of mergers and take-overs. It should be noted that in the 1971 data the margin between net output per worker and the average wage shrinks rapidly in firms with a net output of £75 million or more.

In general, the wage lines have a similar shape to the net output per worker lines but, except for the largest United Kingdom firms, the slope of each wage line is somewhat less than the slope of the net output per worker line.[3] Thus, the general tendency is for the wage share to decline as the size of

[3] The estimated level of the average wage in the smaller firms in Brazil and Korea is biased downwards by the inclusion of working proprietors in the denominator of the fraction, i.e. by using $L$ instead of $E$.

firm increases. This tendency is more marked in Brazil and Korea than in the United Kingdom.

If we judge the average slope of each curve by the slope of the approximately linear section between the enlarged points, and

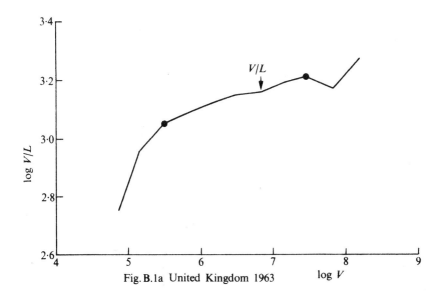

Fig. B.1a United Kingdom 1963

assume that these slopes measure the elasticity coefficients of the underlying functions, we can obtain the estimates shown in Table B.4. These estimates show that both $\beta$ and $\alpha$ are much higher for Brazil and Korea than for the United Kingdom. The figures are consistent with the known facts that both the rate of profit and the rate of growth in Korean and Brazilian manufacturing are higher than in United Kingdom manufacturing.

TABLE B.4
*Estimated values of $\beta$ and $\alpha$ in selected countries*

|  | $\beta$ | $\alpha$ |
|---|---|---|
| United Kingdom 1963 | 1·085 | – |
| United Kingdom 1971 | 1·071 | 1·046 |
| Brazil 1970 | 1·230 | 1·140 |
| Korea 1966 | 1·282 | 1·164 |

In countries like Brazil and Korea, which are experiencing rapid technical change, several different levels of technique are being used simultaneously. Since the larger firms are more likely to be using the more advanced techniques, the differences in labour productivity between firms of different sizes reflect both the effects of economies of scale and of differences in technique. On the other hand, the low values of $\beta$ and $\alpha$ in the United Kingdom probably reflect the relative homogeneity of public techniques employed in that country, as well as other factors peculiar to British industry. Simulations of the growth of firms based on the model outlined in Chapter 9, a few of which are reported in Appendix C, suggest that, on reasonable assumptions about the parameters of the model, it would be impossible to develop a size distribution of firms, even after 75

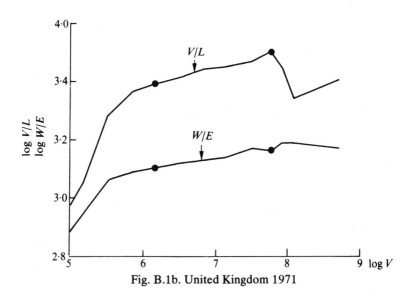

Fig. B.1b. United Kingdom 1971

years of growth, approximating to those which are observed in industrialized economies unless the value of $(\beta - \alpha)$ were at least 0·06. It seems probable, therefore, that most industrializing countries pass through a phase in which the cost advantages of large firms are much greater than those which obtain in fully mature economies.

In drawing these conclusions we are, of course, taking considerable liberties with the data, which cover so few countries and are so unsatisfactory in other respects. By assuming that the slope coefficient of the central portion of each graph is representative of the underlying function it is implicitly assumed that the upward bias in census net output is a constant proportion of true net value added in each size group of firms. But this assumption may be false. It could be tested only by the collection of data of much better quality than any now available from manufacturing censuses.

The results which we have obtained from the census figures are reassuring so far as they go, since they do not contradict the assumption that labour productivity increases with size of firm (except for a few firms near the top of the United Kingdom

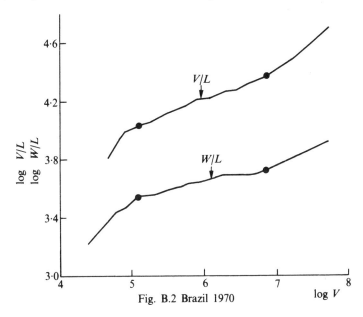

Fig. B.2 Brazil 1970

distribution). Moreover, after allowance for the classification bias, the figures may be consistent with log-linear value added per worker and wage functions. But if we extrapolate net output per worker and the average wage, using the $\beta$ and $\alpha$ coefficients given in Table B.4, we find that the implied ratio of net output to the wage in the one-man firm is 1·6 in the United Kingdom (in 1971), 2·6 in Brazil, and 1·9 in Korea. These figures are biased upwards by the inclusion in net output of the various items mentioned earlier, and by the exclusion from wages and salaries of supplementary labour costs, such as insurance and

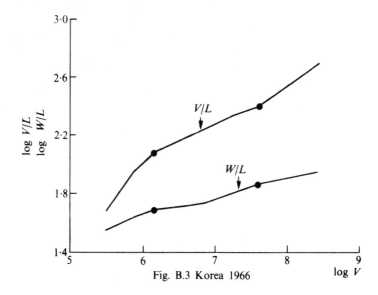

Fig. B.3 Korea 1966

pension contributions, bonuses, holiday money, housing subsidies, and travel allowances.[4] According to the model, we should expect the ratio of value added to the imputed average wage in the one-man firm to be in the region of 1·0. United Kingdom aggregate census data can be adjusted to a more satisfactory basis by using estimates available in the national accounts. If it is assumed that both value added and the wage in the one-man firm should be adjusted in proportions equal to the proportions derived from aggregate census and national accounts figures, the effect in 1971 is to reduce the ratio of value added to the wage in the one-man firm from 1·6 to 1·12. Although no similar adjustment has been attempted for Brazil or Korea, it seems unlikely that the gap in these countries could be bridged in this manner. It seems more probable that this gap

[4] The Brazil and Korea wage estimates are also biased downwards for the reason mentioned in the footnote on page 304.

reflects the existence of a dual economy in these countries, or more accurately a multiple-technique economy. In that case, the functions which are estimated from censuses of manufactures will be dominated by the more advanced techniques and will give little or no weight to the firms using less advanced techniques. They will, therefore, underestimate the degree of difference between productivity in very small, technically backward, firms and larger firms using more advanced techniques.

# APPENDIX C

## SIMULATIONS OF THE GROWTH OF FIRMS

### 1. Methods

For the purpose of the simulations it was assumed that the functions (A.1), (A.2), (A.10), and (A.13) are valid for a single industry or group of industries. Then the rate of profit of a firm of efficiency $\theta_i$ in that industry or group of industries is given by (A.15).

Since I shall report only the set of simulations for which the capital-value added ratio is held constant (i.e. $\gamma = 1$), the relevant formula for the rate of profit is given by (A.16), namely

$$r_i = \tfrac{1}{C} (\theta_i - L^{\alpha-\beta}) \qquad (C.1)$$

It was assumed that in each year each firm adds to its net capital, either from internal or external funds, a fixed proportion, $a$, of its net profits during the preceding year. So we have

$$K_{t+1}/K_t = (1 + ar_{it}) \qquad (C.2)$$

where $K_t$ is the net capital of the firm in year $t$ of its life and $r_{it}$ is its rate of profit in the same year.

But from (A.14) and the assumption that $\gamma = 1$ we have

$$K_{t+1}/K_t = (L_{t+1}/L_t)^\beta \qquad (C.3)$$

Combining (C.1), (C.2), and (C.3) we thus obtain

$$L_{t+1}/L_t = \{1 + \tfrac{a}{C} (\theta_i - L^{\alpha-\beta})\}^{\frac{1}{\beta}} \qquad (C.4)$$

This expression provides the necessary formula for computing the growth of a firm of efficiency $\theta_i$, given the parameters $a$, $C$, $\alpha$, and $\beta$.

In the set of simulations reported here these parameters were assumed to take the following values:

(1) $a = 0.6$ or $0.8$
(2) $C = 2$ in all cases

(3) $a = 1 \cdot 04$ in all cases

(4) $\beta = 1 \cdot 118$ or $1 \cdot 156^{1}$

The parameter $\theta_i$ was assumed to be a normally distributed random variable with $\bar{\theta} = 1$ and $\sigma_\theta = 0.25$. Since $B_i$ is value added in an OMF of efficiency $\theta_i$, this implies that the value added of each cohort of OMFs is distributed with a variance of $\sigma^2_\theta$.

It seems to be normal for the variance of profit rates to be smaller for larger firms than for smaller firms.[2] To allow for this effect, it was assumed that

$$\theta_{it} = 1 + (\theta_{i1} - 1) L_t^{-0.25\beta}$$

where $\theta_{i1}$ is the efficiency of the firm in its first year of operation (as an OMF) and $\theta_{it}$ is its efficiency in year $t$ of its life.

The simulations were divided into two groups. In group 1 the results were fully determined by the previous set of assumptions. But in group 2 the rate of profit was subject to stochastic variations in each year. For this group of simulations the value of $r_i$ in (C.1) was replaced by $r'_i$, where

$$r'_i = r_i + u_t$$

and $u_t$ is a random variable with $\bar{u}_t = 0$ and $\sigma_{ut} = 0 \cdot 2 L_t^{-0.2\beta}$. This implies that the variance of $u_t$ diminishes as the size of firm increases.

It was assumed that in year 1 a cohort of OMFs of size $N_1 = 100$ entered the industry, and in each successive year an additional cohort entered, the size of which increased at a steady rate of 2 per cent per annum. Hence $N_T = 100 (1 \cdot 02)^{T-1}$, where $T$ is the number of the year of observation, counted from the beginning of the process.

Since OMFs in group 1 make no profits and cannot grow unless they have $\theta_{i1} > 1$, in this group of simulations the range of $\theta_{i1}$ used for calculation was restricted to $1 \cdot 1 \leq \theta_{i1} \leq 2 \cdot 5$. In group 2, however, firms with $\theta_{i1} < 1$ may make profits if $u_{i1} > 0$, and the range of $\theta_{i1}$ in this group was extended to $0 \cdot 1 \leq \theta_{i1} \leq 2 \cdot 5$. But since many firms in this group with low values of $\theta_i$

---

[1] The original set of simulations employed a formula containing a parameter $\lambda = (\beta - a)/\beta$, which was assumed to take alternative values of $0 \cdot 07$ or $0 \cdot 1$. The values of $\beta$ given above are those implicit in the assumed values of $a$ and $\lambda$.

[2] See, for example, Singh and Whittington (1968).

make losses, and are consequently obliged to reduce their net capital, it was decided that firms in this group with aggregate net losses over any three consecutive years amounting to 25 per cent on their capital should be excluded from the final sample. The effect of this rule was to reduce considerably the number of new entrants in this group which survived for more than a few years.

## 2. Results

The following tables show percentage size distributions of firms surviving at the end of fifty and seventy-five years, for various combinations of the parameters. Table C.1 contains distributions for which $\beta = 1\cdot118$ and Table C.2 for $\beta = 1\cdot156$. Columns headed I refer to group 1 simulations, using $r_i$; columns headed II refer to group 2 simulations, using $r_i'$.

All the distributions are highly skew and widely dispersed. The degree of dispersion increases with $T$, $a$, and $\beta$, as does the average rate of profit. The effect of the stochastic variation of $r$ is

TABLE C.1
*Percentage size distributions of firms*
$(\beta = 1\cdot118)$

| Size of firm (L) | $a = 0\cdot6$ | | | | $a = 0\cdot8$ | | | |
|---|---|---|---|---|---|---|---|---|
| | $T = 50$ | | $T = 75$ | | $T = 50$ | | $T = 75$ | |
| | I | II | I | II | I | II | I | II |
| Less than | | | | | | | | |
| 5 | 70·34 | 70·21 | 57·15 | 60·21 | 57·66 | 62·64 | 46·84 | 53·99 |
| 5 – | 12·09 | 11·26 | 12·57 | 8·92 | 14·31 | 10·85 | 11·63 | 9·40 |
| 10 – | 8·54 | 9·17 | 9·70 | 12·28 | 9·33 | 7·53 | 8·55 | 5·10 |
| 20 – | 5·52 | 4·66 | 7·93 | 5·95 | 8·22 | 8·40 | 9·53 | 9·27 |
| 50 – | 2·15 | 3·02 | 4·33 | 3·46 | 4·52 | 4·63 | 5·87 | 5·23 |
| 100 – | 0·90 | 1·32 | 3·34 | 3·20 | 2·60 | 3·40 | 4·61 | 3·13 |
| 200 – | 0·41 | 0·25 | 2·32 | 2·00 | 2·14 | 1·26 | 3·68 | 4·22 |
| 500 – | 0·04 | ·10 | 1·30 | 2·09 | 0·70 | 0·82 | 2·49 | 2·75 |
| 1,000 – | 0·01 | ·01 | 0·72 | 1·05 | 0·38 | 0·22 | 2·42 | 1·40 |
| 2,000 – | – | – | 0·45 | 0·65 | 0·13 | 0·20 | 1·60 | 2·62 |
| 5,000 – | – | – | 0·19 | 0·19 | 0·01 | 0·05 | 2·78 | 2·89 |
| Total | 100·00 | 100·00 | 100·00 | 100·00 | 100·00 | 100·00 | 100·00 | 100·00 |
| Average rate of profit (%) | 19·7 | 20·2 | 25·1 | 25·0 | 22·9 | 23·9 | 30·4 | 29·8 |

TABLE C.2
*Percentage size distributions of firms*
$(\beta = 1\cdot156)$

| Size of firm (L) | a = 0·6 | | | | a = 0·8 | | | |
| | T = 50 | | T = 75 | | T = 50 | | T = 75 | |
| | I | II | I | II | I | II | I | II |
| --- | --- | --- | --- | --- | --- | --- | --- | --- |
| Less than 5 | 66·62 | 69·15 | 54·13 | 59·45 | 54·79 | 62·85 | 44·52 | 52·54 |
| 5 – | 13·60 | 10·35 | 11·70 | 10·07 | 12·09 | 10·46 | 9·81 | 6·68 |
| 10 – | 7·67 | 9·28 | 8·87 | 6·83 | 9·98 | 4·49 | 8·12 | 5·54 |
| 20 – | 6·85 | 6·75 | 8·77 | 6·36 | 9·43 | 7·43 | 8·94 | 8·58 |
| 50 – | 2·88 | 2·16 | 4·79 | 4·20 | 4·32 | 3·42 | 4·97 | 3·94 |
| 100 – | 1·40 | 1·35 | 3·19 | 3·55 | 3·64 | 5·76 | 4·29 | 3·04 |
| 200 – | 0·77 | 0·74 | 3·49 | 4·06 | 2·98 | 2·83 | 5·33 | 6·35 |
| 500 – | 0·17 | 0·17 | 1·85 | 1·22 | 1·30 | 1·03 | 3·17 | 2·40 |
| 1,000 – | 0·03 | 0·04 | 1·21 | 1·71 | 0·88 | 1·01 | 2·40 | 2·58 |
| 2,000 – | 0·01 | 0·01 | 1·13 | 1·34 | 0·44 | 0·54 | 2·24 | 2·17 |
| 5,000 – | – | – | 0·87 | 1·21 | 0·15 | 0·18 | 6·21 | 6·18 |
| Total | 100·00 | 100·00 | 100·00 | 100·00 | 100·00 | 100·00 | 100·00 | 100·00 |
| Average rate of profit (%) | 26·0 | 25·6 | 34·3 | 34·1 | 31·1 | 31·2 | 39·9 | 40·3 |

usually to increase slightly the degree of dispersion of the upper tail of the distribution, but at the same time to increase the proportion of very small firms.

While these simulations do not prove that observed size distributions of firms have in fact been generated by processes similar to those assumed in the model, they show that observed size distributions could have been generated in this manner.

For reasons given in Chapter 9 (and discussed further in Appendix B), it is probably unrealistic to assume that $\beta$ remains constant over a long period of time. If $\beta$ declines over time, the effect will be to restrict the rate of growth of firms in the later years, to reduce inter-size profit differentials in those years, and to prevent the average rate of profit from rising to the extent shown in the tables. Indeed, if $\beta$ falls sufficiently, the average rate of profit will fall, despite continued growth in the dispersion of firm sizes. This may be part of the explanation for the apparent decline in the rate of profit in the most highly industrialized countries during the past one or two decades.

# REFERENCES

AHLUWALIA, M. S. (1974), 'Income inequality: some dimensions of the problem', in Chenery, H. and others, *Redistribution with Growth*, Oxford University Press.

—— (1976), 'Income distribution and development: some stylized facts', *American Economic Review*, vol. 66.

ALTERMAN, J. (1964), 'Comment on Lebergott', in *The Behavior of Income Shares*, Studies in Income and Wealth, vol. 27, National Bureau of Economic Research, Princeton University Press.

ANDREWS, P. W. S. (1949), *Manufacturing Business*, Macmillan.

ARROW, K. J. (1964), 'The role of securities in the optimal allocation of risk-bearing', *Review of Economic Studies*, vol. 31.

——, CHENERY, H. B., MINHAS, B., and SOLOW, R. M. (1961), 'Capital–labor substitution and economic efficiency', *Review of Economics and Statistics*, vol. 43.

—— and HAHN, F. H. (1971), *General Competitive Analysis*, Holden-Day and Oliver and Boyd.

ATKINSON, A. B. (1971), 'The distribution of wealth and the individual life-cyle', *Oxford Economic Papers*, vol. 23.

—— (1975), *The Economics of Inequality*, Oxford University Press.

—— (ed) (1976), *The Personal Distribution of Incomes*, Allen and Unwin.

—— and HARRISON, A. J. (1978), *Distribution of Personal Wealth in Britain*, Cambridge University Press.

BAIN, J. S. (1949), 'A note on pricing in monopoly and oligopoly', *American Economic Review*, vol. 39.

—— (1956), *Barriers to New Competition*, Harvard University Press.

BAUMOL, W. J. (1959), *Business Behaviour, Value and Growth*, Macmillan.

BECKER, G. S. (1964), *Human Capital*, Columbia University Press for the National Bureau of Economic Research.

—— (1967), '*Human Capital and the Personal Distribution of Income*', W. S. Woytinsky Lecture No. 1, University of Michigan.

BLAIR, J. M. (1942), 'The relation between size and efficiency of business', *Review of Economic Statistics*, vol. 24.

BLAUG, M. (1968), *Economic Theory in Retrospect*, 2nd edn., Heinemann.

BLISS, C. J. (1975), *Capital Theory and the Distribution of Income*, North-Holland.

BOWLEY, A. L. (1914), 'The British super-tax', *Quarterly Journal of Economics*, vol. 28.

—— (1937), *Wages and Income in the United Kingdom since 1860*, Cambridge University Press.

BRONFENBRENNER, M. (1971), *Income Distribution Theory*, Macmillan.

BUDD, E. C. (1970), 'Postwar changes in the size distribution of income in the U.S.', *American Economic Review*, vol. 60.

CANNAN, E. (1914), *Wealth*, Staples Press, London.

CHAMPERNOWNE, D. G. (1953), 'A model of income distribution', *Economic Journal*, vol. 68.

CHISWICK, B. R, (1974), *Income Inequality*, Columbia University Press for the National Bureau of Economic Research.

COBB, C. W. and DOUGLAS, P. H. (1928), 'A theory of production', *American Economic Review*, vol. 18.

CYERT, R. M. and MARCH, J. G. (1963), *A Behavioral Theory of the Firm*, Prentice-Hall.

DALTON, H. (1920), *The Inequality of Incomes*, Routledge.

DANZIGER, S. and SMOLENSKY, E. (1976), 'Income inequality: problems of measurement and interpretation' (mimeo), Institute for Research on Poverty, University of Wisconsin, Madison.

DAS, T. (1977), *Effects of Demographic Change and Choice of Income Unit on the Size Distribution of Income*, Ph.D. thesis, University of East Anglia.

DAVIDSON, P. (1959), *Theories of Aggregate Income Distribution*, Rutgers University Press.

DAVIE, R., BUTLER, N., and GOLDSTEIN, H. (1972), *From Birth to Seven*, The Second Report of the National Child Development Study, Longman.

DEBREU, G (1959), *Theory of Value*, Wiley.

DENISON, E. F. (1967), assisted by J.-P. Poullier, *Why Growth Rates Differ*, The Brooking Institution, Washington, D.C.

— — (1974), *Accounting for United States Economic Growth 1929–1969*, The Brookings Institution, Washington, D.C.

DOERINGER, P. B. and PIORE M. J. (1971), *Internal Labor Markets and Manpower Analysis*, Heath Lexington Books.

DOUGLAS, P. H. (1934), *Theory of Wages*, Macmillan.

— — (1948), 'Are there laws of production?', *American Economic Review*, vol. 38.

ENGELS, F. (1934), *Anti-Dühring*, Lawrence and Wishart.

FEINSTEIN, C. H. (1968), 'Changes in the distribution of national income in the United Kingdom since 1860', in Marchal, J. and Ducros, B. (eds), *The Distribution of National Income*, Macmillan.

— — (1976), *Statistical Tables of National Income, Expenditure and Output of the United Kingdom, 1855–1965*, Cambridge University Press.

FERGUSON, C. E. (1971), *The Neoclassical Theory of Production and Distribution*, Cambridge University Press.

FIEGEHEN, G. C. and LANSLEY, P. C. (1976), 'The measurement of poverty: a note on household size and income units', *Journal of the Royal Statistical Society, Series A*, vol. 139.

— —, LANSLEY, P. S., and SMITH, A. D. (1977), *Poverty and Progress in Britain 1953–73*, Cambridge University Press.

FISHER, F. M. (1971), 'Aggregate production functions and the explanation of wages: a simulation experiment', *Review of Economics and Statistics*, vol. 53.

FRIEDMAN, M. (1953), 'Choice, chance, and the personal distribution of income', *Journal of Political Economy*, vol. 61.

— — (1957), *A Theory of the Consumption Function*, Princeton University Press.

GINTIS, H. (1971), 'Education, technology, and the characteristics of worker productivity', *American Economic Review*, vol. 61.

GLYN, A. and SUTCLIFFE, B. (1972), *British Capitalism, Workers and the Profits Squeeze*, Penguin.

Government of India, (1976), *National Accounts Statistics 1960–61 to 1973–74*, Central Statistical Organisation, New Delhi.

HALDI, J. and WHITCOMB, D. (1967), 'Economies of scale in industrial plants', *Journal of Political Economy*, vol. 75.

HALL, M. and WEISS, L. (1967), 'Firm size and profitability', *Review of Economics and Statistics*, vol. 49.

HALL, R. L. and HITCH, C. J. (1939), 'Price theory and business behaviour', *Oxford Economic Papers*, vol. 2.

HARCOURT, G. C. (1972), *Some Cambridge Controversies in the Theory of Capital*, Cambridge University Press.

HARROD, R. F. (1952), 'Theory of imperfect competition revised', in *Economic Essays*, Macmillan.

HAUSE, J. C. (1972), 'Earnings profile: ability and schooling', *Journal of Political Economy*, vol. 80.

HEIDENSOHN, K. (1969), 'Labour's share in national income—a constant?', *The Manchester School*, vol. 37.

HICKS, J. R. (1932), *The Theory of Wages*, 2nd edn. 1963, Macmillan.

—— (1941), 'The rehabilitation of consumers' surplus', *Review of Economic Studies*, vol. 9, reprinted in American Economic Association, *Readings in Welfare Economics*, Allen and Unwin (1969).

—— (1946), *Value and Capital*, 2nd edn., Clarendon Press, Oxford.

HUTCHINSON, T. W. (1960), *The Significance and Basic Postulates of Economic Theory*, Augustus M. Kelley reprint.

International Labour Office (1972), *Employment, Incomes and Equality*, Geneva.

JAIN, S. (1975), *Size Distribution of Income: A Compilation of Data*, World Bank, Washington, D.C.

JAQUES, E. (1956), *Measurement of Responsibility*, Tavistock Publications, London (republished by Heinemann, 1972).

JOHNSON, H. G. (1973). *The Theory of Income Distribution*, Gray-Mills.

JOHNSTON, J. (1960), *Statistical Cost Analysis*, McGraw-Hill.

KALDOR, N. (1955), 'Alternative theories of distribution', *Review of Economic Studies*, vol. 23.

KALECKI, M. (1939), *Essays in the Theory of Economic Fluctuations*, Allen and Unwin.

—— (1942), 'A theory of profits', *Economic Journal*, vol. 57, reprinted in Kalecki, M., *Studies in Economic Dynamics*, Allen and Unwin (1943).

—— (1945), 'On the Gibrat distribution', *Econometrica*, vol. 13.

—— (1954), *Theory of Economic Dynamics*, Allen and Unwin.

KEYNES, J. M. (1930). *A Treatise on Money*, vols. I and II, Macmillan.

—— (1936). *The General Theory of Employment, Interest and Money*, Macmillan.

—— (1939), 'The income and fiscal potential of Great Britain', *Economic Journal*, vol. 49.

KING, J. and REGAN, P. (1976), *Relative Income Shares*, Macmillan.

KNIGHT, F. H. (1921), *Risk, Uncertainty and Profit*, Houghton Mifflin Company.

KRAVIS, I. (1959), 'Relative income shares in fact and theory', *American Economic Review*, vol. 49.

KURZ, M. (1974), 'The Kesten-Stigum model and the treatment of uncertainty in equilibrium theory', in Balch, M., MacFadden, D., and Wu, S., *Essays on Economic Behavior under Uncertainty*, North-Holland.

KUZNETS, S. (1953), *Shares of Upper Income Groups in Income and Savings*, National Bureau of Economic Research, New York.

— — (1955), 'Economic growth and income inequality', *American Economic Review*, vol. 45.

— — (1959), 'Quantitative aspects of the economic growth of nations: IV. Distribution of national income by factor shares', *Economic Development and Cultural Change*, vol. 7.

— — (1963), 'Quantitative aspects of the economic growth of nations: VII. Distribution of income by size', *Economic Development and Cultural Change*, vol. 11.

— — (1976), 'Demographic aspects of the size distribution of income: an exploratory essay,' *Economic Development and Cultural Change*, vol. 24.

LAYARD, R. and PSACHAROPOULOS, G. (1974), 'The screening hypothesis and the returns to education', *Journal of Political Economy*, vol. 82.

LEBERGOTT, S. (1964), 'Factor shares in the long term: some theoretical and statistical aspects', in *The Behavior of Income Shares*, Studies in Income and Wealth, vol. 27, National Bureau of Economic Research, Princeton University Press.

LEWIS, W. A. (1954), 'Development with unlimited supplies of labour', *The Manchester School*, vol. 22.

LILLARD, L. A. (1977), 'Inequality: earnings vs. human wealth', *American Economic Review*, vol. 67.

LYDALL, H. F. (1955) 'The life-cycle in income, saving, and asset ownership', *Econometrica*, vol. 23.

— — (1959), 'The long-term trend in the size distribution of income', *Journal of the Royal Statistical Society, Series A*, vol. 122.

— — (1968a), 'Technical progress in Australian manufacturing', *Economic Journal*, vol. 78.

— — (1968b), *The Structure of Earnings*, Oxford University Press.

— — (1971), 'A theory of distribution and growth with economies of scale', *Economic Journal*, vol. 81.

— — (1975), *Trade and Employment*, International Labour Office, Geneva.

— — (1976), 'Theories of the distribution of earnings', in Atkinson (ed.) (1976).

— — (1977), 'Income distribution during the process of development', World Employment Programme Research Working Paper No. WP 52 (mimeo), International Labour Office, Geneva.

— — (1978), 'Some problems in making international comparisons of inequality' (mimeo), paper contributed to the Murphy Symposium on Income Distribution, Tulane University, New Orleans.

— — and LANSING, J. B. (1959), 'A comparison of the distribution of personal income and wealth in the United States and Great Britain', *American Economic Review*, vol. 49.

MARRIS, R. L. (1964), *The Economic Theory of Managerial Capitalism*, Macmillan.

MARSHALL, A. (1920), *Principles of Economics*, 8th edn., Macmillan.

MARX, K. (1946) *Capital*, vol. I, Dona Torr (ed.), from the original English edition of F. Engels, Allen and Unwin.

— — (1909), *Capital* vol. III, F. Engels (ed.), translated by E. Untermann, Charles H. Kerr, Chicago.

— — and ENGELS, F. (1968), *Selected Works in One Volume*, Lawrence and Wishart.

MAYER, T. (1960), 'The distribution of ability and earnings,' *Review of Economics and Statistics*, vol. 42.

MINCER, J, (1970), 'The distribution of labor incomes: a survey', *Journal of Economic Literature*, vol. 8.

— — (1974). *Schooling, Experience, and Earnings*, Columbia University Press.

— — (1976), 'Progress in human capital analyses of the distribution of earnings', in Atkinson (ed.) (1976).

MINHAS, B. S. (1963), *An International Comparison of Factor Costs and Factor Use*, North-Holland.

MOORE, F. T. (1959), 'Economies of scale: some statistical evidence', *Quarterly Journal of Economics*, vol. 73.

MYRDAL, G. (1944), *An American Dilemma*, Harper.

PAGLIN, M. (1975), 'The measurement and trend of inequality: a basic revision', *American Economic Review*, vol. 65.

PARETO, V. (1897), *Cours d'économie politique*, Lausanne.

— — (1927), *Manuel d'économie politique*, 2nd edn., Paris.

PASINETTI, L. L. (1962), 'Rate of profit and income distribtution in relation to the rate of economic growth', *Review of Economic Studies*, vol. 29.

PAUKERT, F. (1973), 'Income distribution at different levels of development: a survey of evidence', *International Labour Review*, vol. 108.

PENROSE, E. T. (1968), *The Theory of the Growth of the Firm*, Blackwell.

PHELPS BROWN, E. H. (1977), *The Inequality of Pay*, Oxford University Press.

— — and HART, P. E. (1952), 'The share of wages in national income', *Economic Journal*, vol. 62.

— — and BROWNE, M. H. (1968), *A Century of Pay*, Macmillan.

PRATTEN, C. F. (1971), *Economies of Scale in Manufacturing Industries*, Cambridge University Press.

PSACHAROPOULOS, G. (1975) *Earnings and Education in OECD Countries*, O.E.C.D., Paris.

RADNER, D. B. and HINRICHS, J. C. (1974), 'Size distribution of income in 1964, 1970, and 1971', *Survey of Current Business*, October.

RADNER, R. (1968), 'Competitive equilibrium under uncertainty', *Econometrica*, vol. 36.

REDER, M. W. (1969), 'A partial survey of the theory of income size distribution', in Soltow, L. (ed.), *Six Papers on the Size Distribution of Wealth and Income*, Columbia University Press for the National Bureau of Economic Research.

RICARDO, D. (1951–73), *The Works and Correspondence of David Ricardo*, P. Sraffa (ed.) vols. I–XI, Cambridge University Press.

RICHARDSON, G. B. (1960), *Information and Investment*, Oxford University Press.

ROBBINS, L. (1932), *An Essay on the Nature and Significance of Economic Science*, Macmillan.

ROBINSON, J. (1933), *The Economics of Imperfect Competition*, Macmillan.

—— (1953), 'The production function and the theory of capital', *Review of Economic Studies*, vol. 21.

—— (1956). *The Accumulation of Capital*, Macmillan.

—— (1960), *Collected Economic Papers*, vol. 2, Blackwell.

RUTHERFORD, R. S. G. (1955), 'Income distributions: a new model', *Econometrica*, vol. 23.

SAMUELSON, P. A. (1947), *Foundations of Economic Anaylsis*, Harvard University Press.

—— (1962a), 'Economists and the history of ideas', *American Economic Review*, vol. 52.

—— (1962b), 'Parable and realism in capital theory: the surrogate production function,' *Review of Economic Studies*, vol. 29.

—— (1971), 'Understanding the Marxian notion of exploitation: a summary of the so-called transformation problem between Marxian values and competitive prices', *Journal of Economic Literature*, vol. 9.

SCHUMPETER, J. A. (1934), *The Theory of Economic Development*, Harvard University Press.

SCOTT, M. FG. (1976), 'Investment and growth', *Oxford Economic Papers*, vol. 28.

SETON, F. (1957), 'The "transformation problem"', *Review of Economic Studies*, vol. 25.

SHACKLE, G. L. S. (1952), *Expectations in Economics*, 2nd edn., Cambridge University Press.

—— (1970), *Expectation, Enterprise and Profit*, Allen and Unwin.

SILBERSTON, A. (1970), 'Price behaviour of firms', *Economic Journal*, vol. 80.

—— (1972), 'Economies of scale in theory and practice', *Economic Journal*, vol. 82.

SIMON, H. A. (1955), 'A behavioural model of rational choice', *Quarterly Journal of Economics*, vol. 69.

SINGH, A. and WHITTINGTON, G. (1968), *Growth, Profitability and Valuation*, Cambridge University Press.

SMEEDING, T. M. (1976), 'The economic well being of low income households: implications for income inequality and poverty' (mimeo), Bowdin College, Brunswick, Maine, United States.

SMITH, A. (1950), *An Inquiry into the Nature and Causes of the Wealth of Nations*, vols. I and II, Edwin Cannan, 6th edn., Methuen.

SMITH, C. A. (1955), 'Survey of the empirical evidence on economies of scale', in *Business Concentration and Price Policy*, Princeton University Press for the National Bureau of Economic Research.

SOLOW, R. M. (1957), 'Technological change and the aggregate production function', *Review of Economics and Statistics*, vol. 39.

SOLTOW, L. (1968), 'Long-run changes in British income inequality', *Economic History Review*, vol. 21.

SRAFFA, P. (1926), 'The laws of returns under competitive conditions', *Economic Journal*, vol. 36.

— — (1960), *The Production of Commodities by Means of Commodities*, Cambridge University Press.

STAMP, J. (1920), *British Incomes and Property*, P. S. King and Son, Ltd., London.

STARK, T. (1972), *The Distribution of Personal Income in the United Kingdom 1949–1963*, Cambridge University Press.

STEINDL, J. (1945), *Small and Big Business*, Blackwell.

— — (1952), *Maturity and Stagnation in American Capitalism*, Blackwell.

— — (1965), *Random Processes and the Growth of Firms*, Griffin.

STIGLER, G. J. (1941), *Production and Distribution Theories*, Macmillan.

SWAN, T. W. (1965). 'Economic growth and capital accumulation', *Economic Record*, vol. 32.

SWEEZY, P. M. (1939), 'Demand under conditions of oligopoly', *Journal of Political Economy*, vol. 47.

— — (ed.) (1975), *Karl Marx and the Close of his System* by E. von Böhm-Bawerk, Augustus M. Kelley.

SYLOS-LABINI, P. (1962), *Oligopoly and Technical Progress*, Harvard University Press.

TAUBMAN, P. (1975), *Sources of Inequality of Earnings*, North-Holland.

— — (1976a), 'Personal characteristics and the distribution of earnings', in Atkinson (ed.) (1976).

— — (1976b), 'Earnings, education, genetics and environment', *Journal of Human Resources*, vol. 11.

— — (1976c), 'The determinants of earnings: genetics, family and other environments; a study of white male twins', *American Economic Review*, vol. 66.

— — and WALES, T. J. (1973), 'Higher education, mental ability, and screening', *Journal of Political Economy*, vol. 81.

TAUSSIG, M. K. (1973), *Alternative Measures of the Distribution of Economic Welfare*, Princeton University Press.

TAYLOR, C. T. and SILBERSTON, Z. A. (1973), *The Economic Impact of the Patent System*, Cambridge University Press.

THATCHER, A. R. (1976), 'The new earnings survey and the distribution of earnings', in Atkinson (ed.) (1976).

THUROW, L. C. (1976), *Generating Inequality*, Macmillan.

United Kingdom Central Statistical Office, *National Income and Expenditure* (annual), H.M.S.O., London.

United Kingdom, Royal Commission on the Distribution of Income and Wealth:

*Report No. 1, Initial Report on the Standing Reference*, H.M.S.O. London (1975).

*Report No. 2, Income from Companies and its Distribution*, H.M.S.O., London (1975).

*Report No. 3, Higher Incomes from Employment*, H.M.S.O., London (1976).

*Report No. 5, Second Report on the Standing Reference*, H.M.S.O., London (1977).

United States Bureau of the Census (1956), *The 1950 United States Census of*

322 *References*

*Population, Occupational Characteristics*, Report P-E No. 1B, U.S. Government Printing Office.

WALRAS, L. (1954), *Elements of Pure Economics*, translated by William Jaffé, Allen and Unwin.

WALTERS, A. A. (1963), 'Production and cost functions: an econometric survey', *Econometrica*, vol. 31.

WEISSKOFF, R. (1970), 'Income distribution and economic growth in Puerto Rico, Argentina, and Mexico', *Review of Income and Wealth*, vol. 16.

WICKSTEED, P. A. (1894), *An Essay on the Co-ordination of the Laws of Distribution*, Macmillan.

WILES, P. J. D. (1956), *Price, Cost and Output*, Blackwell.

WILLIAMSON, J. G. (1977), 'The sources of American inequality, 1896–1948', *Review of Economics and Statistics*, vol. 59.

WILLIAMSON, O. E. (1967), *The Economics of Discretionary Behavior: Managerial Objectives in a Theory of the Firm*, Markham Publishing Company.

# INDEX